SYMBION:

Spirituality for a Possible Future

by

Richard J. Woods, OP

Bear & Company

The publishers of creation spirituality.
Spiritualities for personal and social transformation

Bear & Company Books are published by Bear &
Company, Inc. Its Trademark, consisting of the words
"Bear & Company" and the portrayal of the bear, is
Registered in U.S. Patent and Trademark Office and in
other countries Marca Registrada
Bear & Company, Inc., P.O. Drawer 2860
Santa Fe, NM 87501

Bear & Company, Inc.
P.O. Drawer 2860
Santa Fe, NM 87501
Typesetting—Casa Sin Nombre, Santa Fe
Cover & Interior Design—Bill Davenport & Roger Radley
Printed in the United States by George Banta & Company

**TO Anne McCaffrey
who has seen the future and
knows that it can work...**

CONTENTS

Foreword

Whether forecasting catastrophy or a future bright with promise, observers of recent and current social development agree that the world as a whole is irreversibly embarked upon a voyage of transition from the industrial age to something as different from it as it differed from the preceding agrarian civilization.

Roberto Vacca described the transition period we are now entering as a "Dark Age" heralding a new Renaissance. Similarly, William Irwin Thompson writes of an "Age of Chaos" preceding the emergence of a New Age in which religion, art and science will form a mystical synthesis. Alvin Toffler, who coined the term "Future Shock" a decade ago to describe the impact of entering the transition period, now refersf somewhat vaguely to the "Third Wave." Six years before *Future Shock*, in his brilliant retrospective *The Meaning of the 20th Century*, subtitled "The Great Transition," Kenneth Boulding anticipated Toffler's forecast by his assessment of the third massive developmental period in human history which he call "postcivilization." Daniel Bell wrote of "the post-industrial society," John Kenneth Galbraith of the "new industrial state," Zbigniew Brzezinski of the "technetronic age." Jacques Ellul fulminated, meantime, against the excesses of "the technological society." Most recently, perhaps, Marilyn Ferguson, taking a leaf from Jung, has written with an astrological flourish of optimism about *The Aquarian Conspiracy*.

Despite all this prognostication, celebration and ululation, few of these writers have attempted to probe the coming era with the needs of contemporary spirituality in mind. Yet the need to do so is imperative, for it is only by understanding the implications and consequences of the present transition period that we will be enabled to construct a humanly possible future. And both the understanding and the construction are, when viewed as a whole, what spirituality is all about.

Symbion is, therefore, an exploration of spirituality as a way toward a possibly better future than that predicted by many observers of present global trends. By "better," I mean more humanly livable — a future in which even our own but especially subsequent generations can *enjoy* a world in which truth, freedom, love, justice and peace are elements of every person's experience; a world in which nature and society coexist and sometimes even interpenetrate gracefully and constructively.

Symbion cannot pretend to be a definitive or comprehensive spirituality for the future. But it does examine some areas that already bear on our common destiny, much as a scout peers at territory that he may never tred but that will have to be traversed at some time in the future. It begins, quite literally, where a previous exploration into contemporary spirituality, *Mysterion*, left off: with the future of mysticism. The focus shifts only slightly as we begin to explore a mysticism *for* the future.

In so far as faith in God's presence in the manifold events of life continues to guide our inquiry as the way *and* goal of our efforts to fashion a viably *religious* lifestyle, *Symbion* is indeed mystical in its approach. Further, however, this book attempts to describe elements of a "new asceticism"—a spiritual discipline required of those willing to devote themselves individually and collectively to working for a future worth having.

The name *Symbion* has its own history. Some twelve years ago, as a newly ordained priest, I was involved with the movement for ecological awareness, which had strong connections with anti-war efforts, anti-establishmentarianism and experiments with alternative lifestyles. Flower children were abroad in those days. Being trained in photography, music and communications, I developed a multi-media presentation on the religious dimension of environmental deterioration and ecological responsibility. The theme was "stewardship"—human responsibility for caring for God's gift of creation, particularly in view of accelerating environmental destruction.

In searching for an appropriate title, I began brainstorming the concept of *symbiosis*, a term which I recalled from my college studies in biology. Simply stated, symbiosis means a constructive relationship between two or more dissimilar organisms which provide permanent and mutual services to each other—camouflage and motility, for instance, as with the sea anemone and hermit crab, or food and stimulation, like the fleas that "scratch" the skin of hedgehogs in places where the prickly little animals can't reach. Human beings have such a symbiotic relationship with the intestinal bacteria inside us which help us to digest in exchange for a place to live and three square meals a day. I envisioned our relationship with the natural environment as most properly being one of a similar symbiosis.

I looked up the Greek origin for the word and discovered *symbion* — a neuter noun which generally meant "companion" and could refer to a friend or spouse, someone you live with. With the definite article and appropriate feminine or masculine ending, it meant "wife" or "husband." Human symbiosis, then, refers to a "way of life" (Cf. Acts 26:4) enriched by common and productive interaction with the environment — *both* the natural and the social "world." Another way of expressing it might be "creative intimacy."

Symbiosis is thus an essentially social category, even on the level of simple plants and animals, among whom it is perhaps the closest approximation to true community. It means, quite simply, a shared life of devoted togetherness. Although not found as such in scripture, *symbion* was used in a specifically religious context by St. Polycarp, the disciple of St. John, in his letter to the Phillippians and is also found in the *Vision of Hermas*, a very early Christian work.

Christened *Symbion*, my program went along smoothly and successfully enough until a militant group surfaced in California calling itself the "Symbionese Liberation Army." How they selected the name still escapes me. But as the story of Patty Hearst and the SLA unfolded, the utility of the audio-visual program decreased and it, too, eventually went underground. However, the early Christian vision of a cosmic harmony recreated under the headship of Jesus, the "re-establishment" (*apokatastasis*) of the world, is no less relevant today and certainly no less needed.

Thanks are certainly due and hereby heartily rendered to Michael McCauley and Todd Brennan of the Thomas More Association for their guidance and patience in steering *Symbion* along in its initial voyage as a study series. I also wish to acknowledge the assistance and cooperation of the Dominican Province of St. Albert the Great and the Institute of Pastoral Studies at Loyola University of Chicago, especially Jerome O'Leary, O.P., then its director, for providing me freedom necessary to undertake this journey. Many others have helped me along the way: Sr. Teresa Bielecki, R.L. and Phyllis

8

Robinson, Mistress Aelflaed of Duckworth (Sandra Adams), Steward of the Society for Creative Anachronism, Dr. James Woods, Jr., and Matthew Fox, O.P., for their unflinching confidence and fraternal support. I wish most particularly to thank Mr. Steven Plane for his heroic service at what is to me the still-mysterious word processor on which the final draft of this book was prepared. The meek will indeed inherit what's left of the earth, but those open to the challenges of technological innovation will no doubt prepare the way.

SECTION ONE:
GROUNDWORK

ONE

Other Worlds

In 1977, two space craft were launched from this planet toward Saturn and Jupiter, out of whose powerful gravitational fields they will be flung toward the distant stars sometime after 1986. These Voyager probes carry on board a remarkable document—a record of civilized life on Earth devised as a greeting card to any life forms in the universe intelligent enough ever to intercept and decipher these messages. A product of the creative collaboration of astronomer Carl Sagan, his wife Linda, and a talented group of associates, each of the Voyager messages included sounds and music as well as pictures inscribed on a long-playing record.

In a variety of respects, the Voyager effort at interstellar communication underscores the spiritual crisis facing intelligent life forms on this planet—one which may, some thousands of millions of years from now, evoke a pang of compassion in some other creaturely breast. For among all the evidence of lofty technological and cultural achievements recorded for future assessment by Sagan and his team, there survived virtually no mention of God, the sacred or the religious dimension of human experience.

Two oblique references managed to slip by the screening process devised by the scientists. One was a statement by a African from South Uganda, Elijah Mwima-Mudeenya of Kampala, who said, "Greetings to all peoples of the universe. God give you peace."1/ The other was picture of the Taj Majal—a mosque, but "a monument not to religion, but to love, and thus (it) was an appealing choice."2/

Secular music of Bach, Mozart and Beethoven was included, along with jazz and mundane folk songs from around the globe. But there were no liturgical chorales,

Masses or oratorios; no Gregorian chant, no Negro spirituals; no hymns or native religious canticles. There was no religious art—the Last Supper, for instance, or Michelangelo's paintings from the Sistine Chapel, or the windows of Chartres, or an arabesque from the walls of the Alhambra, or an illumination from the Book of Kells. No Buddhist temple appears, no cathedral, synagogue or lamasery—only the Taj Majal, exempt because a monument to human, not divine, love. (A few gothic chapels did get by—in a picture of Oxford, England—probably because they are unrecognizable to anyone unfamiliar with that beautiful "City of Spires.")

Sagan excuses such pervasive neglect of humankind's highest aspirations and artistic achievements with an astonishing appraisal: "Why not include the houses of worship and artifacts of the three or four major religions? Because there at least a dozen and probably hundreds of major religions on the Earth, and elements of the omitted religions would very likely produce an outcry much more serious than any feared because of non-representation of some tradition of ethnic music."3/ Although the vast majority of the world's peoples are either Christian, Hindu, Buddhist or Muslim, there was room on board for lengthy statements by politicians and other "world leaders"—the President of the United States, a two-page list of senators and congressmen "associated" with NASA, the Secretary General of the United Nations and statements and even poems from fifteen UN delegates. There were none however from the Dalai Lama, the Pope, the Archbishop of Canterbury, the Ayatollah Khomeini, a Buddhist nun or a yogi. One wonders what Mother Teresa of Calcutta would have said, or, were he alive, Teilhard de Chardin.

Thus a monumental account of the product of thousands of years of social evolution on Earth has been sent to the stars lacking significant reference to our effort to respond to the most important questions of all: why are we here? What is the meaning of this vast cosmos? Is there something, indeed some One behind and yet beyond the mysteriously beckoning universe? Is it possible to communicate with such a Presence?

Also missing from the Voyager's records is any allusion to humankind's unique tendency, found almost everywhere on earth (excepting scientific laboratories, psychoanalysts' offices and war rooms): the will not only to ask hard questions, but to worship.

It is easy, of course, to fault scientists and engineers for religious and philosophical naivete. Theologians and metaphysicians are no less biased in their way, and they could hardly have launched a couple of Voyager rockets! But it is still worth considering the possible impact such a record of human civilization, devoid of indications of religious longing or achievement, might have on an advanced, alien civilization.

For instance, the hapless secularism of the Voyager probes ironically and fittingly became the butt of a cosmic joke in the film Star Trek: the Motion Picture. Having been swept up by a black hole and flung to the edge of the universe, one of the capsules encounters a "race" of purely mechanical but intelligent beings, who reprogram the space capsule and send it back "home" to report its findings and "become one with the creator." The Voyager has become a mystical machine with almost unlimited power and intelligence and a voracious appetite for unitive experience.

Consider another possibility:

The Reception Committee: A Space Fantasy

Galactic excitement mounted as the confederation's Supreme Council ended their intense debate concerning the fate of the newly discovered planetary civilization. Exceptionally stringent action had been urged by the joint military commanders. Yet cleansing an entire planet was a rare and extreme measure—so extraordinary that although allowed for by unanimous consent of the Council, no one could find a record of it having ever been executed. Yet this was no ordinary situation. No one could find a record of anything quite like it in galactic history.

Finally, Arch-president Xanthos presented himself by holograph to the expectant myriads of citizens tensed in anticipation of the long-awaited announcement.

"Peoples of the Galaxy: the Supreme Council has finally arrived at a decision regarding the third planet of the star system in the 197th sector, called Yrth by those who sent the exploratory vehicle we recently intercepted.

"This was truly one of the most serious and unusual encounters in the 200,000-year history of the confederation. From the evidence placed on board the spacecraft, it seems clear that a planetary civilization has developed with a total disregard for religion and a profound ignorance of the All-Holy. In every other galactic culture, religion occupies the highest place and embodies the most cherished aspirations known to living beings. Obviously, contact with a thoroughly atheistic civilization equipped with aggressive instincts as well as powerful weapons could be disastrous for the peace-loving and largely defenseless civilizations of the galactic confederacy.

"Strong arguments were pressed that total and immediate annihilation of this darkened planet would be the simplest and indeed the most merciful solution. Fortunately, its contamination has not yet spread.

"An alternative proposal suggested than an intensive educational campaign might conceivably overcome Yrth's grave and dangerous blindness. Given its apparent expansionist intentions, however, such a program could take far too long, even if successful—and there is no guarantee that missionary activity of this kind would in fact succeed.

"In the midst of these discussions, a small and previously overlooked item in the record of cultural artifacts and ambitions was brought to our attention by a language analyst. It might well represent evidence of a rudimentary or vestigial religious sense. The simple expression: 'God give you peace,' <u>could</u> point to a pervasive if tenuous belief in the providence of the All-Holy.

"Therefore exterminating the population of Yrth was ruled out for the time being, at least until it can be determined whether the sense of the All-Holy is increasing or decreasing. In the meantime, in order to prevent contamination one way or another, it has been decided to place Yrth under quarantine for 500 years.

"Although the pictures and sounds encoded and stored aboard the spacecraft were ostensibly an invitation to respond, it was decided that no communication of any kind be made with the inhabitants of planet Yrth. We can only be grateful that we intercepted this message before any actual contact was made. Further, no visitations will be permitted except for authorized investigative expeditions to determine the status of religious sensibility.

"For the sake of preserving universal harmony and concord, the inhabitants of Yrth must continue for the indefinite future to work out their spiritual destiny in ignorance of and isolation from all other intelligent life forms in the universe."

–O–

Still another scenario might involve the dilemma of a far-distant civilization which, like ours, had waited hopefully for perhaps thousands of years for a word from "beyond." Faced with the misfortunes of existence, with mysteries concerning the origin of the universe and its end, the problem of evil, possibilities of transcendence, the challenge of finitude and death, the quest for meaning—would not these <u>religious</u> stirrings provide a key item in the recognition of kindred spirits, evidence of higher forms of concern? We might even have some Good News for them.

Again, if we intercepted a record similar to that on the Voyagers describing the civilization of an alien world devoid of religious values, beliefs and customs, as well as "artifacts," would we welcome such beings willingly into our homes? Consider the vast uneasiness of the American people confronted merely by the expressed atheism of "godless Communism" in the U.S.S.R., Cuba and elsewhere. Our earthly xenophobia would hardly fare better when translated into stellar terms!

But perhaps the scientists among these intelligent creatures, like our own, would merely be reticent and even embarrassed by the irrepressible religious instincts of their people. What then? Would there be time enough to discover a mutual bondedness before we decided whether or not to have each other as dinner?

And, finally, what if the religion of the "aliens" (us or them) was itself repugnant to those making contact, much as happened on this planet when Catholic Romans met heathen Gauls and Saxons, or Spaniards fell upon the Incas, Aztecs and Mexica or Protestants encountered the "idolatrous" Mohicans and Hawaiians? Could there be wars of persecution such as have bloodied this globe for centuries as Hindus, Assyrians, Moslems, Romans, Jews, Protestants and Catholics butchered each other in the name of the God who is love?

Perhaps it is just as well that Carl Sagan "edited" the sections on religion out of his records. Perhaps we had better get our own temples, mosques, basilicas, synagogues and meeting houses in order before we start preaching to the star-dwellers. Perhaps this is, after all, the real crisis of contemporary civilizations: how is it possible to be a religious person today. . . and more importantly, tomorrow?

For, unlike Sagan, I believe that in spite of its misapprehensions, religion is a strategically important component of a viable pattern of life and, in fact, will become more so in the future. Significantly, at the World Future Society's First Global Conference on the Future held in Toronto in July, 1980, fifteen presentations were specifically devoted to religion as a force for a more humane future. Even in other presentations, religion was frequently cited as a major influence on future lifestyles. For example, William O. Comboy, professor of speech communications and human relations at the University of Kansas, Lawrence, observed that the public itself considers religion to be one of the five most powerful forces in shaping the course of society. (The others are government, business, education and technology.) During the conference as a whole, Thomas Merton and Teilhard de Chardin were frequently mentioned as leading religious "futurists."

Future Focus

Social scientists, philosophers and a scattering of theologians have increasingly concentrated on studies of the future in order to illuminate the present situation. These "futurists," such as the five thousand who gathered that July in Toronto, realize that unless we begin now to plan responsibly and humanely for the next century, millions of people will not only fall prey to unprecedented ecological cataclysms and human-made disasters, there may be no future for the majority of them at all.

For the first time in human history, .ııs generation has been able to rise sufficiently abovє the social process itself to be able to perceive that process in its broad outlines and to exercise a measure of control over its workings, even to give it some direction. Our attempts have so far been largely fumbling, but it is clear that we now have (or shortly will have) the capacity consciously to redirect the course of history. This may be the most evident proof of the essential difference between human beings and other living creatures on this planet.

Scientific research has already provided an amazing range of constructive technological advances in critical areas of life. Deadly diseases once rampant throughout the world, such as smallpox, have been eradicated. Agricultural breakthroughs promise sufficient food for all the world's peoples. New forms of cheap and ecologically responsible energy sources are being developed which can open up undreamed-of possibilities for all of humankind. Accelerating electronic communications developments have made world-wide exchange and education possible.

What science and its technological application have not done, and perhaps will never do, is to provide the will freely to share the benefits of "modernity" with all peoples everywhere. Science and technology can devise new and ever more frightful weapons of war, but they cannot invent a tool for making peace and justice. The realm of human decisions, values, prejudices, beliefs, fears and ideas has proved to be impervious—sometimes dangerously so—to progressive innovation. If anything, new weapons of destruction have made the old hatreds more lethal.

It is quite probable as a consequence that only a revolution in human values can prevent mutually assured destruction within two decades. That these are the stakes seems clear to most futurists. But such a return to human dignity, freedom, creativity, justice and love as the heritage of all Earth's children can only be achieved by the development of an "appropriate technology"—of the spirit. That is to say, a mystical spirituality for the future, as an effective return to the presence of God among us, with its behavioral implications for the natural and social world.

Breaks with the Past

Among the other valuable insights about the future found in Pauwels and Bergier's prophetic 1963 book, The Morning of the Magicians, was the prediction that the future will be more like the past, even the ancient past, than it will resemble the present. Perhaps the most important lesson we have to learn about our contemporary situation as it hurtles us with increasing velocity toward the future is that rapid social change, as a function of fundamental shifts in basic technology, creates a sense of abrupt discontinuity with the past.

As the recent development of "catastrophy theory" shows, apparently unprecedented, sudden and dramatic change is not without antecedent conditions, nor is it totally unpredictable—if we know what to look for! The fact is that most abrupt shifts in our lives, collectively and particularly, occur seemingly without warning—seemingly because we are not attentive to the signals of coming change. We do not know how to read the signs of the times, as Jesus noted so long ago. Thus, we experience the onset of a cold, for instance, as a sudden realization that we are already ill, even though, in hindsight, we realize that we were dimly aware of it before the state of our bodily indisposition crossed the threshold of conscious awareness.

Friedrich Engels described this curious tendency of slowly accumulating changes to erupt suddenly into consciousness in his famous "law" which states that increasing quantitative changes will become manifest as a qualitative change when a point of critical transformation is reached. Thus, as water is heated, there is little apparent change until just before the boiling point is reached, when the pot explodes into activity. Similarly, a supersaturated solution will crystallize almost instantaneously after a long period of apparent inactivity. In both cases, undetected incremental change suddenly produces drastic transformation. It is important to note that the threshold of state-change is also a threshold of "visibility" or consciousness.

In society, too, small but powerful changes accumulate incrementally and thus unobserved until a critical mass is reached and a chain reaction occurs, sometimes as a panic, a riot or a revolt. On a less dramatic scale, fundamental changes in the way people think, behave and value things can suddenly crystallize into new patterns of activity and consciousness, a "paradigm shift" which is the result of an apparently total reorganization of our models of life. Physiologically, something like this happens at puberty and menopause.

A major paradigm shift in society can produce a profound sense of discontinuity—a sudden break with the past is often very disconcerting. Many social scientists and most futurists believe that we are undergoing such a massive paradigm shift today, especially in the West.

Anomie and Spirituality

Some years ago, Peter Drucker pointed to discontinuity as a cardinal feature of our era. Links with the familiar past grow tenuous under pressure from an ever-increasing rate of technological change. When these links break, or appear to, we are left with an aching sense of disconnectedness, facing a future shorn of customary traditions and routines.

At such moments, we become painfully aware of our need for rootedness. It is not by chance that just as the Mormons became preoccupied with tracing genealogies after their explicit break with traditional Christianity in the nineteenth century, Americans in the late twentieth century have become preoccupied with rediscovering their roots. The success of Alex Haley's book of that name testifies to the power of our sense of connection, especially when confronted by the forces of discontinuity.

There can be little doubt that the world as a whole is facing a variety of crises that threaten every previously held belief, value and pattern of behavior. As the future bears down on us, political and moral confusion already abound. Economies totter and collapse. Terrorism, assassination and coups strike right and left alike. Religious values are severely challenged in the Middle East, Northern Ireland, Africa, Southeast Asia, China and elsewhere. Worldwide pollution threatens all peoples with increasing disease and misery. New epidemics, such as Legionnaires' Disease, worry the medical profession with the spectre of global plague spread by jet transportation. Widespread famine threatens the world's poor while spiraling inflation further depletes their meager savings (if any) and even the rich feel imperilled. Democracies form strange alliances with dictatorships. Novel forms of communication, transportation and calculation have created whole new industries, professions and pastimes. Overpopulation and mass migration, some of it the grim harvest of "small" wars, result in serious problems of dislocation.

We scarcely have time to adjust to one crisis when another is upon us with the force of what Alvin Toffler called "future shock"—endangered nuclear reactors, terrorist hostages, wayward signals in our "defense" system, drought, exploding nuclear missile sites, even earthquakes, hurricanes and volcanic eruptions. We suffer from what another perceptive critic called "rapidation" a decade ago.

The psychological effect of the perceived breakdown of traditional ways and means of achieving social goals is known in social science as anomie. A French word introduced by Emile Durkheim at the turn of the century, "anomie" is based, in turn, on the Greek word anomos, which literally means "lawless." It is found, for instance, in the writings of the Evangelist, St. John.

Unlike St. John, Durkheim and his followers implied no moral judgment by anomie. They used it to refer to a depressing and dread-filled sense of normlessness, a loss of standards and values, which in turn manifests itself in various forms of "coping" strategies. For the basic question facing a society in the throes of rapid and profound changes which seriously stress its goals and values and the traditional ways of realizing them, is, like that of the passengers and crew of a storm-wrecked ship, one of <u>survival.</u>

Concretely speaking, what do we need in terms of a contemporary spirituality in order to survive the chaos of the present situation? There is no simple answer. But in general, it strikes me that as members of a planetary society, we need what we have always needed in less global crises: a renewed sense of purpose and meaning in life, hope for the future, an ability to laugh, play and celebrate, a strong awareness of community bonded-ness, the capacity to create and enjoy, freedom from dire want and disease, the opportunity to participate freely in decisions determining how we shall live together, access to education, the chance to work, to love, to share the fruit of our labor with others in peace and without fear of oppression and, not least, the power to experience personal transcendence in moments of reflective awareness and active worship of God.

<u>How</u> we can preserve and fulfill the deepest values and highest aspirations that have motivated humankind through its pilgrimage toward the future in the face of declining resources, battered economies and similar en-tropic forces, and do so <u>well,</u> is the concern of the following chapters. It <u>can</u> be <u>done,</u> I think. And not least by occasionally <u>retrieving</u> lessons from the distant past to help us through uncertain moments to come. This is, in fact, a requirement of a truly contemporary spiri-tuality, as Pauwels and Bergier realized twenty years ago: ". . .as a preliminary to understanding the present, one must be capable able of projecting one's intelligence far into the past and far into the future."<u>4/</u>

TWO

Environment and Spirit

The human spirit is the candle of the Lord.
—Proverbs 31:19

Several years ago, an advertisement for the film Zardoz aptly expressed the sense of malaise that has recently gripped most of us as we look toward the closing decades of the twentieth century: "I have seen the future. And it doesn't work."

Of course, we can "see" the future only as a projection of the present based on our understanding of the past. Moreover, unpredictable surprises will always change the actual future from its imagined form, despite sometimes unusually perceptive prognostications by prophets and creative writers such as Jules Verne. But, as we shall see in the next chapter, unlike Verne, who was blessed with an optimistic belief in progress, his literary descendents often seem to be a gloomy lot as they peer ahead—from George Orwell's 1984 and Aldous Huxley's Brave New World to the even bleaker prospects forecast by Jacques Ellul, Harlan Ellison and others. Whatever surprises lie ahead, they warn us, are as likely as not to be unpleasant.

Time's Riddle

As a projection of contemporary fears and hopes, the future does not really exist. We are largely frightened by the vision of our responsibility for present decisions, power and action (or inaction) in terms of future implications. And a growing chorus of voices seems to be telling us that we should be afraid.

In the present era, they say, humankind is already entering upon the greatest crisis of its history, the full magnitude of which will be comparable, perhaps, to the

Great Flood of prehistorical or mythological memory. As with the Flood, moreover, we are bringing this crisis upon ourselves, as much by foolishness as by our sins. Fire from heaven may be the way our punishment will be recalled in some distant, post-historical myth. But there may be no myth. The desolation of Mars may presage the future of Earth. For like the Flood, the present crisis endangers not only the future of the human race on this planet, but that of other animals as well and even of plant life.

The present crisis is total because it is environmental: it affects every aspect of life on this planet. And because the crisis is environmental, the issues concerning spirituality as a way toward a possible future are also environmental. They deal with our manifold connections with social and natural elements and forces throughout the world. However, the primary question an environmental spirituality must face is whether a religious approach to life has in fact anything worthwhile to offer the future of this planet. Can religious awareness converted into action make a positive difference? An affirmative answer is by no means obvious.

For instance, even religious enthusiasts of Carl Sagan's spectacular television series Cosmos failed to note that his opening definition of the cosmos itself—"all there ever was, or is or ever shall be"—neatly excludes from the discussion both God and the religious dimension of human experience. For the truly secular humanist such as Sagan, there is neither God nor Spirit nor anything else in the universe than cannot be reduced to matter and energy. In such a vision of reality, what else could religion or spirituality contribute except mystification?

Materialism, humanistic or otherwise, is undoubtedly one of the "principles of this world" that sorely vex the spirit today. The atheistic premise is easily swallowed along with the pretty pictures and special effects. But sooner or later, the hook of despair will be set.

The alternative thesis—one espoused here—is that only the recognition of the spiritual nature of the human person and society, together with the disciplined cultivation of that spiritual dimension, will make a future worth living humanly possible. To be able to do so, such a disciplined attitude must address the major aspects of the overall environmental crisis, both social and natural. It must look unflinchingly ahead as well as back to the familiar past. Thus, rather than hairshirts, flagellation, pilgrimages and the hyper-development of particular habits or "virtues" dictated by the necessities of monastic life, the "new asceticism" will inculcate the appropriate attitudes, values and behavior that alone can enable modern humankind to survive collectively what Robert Vacco calls "the coming dark age."

The Candle of the Lord

"Spirit" and "spirituality" are commonplace words today, even among technocrats and scientists with no particular religious bent or belief. One of the cardinal purposes of the messages placed aboard the Voyager spacecraft, we are told, was "to expand the human spirit."1/ Likewise, as Dr. Harold Bloomfield recently observed in regard to health care, "Within holistic medicine, spirit is a pragmatic concept, not religious or mystical. Holism implies that human life is more than the sum of mental-emotional states, such as thoughts, perceptions and feelings, and physical parts, such as brain, heart and intestines. Spirit refers to that which gives meaning and direction to your life."2/

"Spirituality" is not itself a biblical concept. The word was coined by French theologians only a few centuries ago to refer to what St. Francis de Sales called "the devout life." To the Greek Fathers, it was "mystical theology." To the theologians of the Middle Ages, it was simply the Christian Life as a whole. But "Spirit" has a far more ancient history, indeed a religious and mystical one. Our familiar word comes from the Latin spiritus, which meant "breath" or, more simply, "wind."

From the most ancient times, these words—associated because they both were forms of air—were used to symbolize (and sacrament) the highest value in the cosmos, life itself—the life of God as well. (We still speak of "getting a second wind" or a "spirited" horse.)

It was spirit-ruach in Hebrew—that hovered over the formless void in Genesis 1:2 (cf. Acts 2:2). The same word was used for "wind" some ninety times in the Hebrew bible. But it is because God breathes into the human form he has made that it becomes a living being (Gen. 2:7).

In the Greek translation of the Hebrew bible, the Septuagint, ruach was translated by the Greek word pneuma some 232 times, which is not surprising since pneuma, also, literally meant "wind" and "breath," surviving in such English words as pneumatic and pneumonia. But when used of human beings, pneuma like ruach meant in theological terms "that in virtue of which man is open to and transmits the life of God (Rom. 8:16, cf. I Cor 2:10f.) . . ."3/ Similarly, in recent times, the Jewish philosopher Martin Buber referred to the human spirit as the capacity for relationship. Even earlier this century, the American religious thinker William Ernest Hocking described the unique human character as "openness to experience." Karl Rahner's interpretation of the medieval concept of "obediential potency" is similar.

All these descriptions point to the peculiarly human capacity for receptivity and transcendence—a radical receptivity toward others, including pre-eminently the Other, the ground and field of all experience, and, as well, an equally radical ability to reach beyond ourselves, to "go out" to others in love and trust.

Spirit, then, is the basis of all human society—not only with other human beings, but with all of creation and, ultimately, with the Creator. Spirit is the ecological principle par excellence.

Spirituality, consequently, refers first to the most fundamental character of a human person, the radical quality of being spirit, spiritual. Second, spirituality also means the whole constellation of beliefs, values, attitudes and behavior connected with that unique character as it appears in human experience, especially in the collective traditions of a community or a people. Thirdly, spirituality most specifically means the concrete and historical forms of life articulated by religious leaders and teachers such as the Buddha, Jesus, Shankara, St. Francis of Assisi, St. Teresa of Avila, and Mother Teresa of Calcutta, and followed by their disciples. Finally, from a developmental perspective, acquiring or cultivating "a" spirituality can most easily be understood as the way in which a person activates the radical human capacity for transcendent receptivity in actual encounters in the world or nature and society. This includes the particular way in which individuals embody a specific spiritual tradition, such as Hinduism, in their own unique situation.

The most "real" spirituality is thus found in concrete human experience—yours and mine—as we enter the age-long dialogue with our predecessors on our way to the future. In less formal terms, spirituality means how we live, the quality of our life as we apply religious insight to our day-to-day situation in the world. It is not, however, merely concerned with issues of good and evil, or avoiding sin and acquiring virtue, as morality is. It is not preoccupied with prayer and ritual, such as liturgy is. It is not speculative or focussed on the intellectual content of dogmas, such as systematic theology is.

Spirituality is concerned with all of these things to some extent, but only in so far as they bear on our life as we live it. Further, there are as many spiritualities in this sense as there are people conscious of their responsibility to integrate their lives in reference to God's self-gift as our Creator, Redeemer and Destiny, as the underlying Presence of our lives. We can speak, therefore, of the spirituality of housewives and truck drivers, or college professors and cloistered nuns, of school children and prisoners. Spirituality is always concrete, personal and situational. It is also developmental. It changes as we do. The spirituality of a fifteen-year-old is inadequate for a fifty-year-old.

Forces and Vectors

As a matter of daily life experience, spirituality is susceptible to the manifold pressures and forces of the world around us. . .and within us. But in two respects, contemporary culture, our world, intrudes upon the spirit differently from that of all previous periods in world history. The first is the incredible density and variety of information we are constantly bombarded with. The second is the speed with which it occurs. Nevertheless, boredom is also a fundamental problem in our society, especially among the young. A sense of particular and national purpose escapes our grasp. Swamped with high-speed information, commercial messages, driving disco and rock music, frustrating and confusing news reports, we are people in search of our souls, as Carl Jung realized fifty years ago.

The struggle to attain a sense of wholeness has never been more difficult or more desperate. The temptation to capitulate to the forces impinging upon us is strong—to allow ourselves to be shaped by the communications media particularly in our ideas, attitudes, values and behavior. Twenty-five years ago and more, Bishop John Robinson cited this struggle as the dominant issue of a future spirituality. In referring to Maisie Ward's study of de-Christianized France, he noted, "The powers of the individual to act, or even to think, to any significant degree in independence of or against his social milieu are constantly being reduced."[4] He goes on to say, "The redemption of man today means his release to become, not an individual—for in independence he is powerless in the face of the giant State—but a person, who may find rather than lose himself in the interdependence of the community."[5]

These sobering statements amply illustrate a central feature of spirituality easily overlooked in the past: its essential social character. All spirituality represents an unavoidable transaction between the particular individual and the social group, whether we recognize it or not. If we do not recognize it, we are inevitably shaped by our culture, becoming little more than passive embodiments of its values, behavior, ideas and beliefs. If, however, we recognize the elements and process of social determination, we can to some degree disengage ourselves from their control and take command of the course of our life.

Thus we will either develop a spirituality or we will reflect one, that of our social group. There is no middle ground short of madness. Even the creation of an explicit personal spirituality will inevitably reflect social factors. The main difference involves the amount of choice we exercise concerning our life-pattern: which cultural elements we deliberately incorporate or reject, and how the way or style we elect shall shape the contours of our history. That story will ultimately reveal itself to be a vector, the combined result of competing forces of socialization and individuation.

Sadness and Hope

There are various avenues to a renewed sense of God's presence in the tasks and trials as well as the joys of everyday life in an increasingly jittery world. The first and indispensible requirement among all of them is waking up, becoming and staying alive to the real possibilities of a future worth living, possibilities both promising and problematic.

One of the most powerfully deadening forces of the principalities and powers who originate the darkness of this world (Eph. 6:12) is despair. This is not merely depression, but a cosmic pathology of the spirit which numbs the whole person. It is the anxious sense of dread (angst) anticipated by Kierkegaard in the last century and explored by Heidegger and Sartre in our own. The soul-eating disease of modern life, it is closely related to the sense of anomie described above, the felt awareness of the breakdown of social goals and means. Apathy, a passive surrender to inexorable decay, is one of the more likely consequences of anomic disintegration.

This listless attitude, a dulling of both mind and body, was called akedia by the ancient Greeks. In Christian times, it was rendered acedia in Latin and later, accidie in medieval English. By that time, it was associated with excessive ascetical practices such as fasting, wearing hairshirts and scourging oneself, behavior itself often the likely product of pervasive anxiety, ataraxia. Accidie, boredom, was sometimes also identified with the "cardinal" sin of sloth, a kind of sadness by which someone becomes sluggish (tardus) in spiritual activities because of bodily weariness.6/ Today, one reason for our frustration and boredom is the sensory and mental overload we inevitably experience from exposure to constant information, noise and pressure. The freshness of things increasingly escapes our attention. Social relationships are easily strained and quickly broken. Divorce, spouse- and child-abuse, alcoholism and drug addiction contaminate our efforts to achieve personal and social harmony.

Routine and monotony are not alleviated by the heightened tempo of the noise around us. One film is like another. Television still wanders in its vast wasteland of the spirit and mind. Our fears and insecurities are fed by incessant news reports on the latest crises here and abroad—about which we can do nothing. The resulting depression which tends to immobilize so many of us as we look ahead toward seemingly ever-bleaker possibilities and threatening catastrophies thus stems less from exaggerated austerity than the powerlessness engendered by inadequate spiritual resources in the face of constant and overwhelming stimulation. Even Russian roulette can become boring if the chamber spins indefinitely but the revolver never fires. Our dilemma is global, moreover;

we have placed nuclear warheads in our revolvers.

The anxious sadness of contemporary despair can be
defined, as Savary and Berne suggest, as "the loss of the
assumption that you (or the human species) will ever
pull through. It is awareness of the possibility that the
'experiment' that is you (or the planet) may fail."7/
Such a mood can be passing, as when I note the loss of
some of the lesser treasures of life—private spaces,
public walks, hidden glades, fine buildings, the thousands of subtle idiosyncrasies that make up cultural
particularity and a sense of identity. The conversion
from the English to the metric system, while a gain in
uniformity and therefore ease, speed and interdependence, is also a loss of diversity and therefore richness.
The sadness with which some of my Welsh friends
describe the progressive erosion of their language and
customs is genuinely moving. For many people, the loss
of Latin from the Mass or of Jacobean English from the
Book of Common Prayer was a similar tragedy.

Such commonplace elements of our lives, once as
familiar and remarkable as the air we breathe, become
visible in all their fragile vulnerability when their
threatened demise illuminates the nature of "progress."
Similarly, the loss of a rare species of cactus in New
Mexico, or of a wildflower in Indiana, the timber wolf
or the great whales—all speak of the tragic dimension
of temporal existence and human insecurity. Yet the
reprieve of the little fish known as the snail darter,
imperilled by the construction of an unneeded dam,
represents a signal triumph of the human spirit. There
is still room for hope.

The sun breaks through. The moon suddenly illuminates
what moments before were just snow drifts, creating a
million glittering crystals. Spring brings an unexpected
blossom to our attention. A bird sings. A friend calls
from across the country just to say hello. A child's
artwork light up a wall. Our hearts leap and throats

constrict in the last five seconds of a hard-fought Olympic hockey game. The world comes alive.

And there are what William Ernest Hocking called "unlosables"—values, traditions, events—specific items which will survive as long as human beings preserve civilization itself—Handel's Messiah at Christmas, vast dragons dancing for the Chinese New Year, the Taj Majal. But even these treasures are vulnerable to decay, and if they are not actively preserved, they, too, will die. And here lies the point. We must appreciate before we can act responsibly, and to appreciate, we must care. Preservation and prevention are human qualities as deep as innovation and departure.

Thus, as we witness a plethora of books and programs about coming global catastrophies, we can be rendered more and more desperate, more depressed, less able to do anything. Anger can help. When people get to the point where they cannot take "it" anymore, they can fight back and break through the psychological barricades of immobility. But angry activity is short-term and hazardous, and often counter-productive. The alternative is a creative breakthrough with constructive intent and positive results.

Jung was right, of course. The true crisis of the modern world is a crisis in spirituality, the loss of soul. How is it possible for us to regain our souls? To become—and remain—open and to grow in a world seemingly calculated to turn us into robots? Another way of putting it is how can the reality of God's presence affect my everyday life? What can I do to become more aware of that presence and allow it to become more effective in my attitudes and behavior?

Toward a New Asceticism: the Ecology of the Spirit

The answer to the malaise of civilization is a spirituality of deep caring and willingness to act, even to sacrifice, in order to protect and enhance what matters most and to let the rest go. Our new asceticism must be a remedy for accidie, not its prolongation. It must help us "cleanse the doors of perception." It must free us from the boring dullness of spiritual torpor and enable us to act, not in anger or frustration, but in full awareness of our responsibility and our power to succeed.

Long a suspect word in the Protestant lexicon, in recent years "asceticism" has received a largely and deservedly bad press even among Catholic spiritual writers, especially those nurtured on ascetical theology before the Second Vatican Council.

Ascetical comes from the Greek askesis, which meant the training or discipline of Olympic athletes. In the early Church, spiritual askesis was attributed to the "athletes of Christ"—the "champions" who, deprived of martyrdom, attempted to develop themselves to the fullness of their abilities as witnesses to the Faith, often by exacting and even heroic "exercises."

We smile today, if perhaps a little lamely, when we look back at these patristic Arnold Schwarzeneggers of the spirit. But we do not smile at the remembrance of an asceticism that was artificial, largely irrelevant to ordinary life, uniform, picayune, and very often a covert form of social manipulation. Our spiritual training for the future must be vastly different if it is to equip us to care deeply and act responsibly in a world growing ever more tense and confused. Such "asceticism" must be more like the development of the skilled control of the artist, the scientist, the craftsperson, the athlete. It will have to be, first of all, self-discipline—not egoistic or masochistic self-absorption, but the cultivation of inner resources and skills needed for effective living in the coming years, including psychological stamina. This in turn requires positive self-control—not just restraint, but the ability to think and act with purpose and a measure of immunity to what will be increasingly stronger pressures to conform, to adopt unconsciously the dominant values, norms, and patterns of behavior fostered by commercial interests and enforced by mass communications media. Being physically "in shape" is a necessary condition, for such physical fitness is easily depleted. A viable spirituality for the future will begin with our "bodied" situation and never lose sight of its priority.

Such a spirituality will also take us beyond individualism. It will become increasingly less appropriate in coming years to speak of "my" spiritual development or concerns. If we do not grow together as a community, "I" will neither develop nor likely even survive, much less flourish. The social dimension of spirituality will be practical and largely physical, moreover—energy conservation, joint projects such as producing and preserving food, and other forms of bodily collaboration.

The age of individualism, rugged or squeamish, is over. As in ancient Greece and Rome, spiritual self-preoccupation is possible only for the rich, well-born and powerful because the liberal accomplishments of aristocratic societies rested on the collective misery of the masses. In the future, any spirituality which is not essentially egalitarian and democratic will have little to offer Christians hoping to be free. As Meister Eckhart preached six centuries ago, in Christ all are now aristocrats of the spirit.

Every authentic human discipline is a training program for further excellence. And all of them have both a negative and positive side—renunciation and concentration. Spirituality is no exception. Non-essentials, irrelevancies, "fat," must be trimmed away before it is possible to develop desired capabilities and talents. The "negative way" precedes and for a time accompanies the "positive way." And there is always need for "refresher courses."

In each of the "ascetical" areas we will explore in the following chapters—food, crafts, music and others—we will thus consider both the need for "detachment," for clearing, as well as the need for reattachment or focussing. Here, as elsewhere, William Ernest Hocking's

34

"ascetical principle" will guide our journey: all detachment is for the sake of reattachment, all turning away
is also a turning toward.

THREE

Future Watching: Utopia and Apocalypse

When the High Lama asked him whether Shangri-La was not unique in his experience, and if the Western world contained anything like it, he answered with a smile: "Well—yes to be quite frank it reminds me very slightly of Oxford."

—James Hilton,
Lost Horizon

As the tense first year of the eighties ended, predictions of grim times ahead seemed to dominate the publishing industry. Titles such as How to Prosper During the Coming Bad Years and The Third World War: August 1985 were pushed aside on best-seller lists by The Coming Currency Collapse, The Coming Real Estate Crash and Jeremy Rifkin's gloomy Entropy.

Something of a balance was struck by the appearance of Marilyn Ferguson's The Aquarian Conspiracy, Alvin Toffler's The Third Wave and Kirkpatrick Sale's Human Scale. Even Rifkin expressed a guarded sense of hope, as had Theodore Roszak in Person/Planet. Overall, however, the enduring literary impression was that the calamities predicted in 1971 by Roberto Vacca in The Coming Dark Age were not far off. The electrical failure that blacked out over 100,000 square miles of the American West just then did not provide much of a counter omen. (Vacca's premonition of the imminent collapse of large technological systems was written in the wake of the devastating New England blackout of 1956.)

At the same time, the hands of the famous "doomsday clock" on the cover of the Bulletin of the Atomic

Scientists moved closer to the zero-hour of nuclear war than at any time since 1953. It had become alarmingly evident, moreover, that such a war could be detonated by a minor systems failure such as that which had darkened Utah. Two of these nuclear "accidents" had been narrowly avoided only months before.

Godspel and Badspel

Future projections have generally tended to fall into two very distinct camps: optimistic or pessimistic. By and large, however, the future seems to have been foreseen as bad news rather than good news. Today, increasingly weightly issues still divide observers into highly polarized schools of thought. But it has become increasingly unlikely with each successive forecast that we can predict a future of bliss or woe on the basis of accumulated facts or the logic of argument alone. However, we need not be able to decide in advance who is right to benefit from the serious work of these experts. Furthermore, as we attempt to chart a way ahead that is both sane and humanely Christian, it is well to bear in mind that the tendency to foresee doom as well as to "hope against hope" is not entirely an assessment of real futures. It is equally or even more a way of describing our present situation and the immediate past in terms of goals, values and aspirations. Thus our prognostications are a reflection of our spirituality, as has generally been the case over the brief centuries of recorded history.

Tenses: Present, Past and Future Perfect

Inflection is one of the more fascinating aspects of language in that it gives us power over time. Irrelevant as that might seem, our ability to think, speak and write in terms of the past and the future establishes the basis of imagination and the theological virtue of hope, as well as guilt, remorse and the possibility of repentance and conversion, that is, of change.

By talking about what was, what could have been, and what will or even might be, we illuminate our present situation as both rooted in the past and laden with future consequences. Thus how we talk about our concrete history, imaginatively construed, also suggests how we are liable to behave in the future. This curious human tendency is seen most easily in our irrepressible urge to tell stories, and its deeper correlative, myth-making.

When we delight a child by intoning "Once upon a time," even if we pretend to be talking about a galaxy long ago and far away, we are engaged in creating realities alternative to our present situation and therefore suggesting further possible courses of action. On the other hand, the adventures of Luke Skywalker appeal to a new generation of youngsters because he is, as Joseph Conrad would say, one of us. He lives in another universe, yet he embodies in a special way something possibly tenuous, obscure and fleeting, but nevertheless something of ours. Perhaps our hopes and dreams, perhaps an awareness of our ultimate situation, being caught up in a titanic struggle between good and evil on some level of development we only dimly perceive.

Among adolescents and young adults, the increased popularity of epic fantasy and heroic romance—the Lord of the Rings, the tales of Conan the Barbarian, the whole gamut of "sword and sorcery" diversions from pulp fiction to elaborate, sometimes computerized games of "Dungeons and Dragons"—points in the same direction. They involve us in a past that never was and a future that never will be—except as an intimation of our own sense of place (or displacement) in a scheme of things only remotely like the secure world of our own real history. By so doing, however, they open up new realms of human potential—not all of it necessarily beneficial. But overall, creative fantasy, like fairy tales, is a constructive way of dealing with possibilities, an especially valuable pastime in a era of severe social stress.

The Vision of Camelot: Myth Maketh Man

Myth-making is a more profound form of storytelling in which a people, rather than a particular person, tell their own story in symbolic form. As a group endeavor, the story belongs to everyone and thus to no single individual. It exists outside the time-frame of a single life and thus has often seemed almost eternal. But as a collective product, myths change in time, as they are retold to meet new challenges to a people's sense of identity and destiny.

The story of King Arthur is such a myth—based in fact on a real historical figure, but elaborated over the centuries far beyond the original events in order to satisfy other purposes. Like all myths, the story of Camelot and the Vision of the Grail, together with the older legends of Arthur and the Knights of the Round Table, tell us (at least us Western Europeans) something about who we are and what we would be. It describes a "Golden Age" in which justice, friendship and peace flourished, and how that great achievement was destroyed by envy, ambition and betrayal. Like its great prototype, the Garden of Eden, it ends with the promise of a new Golden Age, a return to what was. For Arthur—the "once and future king"—would come again in our greatest hour of peril. And we will regain what we had lost.

In truth, Arthur has returned again and again, as his story was told and retold century after century in ever new guises to remind us of that noble dream. It was apt and tragically moving that the short presidency of John F. Kennedy was interpreted even before his death as a version of Camelot, which was not by chance the title of a popular musical of that era and one of Kennedy's personal favorites. With his whole complex of faults and virtues, John Kennedy was indeed an "Arthur Redivivus."

This example of a contemporary embodiment of myth illustrates other features besides the theme of the Golden Age—whether in the past or in the future or both. It shows us the danger of power and the bane that follows greatness. In most of the great myths that tell of the origin and destiny of peoples, there is a tragic crisis which dooms the characters (and us, their progeny) to wander all but trackless in the wreckage of a once grace-filled Creation. Here, in one form or another, is the human predicament—the longing for a pleroma, a "filled-time" of peace and plenty in the midst of a struggle to maintain a grip on decency, sanity and sufficiency. But remembering who we are in terms of who we were helps us to prepare for who we will be, or can be: the Children of God, living happily ever after in the New Jerusalem.

Such myths, stories and legends have come to embody elements of a distinctive kind of literature over the ages, one which is profoundly spiritual, though often unrecognized as such. For it illuminates the character and aspirations of peoples in often deceptively simply symbols and dramatic episodes. This type of literature, which includes some of the world's most cherished stories, has both apocalyptic and utopian elements. A late marriage of the two within the last century has generated two new forms, science fiction and epic fantasy. All are important spiritual methods of assessing the present in terms of the future conceived of as an imaginary past. All also incorporate both optimistic and pessimistic elements, godspel and badspel, balanced in dramatic and sometimes theological tension. A brief glance at both the older and younger forms will help us frame our inquiry as we begin our investigation of a spirituality for a possible future.

Visions of Doom and Triumph

Apocalyptic literature developed out of Israel's longing for the eventual establishment of the Kingdom of God. Since the mid-nineteenth century, it has been the domain of a branch of theology called eschatology, from the Greek words meaning "discourse on the last things." Conventionally, eschatology deals with death, judgment, hell and heaven, that is, the final destiny of each person, more significantly, the human race as whole and, indeed, all of Creation. As it began, however, eschatology meant the particular way in which Judaism understood the future with regard to its present distress.

Most scripture scholars believe that apocalyptic literature developed out of the eschatological preaching of the prophets after the era of official prophecy ended with the fall of Jerusalem in 587/6 BC. The earliest examples are found in portions of Isaiah (13, 24-27), Ezekiel 38 and 39, Amos 5 and 9, Zephaniah, Zechariah, Joel and especially Daniel 12 and 13. The function of apocalyptic, like the mission of the exilic prophets, was to strengthen the Jews in times of persecution, particularly that of the Graeco-Syrian Seleucid dynasty which attempted to extirpate Judaism in the second century BC, provoking the great Maccabean Revolt of 165 BC

The major apocalypses of this period are part of a huge mass of literature that was not incorporated into the Jewish or Christian canons of Scripture, including the Books of Enoch, 4 Ezra, the Assumption of Moses, Jubilees, the Ascension of Isaiah, and 2 and 3 Baruch. Apocalyptic elements are also found in the synoptic gospels (Mt. 24 and 25, Mark 13 and Luke 21) and in the epistles, notably I Cor. 15, 2 Thessalonians, 2 Peter and Jude. But the Book of Revelation (the Apocalypse) is the major and only complete work of this genre in the New Testament. It is believed to have been written to encourage Christians suffering under Nero's persecution. (There were many non-canonical apocalypses then as now, of course. The Qumran scrolls, first discovered in 1947, contain a number of important apocalyptic fragments which have shed light on the Essenes and other Jewish sects of this period.)

Basically, apocalyptic literature attempts to strengthen hope in God's providence and the eventual triumph of his people over their enemies. The central theme is contained in a highly symbolic revelation (hence the name—apocalypsis means "revelation") concerning the future which is granted to a seer such as Daniel or John—important figures from a preceding age of faith. Since apocalypses are usually set in the past, the future of tribulation they describe would be the present for their readers, and the eventual triumph just beyond the morrow.

The characteristic features of the apocalyptic future include a great war between the forces of good and evil; a division of history into measured "ages," each more dismal than the previous, leading to the last, present age—a time of persecution of the faithful; the advent of the great apostate—for Christians, the Anti-Christ; his defeat after a bloody battle by divine intervention; followed by a restoration or recreation, including the Judgment of the Nations and the establishment of the Messianic Kingdom.

The religious vision underlying this scheme presumes a radical dualism between good and evil. But it also expresses confidence in the eventual triumph of goodness and the unification of history as a manifestation of God's mysterious plan for human salvation. There is nothing particularly Christian about all this, although it is a scheme susceptible of a Christian interpretation, as the Book of Revelation demonstrates. It is, rather, a fundamentally human way of keeping faith.

With the fall of Jerusalem in 587 BC, again in the progressive disasters of 70 and 135 AD, and through subsequent ages, it became evident to many that human efforts alone would forever remain utterly inadequate to usher in the heavenly kingdom so ardently desired. But fidelity to the end, often a most bitter one, could be justified by appeal to God's vindication—a divine achievement of what human efforts had lost. Human pessimism thus had as its correlative a divine optimism, but one that tended to transcend human history. And thus apocalyptic became associated with a radical and tragic loss of confidence in human institutions as the price for hope.

As an example of human trust at its highest pitch, the apocaplytic sense of eventual vindication has endowed men and women with heroic courage in the midst of catastrophe—from the decimation of the Jews in the second century and the Roman persecution of the early Christians to the European wars of religion in the seventeenth century, the military slaughter of Native Americans in the nineteenth century, the pogroms and gas chambers of the Third Reich and even the tortured confidence of the Jonestown victims in the twentieth. As a way of constructively interpreting such events at a later time by survivors and historians, the apocalyptic frame of reference fans the spark of hope with the promise of justification and even emulation. Nevertheless, the question must be raised whether apocalyptic literature does not ultimately undermine human initiative and agency as the possibility of shaping future events is tacitly relinquished into the hands of those acknowledged to be under the sway of evil.

No Man's Lands: the Utopian Vision

The literature of Utopia is at least as old as Plato's Republic, but it was named by St. Thomas More when he published a treatise by that name in 1516. Although it is superficially a portrait of an ideal realm whose saintly citizens followed both natural law and natural religion, More, like Plato, was indirectly satirizing the institutions of his own time. And subsequent utopian writing continued to be an interpretation of the present in terms of a "no-place" (in Greek, u-topos) which is equivalent to the "no-time" of apocalyptic.

As a literary form, utopian projections came to contain a temporal element in the postulation of a lost Golden Age and a hoped-for future in which human beings would regain Paradise. The later Arthurian legends were thus partly utopian. Other famous utopias were Francis Bacon's New Atlantis (1626), Jonathan Swift's Gulliver's Travels (1726), Samuel Butler's Erewhon (1872)—being "nowhere" spelled backwards—and even Daniel Defoe's Robinson Crusoe (1719). James Hilton's romantic novel Lost Horizon (1933) represents a more recent approach, with its now immortal account of Shangri-La.

Wormy Apples

The modern era upped the satirical ante of the classical utopians with the development of cautionary anti-utopias. More pessimistic than their predecessors, anti-utopians foresee not the recovery of a Golden Age, but the advent of an even worse state than that we are in. As a covert satire of the present, anti-utopian literature simply projects contemporary trends into an apparently care-free future, if one actually almost apocalyptic in its absence of hope.

Two films provide early examples—Fritz Lang's Metropolis and Charlie Chaplin's Modern Times. The most important anti-utopias of the early twentieth century were penned, however, by two remarkable Englishmen: Brave New World (1932) by Aldous Huxley, and 1984 (1946) by George Orwell. Both have been mistaken for science fiction, which they resemble. They are in fact socio-political diatribes couched in the form of futuristic novels. The view of the future they present, moreover, is chilling and, as Huxley pointed out in his 1957 postscript, Brave New World Revisited, very possible.

With uncanny realism and prophetic instinct, Huxley wrote in his introduction to the 1946 edition of this novel, "A really efficient totalitarian state would be one in which the all-powerful executive of political bosses and their army of managers control a population of slaves who do not have to be coerced, because they love their servitude."[1]/ The same year, Orwell (Eric

Blair) published his grimly anti-utopian 1984, fulfilling
Huxley's premise to the letter.

Toward the end of his story, the main character is told
by the man responsible for this social reconditioning, a
figure of benign authority whom he has grown perilously
close to loving, "But always—do not forget this,
Winston—always there will be the intoxication of
power, constantly increasing and constantly growing
subtler. Always, at every moment, there will be the
thrill of victory, the sensation of trampling on an
enemy who is helpless. If you want a picture of the
future, imagine a boot stamping on a human face—
forever."2/

Revised Standard Version

Several other twentieth-century authors have looked at
the future in terms of utopian and anti-utopian
possibilities. H.G. Wells was perhaps the earliest.
Things To Come is still a minor classic (as is the film
based on it). The War of the Worlds is an apocalyptic
anticipation of undesirable contact with alien life forms
devoid of sensitivity and compassion that is still
superior to Alien itself. Arthur C. Clarke's brilliant,
wistful Childhood's End addresses the same topic, but
considers the alternative of contact by a highly
developed race of great compassion and sensitivity, but
with conceivably even worse results.

Although science fiction and epic fantasy represent the
twin offspring of apocalyptic and utopia, many examples of the parental varieties still appear. In the
halcyon 'fifties, Philip Wylie's novel When World's
Collide, an exercise in early catastophism, was brilliantly translated into film by George Pal, who had
made film history shortly before with his still-gripping
Destination Moon. (Later, Pal filmed Wells' The War of
the Worlds and attempted a less successful version of
Atlantis the Lost Continent, blending anti-utopian and
apocalyptic elements in a broth of allegory.) In the
early seventies, Hal Lindsey concocted an explicitly

apocalyptic jeremiad, The Late Great Planet Earth, a fundamentalistic projection of the Book of Revelation through a reactionary political lens. Lindsey's repudiation of liberal culture and civilization was a highly lucrative play to a new generation of evangelical dropouts frightened at the prospect of their brave new world.

The eschatological fever of the seventies was fed by other sensational films and novels—The Poseidon Adventure, The Towering Inferno, Earthquake, The Omen and a welter of cheap "ecological" thrillers following Hitchcock's The Birds, in which nature—in the form of frogs, bees, ants, moths, sharks, piranha fish, bears, dogs and even rabbits—rises up and nearly destroys civilization.

Utopian fantasies have become rare in comparison with anti-utopian projections, although Lost Horizon was remade into a soggy musical comedy and Camelot had its film come-uppance. Conversely, thought-provoking anti-utopian "entertainments" flourished for a time: Harlan Ellison's sardonic A Boy and His Dog, which exacts enormous revenge on the mid-century by calling its subterranean anti-utopia "Topeka"; Soylent Green, a modest proposal for vegetarianism; Zardoz and a remake of its adumbrated predecessor, The Wiz. (Even Oz has its serious drawbacks for a native Kansan.)

Novels of the period which pointed ahead faltering were led by two superb works of contemporary fiction, Ray Bradbury's Farenheit 451 and Anthony Burgess' A Clockwork Orange, both of which were more or less successfully translated into films. At least for those of us who read and go to the movies, the feeling that something was amiss in the future was hard to escape by the end of the seventh decade of this century.

Future Imperfect: Science Fiction and Epic Fantasy

Some years ago, Kingley Amis sagaciously entitled his fine study of science fiction New Maps of Hell, illustrating the eschatological if not apocalytic dimension of the new genre. Much science fiction is just that, a fictitious projection of existing scientific knowledge and technique into a freely constructed future. Much of the literature produced by Jules Verne in the last century falls in this category, as have many works by more modern writers such as Isaac Asimov, Arthur C. Clarke and Robert Heinlein. But satire and the dialectic of ideas have also found expression in the science fiction of Philip Jose Farmer, Ursula K. LeGuin, Kurt Vonnegut, Anthony Burgess, Ray Bradbury and, perhaps most recently, Doris Lessing.

For almost a century, futurists have turned to science fiction to plot possible consequences of technological interventions on human culture. Writers from H.G. Wells to Frank Herbert have, in turn, cautioned us against the dangerous potential of advanced technologies in the hands of morally defective societies. And, as the lay theologian C.S. Lewis more stringently reminded us in his own science fiction trilogy, all human societies are in fact defective. Consequently, if moral rearmament does not out-strip weapons development (among other things), we will not have much of a future to plan for.

Often, even from the beginning, science fiction themes have been overtly religious, and in this respect can also be considered eschatological. A fine example of such a work is the unusually precognitive novel by the son of the Archbishop of Canterbury and later papal chamberlain to Pope Pius X, Fr. Robert Hugh Benson. Lord of the World, the only novel of Benson's set in the future, deals with the coming of the Anti-Christ and the end of the world. First published in 1907, Benson's book is still far more incisive and intelligent than the silly Omen trilogy or Hal Lindsey's ravings. Not only a theological diatribe, Lord of the World is also a scathing satire on social progress and religious liberalism. It is not, however, shrill or cold. It is even curiously utopian. Like colonial Williamsburg, Benson's Rome is deliberately regressed to mid-nineteenth century status, which he conceived to be the apogee of papal glory. Significantly, however, his eternally Victorian city is bombed to smithereens by a vast squadron of imperial aircraft (described, incidentally, a year before Kitty Hawk).

The purest example of epic fantasy in an apocalyptic vein remains J.R.R. Tolkien's great trilogy The Lord of the Rings (1954-55), which spawned a host of imitative trilogies after its rediscovery in the mid-'sixties. As a philologist (like his friend C. S. Lewis, whom he brought back to Christian faith) Tolkien was not only expert in comparative mythology, which he plundered extensively for his plots, but also a skilled exegete who collaborated on the Jerusalem Bible. His trilogy, not surprisingly, contains almost every element of true apocalyptic literature except a divine revelation itself. (And this was supplied ingeniously in Tolkien's posthumous and beautiful "prequel," The Silmarillion.) It is also replete with heroes, wizards, monsters, elves and the whole panoply of high magic. It is this element which predominates the currently popular derivative strategy game "Dungeons and Dragons" with its own host of imitators.

The return to magic, even vicarious magic, on the part of a growing segment of the new generation is a phenomenon not to be idly dismissed. At least it points toward a pervasive quest for a sense of power-control over natural and even supernatural events. Mythical, imaginary settings do not completely obscure the deeper fact that among the young there is developing a sense of powerlessness in the presence of an uncertain future. The lesson the young can learn from Tolkien, if they attend well, is not how to obtain power, but how to relinquish it when called to.

Falling Stars

The most recent specimen of apocalyptic disguised as science fiction is the Star Wars saga of filmmaker George Lucas. Like Tolkien, Lucas peoples his universe with wizards and despots, magic and monsters as well as space ships and laser weapons. Beneath it all, the main action centers on the decisions of weak, fallible (and failing) human beings caught up in a titanic struggle between the forces of good and evil, light and darkness. Instinctively, the young find in these films an apt metaphor for the world in which they live now.

Also like Tolkien, Lucas sees as the central issue of our drama the struggle for power as an end in itself. More Christian in his approach than Orwell or Lucas, however, Tolkien suggested that salvation lies in the ultimate renunciation of power. All such power, even when necessary, tends to corrupt, as Lord Acton taught over a century ago. The more unlimited the power, the greater the corruption. Only those who have no interest in power for its own sake—Gandalf the White, Obi-Wan Kenobe, Yoda—can exercise it without creating worse problems. And even in such cases, a price must be paid in terms of human suffering—a lesson from the Tao.

The futile totalitarianism of 1984 is a more likely threat for the immediate future than the dastardly imperial slavery of Darth Vader or the Empire in Frank Herbert's Dune novels, which are perhaps more parabolic than predictive. The particular horror of Orwell's vision of an earthly hell is that in many respects it has already begun to appear, as the subversion of the media and subtle uses of propaganda have demonstrated for over a decade.

Perhaps the most telling and accurate of these prognostications, and for our purposes the most exemplary, is a novel published in 1959 by Walter Miller, Jr., A Canticle for Leibowitz. It has been in print for all these years and has sold over a million copies, though widely unknown outside science fiction circles. Deeply human, funny, immensely tragic, Canticle is an eschatological, apocalyptic, anti-utopian saga spanning three thousand years of history. On some deep level of meaning, it is possibly the most profound study of the Church written in this century. The message it holds out to us is ultimately on one of hope, not in power or in might, but in the Spirit of the God of Love.

Unlike many of the stories and films we have surveyed, Miller's book is also attentive to real problems such as an increasing shortage of energy supplies. Significantly in this respect, Miller's focus on the monastic solution to a Dark Age (the Albertian Order of St. Leibowitz) was echoed by Roberto Vacca's suggestion in The Coming Dark Age. Harkening back to the centuries so tagged by Renaissance writers impatient for the glory of classical Rome, Vacca envisioned a new kind of monasticism like the Celtic institutions which preserved the learning and culture of the West from the fifth to the tenth centuries:

"These groups I am contemplating—conservers of civilization and catalysts of a future renaissance—should have characteristics in common with the monastic fraternities, if only because they would have to differ profoundly in constitution and purpose from the way of life, the distress, and the disorder prevailing in society outside."3/

To understand Vacca's point, and Miller's, we must again follow the injunction of Pauwels and Bergier and return to the past, which may well resemble our future more than does the present. And in this instance, the hint of an explanation comes again from Arthurian Britain with the rise of Celtic spirituality and the vision of Camelot.

FOUR

Toward a New Spirituality:
A Fifth-Century Suggestion

It is especially ironic that an era such as ours of rapid technological change and unpredictable social upheaval finds in the remote past paradigms that can help us prepare for a future of scarcity. This need not imply that history is circular and that we are somehow condemned to repeat past experience. But it does suggest, as Pauwels and Bergier claimed, that the future will in many respects resemble previous situations more than it does the present. If so, we can learn from past successes and failures how to aim for a better future.

For some years, I believed that the twentieth century bore a remarkable resemblance to the fourteenth. Both were characterized by unusual natural cataclysms, apocalyptic expectations, devastating warfare on an unprecedented scale, rapid social change, heavy taxation and resulting citizen revolts against them, a resurgence of Islamic militancy, the breakdown of political and ecclesiastical order, the rise of religious sects, and especially the flowering of mysticism among lay people and religious. Barbara Tuchman's masterful account, A Distant Mirror, provided welcome corroboration of my intimations.

In searching for a paradigm to account for such remarkable coincidences, I recalled a psychological concept used by psychological students of mysticism such as Prince and Savage, Deikman and Barron.1/"Regression in the service of the ego" was identified by Ernst Kris in his Psychoanalytic Explorations in Art 2/as a phase of development, especially in artists' experience. He observed that present obstacles to growth are overcome by a temporary and often unconscious return to earlier forms of behavior associated with a previously successful breakthrough in the developmental process. Such regression is a fairly common phenomenon, it seems.

For example, when beginning school, children confronted by the demands of grammar, syntax, spelling, arithmetic and so on may revert to bed-wetting, thumb-sucking and baby-talk until they have gained sufficient confidence in their ability to surmount these frustrating challenges to learning. It is something like pole-vaulters and high-jumpers backing up to obtain sufficient speed and momentum to launch themselves over the hurdle. The more difficult the goal, the farther back the runners must retreat.

Groups seem to behave in the same way. Faced with sudden challenges, whole societies tend to interpret present experience in terms of past accomplishments as a prelude to a possible future consistent with traditional goals and values. The greater the challenges, the farther back they reach for historical models.

Americans have recently experienced this phenomenon in several forms, such as a nostalgia for the 'forties and 'fifties—a time of remembered national challenge and successful response in both hot and cold war as well as peaceful prosperity. In 1976 we recalled our revolutionary beginnings with bicentennial celebrations. Office-seekers have again campaigned under the portraits of heroes like Lincoln, Jefferson, Roosevelt and Truman, evoking successful campaigns of the past by the adroit use of slogans and images. The recent popularity of Western wear and mechanical bucking bulls, the "urban cowboy" syndrome, celebrates the glory days of the Wild West, when a New Frontier was tamed and Law and Order prevailed under valiant sheriffs and legendary marshalls. It was not by chance, I think, that Americans elected to the presidency a man whose professional career consisted largely in portraying such heroes in films and television.

52

The Return of the King

Americans are by no means unique in this respect. Every people celebrates their past achievements formally and informally—burning images of Guy Fawkes in England, having Bastille Day parties in France, commemorating the Battle of the Boyne with mock battles and Orange Parades in Ulster. Such historical reminders are cultural reinforcements, celebrations of tacit hope in the future, not the past. As such they are part of the normal order of social life. On the other hand, unpredictable crises and challenges likewise summon up memories of past victories, but in a more spontaneous fashion. In both cases, people reach back into their past for the most appropriate examples in order to glean a hint as to the character and importance of present events.

The recent enthusiasm among youngsters for "dungeons and dragons," swords, sorcery and warrior-kings suggests that our current regression in the service of the collective ego is now taking us back beyond the fourteenth century to an even more primitive world, the age the Renaissance called "dark"—and not without reason.

The search for ideals and heroes from an era in which western civilization collapsed in the face of barbarian invasions and the fall of imperial Rome tells us this: the challenge we are now facing is far more serious than that of the fourteenth century. It is a challenge that involves the whole of western civilization—its basic values, goals and fundamental institutions. We face, in short, a global crisis, and not merely on a political or religious level. We have been confronted by a manifold crisis at once economic, social, ecological, educational and aesthetic.

Such a vast array of problems is not only apocalyptic in its scope, it is also unimaginable except in terms of myth and symbol. For we seem to be embroiled whether by accident or design in a conflict between great and yet unseen adversaries influencing both natural and social events—some Darth Vader vs. Obi-Wan Kenobe, Sauron vs. Gandalf, Morgan le Fay vs. Merlin. Like Luke Skywalker and a young Celt centuries ago, we reach out imaginatively for improbable weapons as we join the fray—archaic swords, second sight. Arthur has indeed come again.

Merlin and Arthur warrant comparison with Ben Kenobe and Luke Skywalker in many respects. But our regression to the Dark Ages, though perhaps mythical in its expression, has a far sounder foundation in fact—the real triumph of Arthurian Britain. This accomplishment can best be seen as having two branches: the political achievement of Arthur himself, and the spiritual achievement of the Celtic monks to whom Vacca refers us. It is they, not the frontier marshall or the Boston revolutionaries, who are our true contemporaries.

Crisis in the Fifth Century

By the end of the second century, the Roman Empire had expanded to the limits of the known world, although remote regions such as Ireland, Scandinavia, most of Africa, northeastern Europe and central Asia remained outside the frontier. It had become at least nominally Christian by the fourth century. But then its central structure began to break down under sheer vastness of administration. Barbarian hordes began to cross the frontiers without challenge and imperilled the City of Rome itself. Eventually, the focus of government and culture shifted east to Constantinople, the capital of the Eastern Empire, as the darkness of barbarism gradually overshadowed the once brilliant Eternal City. By 476, the Western Empire was only a clutter of petty kingdoms dispersed in a desert of continual warfare.

On the edge of the Western Empire, the island called Britannia was the farthest colony from Rome and an important one. It included southern Caledonia (Scotland, called Alba by its native Celts), Cambria (Wales—known later as Cymru, "the community") and even

Britannia Minor (Brittany, the Celtic Armorica) across the channel. Scouted by Julius Caesar in 55 BC, subdued by Claudius and Vespasian in 43 AD, fortified by Hadrian and Antoninus in the second century, Britain (or Prydein and sometimes Albion in the language of its own people) was a thoroughly Romanized part of the Empire.

Celtic Christianity

The Christian faith entered Britain as early as 37 AD according to the sixth-century Welsh monk, Gildas. However, the first Apostle of Britain known to us is St. Ninian (360-432). Although he founded several monasteries in addition to his headquarters in southwest Scotland, Candida Casa, Ninian chiefly labored as a missionary preacher among the pagan Picts of the North. Ireland (Eriu or Erin to the Celts, Hibernia to the Romans) was evangelized later than Britain, since it had never been part of the Roman world. Its first missionaries were probably British, including the obscure St. Palladius, sent to the Scots by Pope Celestine I in 431 (the homeland of the Scots being, at that time, Ireland). St. Patrick (390-461), the Apostle of Ireland, was also a British Celt, either Welsh or Cornish. Captured and taken to Ireland by pirates at 16, he managed to escape. Once home again, Patrick heard the call of the pagan Irish. He became a priest, a bishop, then returned to Ireland to evangelize his captors.

Monasticism arose in Britain and Ireland independently and as early as it did on the continent. According to legend, Ninian had been known to St. Martin of Tours (326-297), who established monastic settlements in Gaul during the fourth century. Celtic monasticism took root just as the Empire began to crumble. The legions had gradually been withdrawn from Britain to garrison outposts more seriously threatened by barbarian advances on the continent. Then, in 367, the country was attacked in concert by Picts, Irish Scots and Saxons from across the North Sea. The invaders were repelled, but only after a two-year struggle. But by then, the end of the Roman Britain was already in view. By 425, the island was without Roman military protection, though still Roman in its ways. That is, the citizens of note were committed to a Christian Roman view of life, with its emphasis on order, culture and stability. To the cultivated Britons of the fifth century, civilization—civitas—was still Romanitas.

The Saxon Invasion

Pirate raids and minor invasions by Saxons, Angles and Jutes had occurred long before 367. But now, settlements were following. With the occupation of the southeast and eastern coast, the destruction of Celtic Britain had also begun. Deprived of the legions, Britain fell before the invaders foot by foot. Villas were deserted, wattle churches and monasteries plundered and burned. The Roman Christian civitas was on the verge of the same devastation that had turned Europe into a wasteland under the Huns, Vandals, Goths and Franks. Then a young warrior appeared who was able to regroup the faltering Britons long enough to stop the pagan advance and thereby earn a lasting place in British memory and legend, and, indeed, those of the world.

Arthur the Celt

Most of us know an Arthur whose image has been distorted over the centuries by the magnifying lenses of writers eager to exploit his adventures for their own purposes. In their view, the Celtic chieftain came to embody ideals of twelfth-century chivalry, fourteenth-century courtesy, sixteenth-century heroism, nineteenth-century romanticism and rectitude, and twentieth-century political idealism.

It is not easy to peel off the layers of significance attributed to Arthur by later generations, but it is necessary to try to do so in order to assess his original contribution to European civilization. The earliest literary sources are contemporary with Arthur himself—

or nearly so, by our time-scale. Some contain only hints
or a name: Gildas' De Excidio Britanniae (the Downfall
of Britain—c. 550), Aneirin's great poem Y Gododdin (c.
600), early legends found in the eleventh-century
Mabinogi, the Triads of Britain, the monk Nennius'
Historia Britonum (c. 820) and the Annales Cambriae,
copied from the much older sources around 960.3/

To these and other even more obscure materials must
be added the growing evidence concerning Arthurian
Britain unearthed by the archeological team headed by
Leslie Alcock and reported by him and Geoffrey Ashe in
a remarkable series of books, including Arthur's Britain,
The Quest for Arthur's Britain and Camelot and the
Vision of Albion.

Scholars such as Ashe concur that he was born in Wales
or Cornwall about 470. He was neither a king nor even
of royal ancestry. A Celtic clan chieftain of noble
birth, he became the dux bellorum—war-leader of the
British kings who had previously divided the island
belligerently among themselves. He was thus a kind of
overlord or military commander.

Thoroughly Celtic, Arthur was also committed to
Romanitas. He summoned his followers to the standard
of the late Empire, the great red dragon which would
someday become the national emblem of Wales. From
this symbol, Arthur took the little Pendragon, "Chief
(or Head) Dragon." Other British kings, such as the
formidable Maelgwn of Gwynedd, were also called
"Dragon." But Arthur was the Pendragon.

His use of cavalry was also borrowed from the Romans,
a strategy which enabled him to move rapidly,
outmaneuvering his horseless foes as well as terrorizing
them with a relatively small number of seasoned
cavaliers or "knights" as they were called by the Anglo-
Saxons. His chief lieutenants seem to have been Cei
and Bedwyr (Anglicized as Kay and Bedivere). In a
series of twelve crucial battles, crowned by a stunning
victory at Mt. Badon in 520, Arthur so thoroughly

routed the Saxons that for a generation or more, Celtic Britain remained secure from further invasion. But Arthur himself, no doubt war-weary and prematurely aged from years of constant battle, did not survive the treachery of feud and civil war among the Celtic princes. According to the Annales Cambriae, he fell at the Battle of Camlan with another warrior named Medraut, who seems to have been the original Mordred. Whether son or nephew, friend or foe, we have no clue.

Rex Quondam, Rex Futurae

Of the other elements of Arthurian lore, we can say that it seems likely that the stone and wooden fort on Cadbury Hill in Somerset may have been the original Camelot, Arthur's headquarters. Archeological evidence points in that direction, but cannot prove it. There is also a strong tradition that his wife was named Guennuvar or Gwenhwyvaer, "Englished" as Guinevere.

Both Arthur and Guinevere were buried, it is still held by many, at Glastonbury Abbey, one of the oldest Christian sites in England. In 1191 a tomb was discovered there containing the bones of a man and woman and bearing the inscription on cross inside the oak coffin: "Here lies the famous King Arthur, buried in the Isle of Avalon."4/ The bones were removed to a new grave, but were scattered by order of Henry VIII at the dissolution of the monastery. As Glastonbury has traditionally been associated with Avalon, "the Isle of Apples," Arthur's burial there may well have been factual, although again, archeology cannot prove it.

The rest is mainly legend, told and retold with embellishments over the centuries to answer the need of later generations seeking hope and an ideal from the Golden Age of Britain's past. Arthur was the King against whose stature all future kings would be measured until he would reappear, it was said, in the darkest hour of Britain's peril.

Arthur's Triumph

The campaign against the invading Saxons in order to preserve civilized Britain did not long survive Arthur. The Celtic defense crumbled by 570 in the face of a Saxon advance begun as early as 550. But Arthur's achievement is no less for that, for it obtained for the only other force capable of turning the pagan conquest the needed time to launch another kind of campaign. Where the sword ultimately failed, the cross did not. What is perhaps most remarkable about the victory of Celtic Christianity is that its expansion into Anglo-Saxon England was unplanned and unsystematic—a spontaneous outreach to the Saxons and Picts, and beyond them even to the new barbarians ruling Europe. The weapons of the monk-missionaries were the love of God and a zeal to spread not only the light of faith to a people who sat again in darkness, but the light of learning as well.

Salvation in the Wilderness: The Irish Conquest

Monasteries had flourished in western Britain for over a century before the Battle of Camlan. In Ireland, even more thousands of young men and women had flocked to the "deserts" of small remote glens and small islands to seek the presence of the living God.

Unlike continental monks, the Celts were free to wander, if more austere in their lifestyle. They mingled with kings and bards, peasants and soldiers. And from the beginning, British and Irish monks and nuns traveled great distances on foot to preach the gospel to pagan Picts, Scots, Saxons and the Germanic tribes across the channel. Many met a martyr's death at the hands of the tribes, pirates or, later, marauding Vikings.

The monks' ceaseless wandering was sometimes undertaken as a penance imposed by their anmchara - "soul-friend" or confessor. In other instances, probably the great majority, this "white martyrdom" was a voluntary gesture of generosity and renunciation, much like the hermits' "green martyrdom" of perpetual exile.

The respite won by Arthur's military exploits enabled the monks, particularly the Irish, to complete the conversion of the invaders. British monks, thousands of whose number had been mercilessly slaughtered by the tide of pagans, were perhaps understandably less eager to join in the evangelization effort. Nevertheless, many labored with notable success to win the invaders to Christ. Irish and British missionaries thus approached from the north and west. Meanwhile, the mission of St. Augustine of Canterbury had also begun auspiciously if slowly in 597, moving up from the southeast. The triple missionary onslaught resulted in the nearly total conversion of the Saxons, Angles and Jutes in less than a century. In fact, at the Synod of Whitby in 663, the Anglo-Saxon Church had become strong enough even to dominate the Celts and bring their church into closer conformity with Roman practices, and, more significantly, under English authority. Similarly, the last great military rally of the Celts ended in defeat with the death of Cadwallon in 633.

Thus by the time eastern and central Britain had fallen under Saxon control, the conquerors had embraced not only Christianity but a highly civilized way of life, much of which they learned from the monk-tutors. The Saxons also inherited the ideal of a unified realm, once the dream of Albion in the mind of a young Celtic warlord. Under Alfred the Great (849-99), that ideal was all but attained despite the new and furious assaults of the Viking Danes. Like the old Saxon pagans, these barbarian freebooters plundered and destroyed churches and monasteries, burning priceless manuscripts and removing beautiful works of art lovingly created by Celtic monks. Like Arthur before him, Alfred finally defeated the invaders and began a new effort to spread the light of learning as well as faith. By the twilight of the Saxon monarchy in 1066, the English church had given the calender three martyred king-saints and a host of holy commoners.

The Lamp of Europe

The great achievement of the Celtic monks in converting the Saxon hordes to the gospel and implanting in them the elements of Christian culture was in the long run less enduring and even less important than the work that followed and indeed grew out of it.

From the beginning, Celtic monasticism had been embued with a love of learning and art exceeding even that of Benedict's sons and daughters. Their primary work was the study of scripture together with the commentaries on the great Greek and Latin Fathers. Some of the greatest treasures of the period are the illuminated Gospels from Kells, Durrow, Lindisfarne and elsewhere. But the classic pagan authors and poets of antiquity were also loved and imitated, especially by the Irish, who never shared the antagonisms of Christians once subject to persecution by Greeks and Romans, a hostility that vitiated much of the continental scholarship of the times. Music, art, calligraphy, rhetoric, geometry, grammar and astronomy were taught and perfected in the monastic schools, which thus became the repository of western civilization and culture for several centuries.

Another and greater accomplishment of Celtic spirituality thus eventuated from the migration of the monks to the continent in the seventh and eighth centuries. Monasteries were founded from Burgundy to Bobbio in Italy, including the great monastery of St. Gall in Switzerland. Soon, monks were teaching art, music and literature as well as carrying out the missionary work of converting Franks, Goths and Lombards.

Perhaps the monks' greatest impact was made through the Frankish court, beginning with that of Charlemagne, who, like Arthur two centuries before, had established a successful front against pagan and now Saracen expansion in the West. But where Arthur himself had at best a friendly relationship with the

Church, Charlemagne was able to encompass both Church and State within the realm of a new "Roman" Empire.

Alcuin (735-804), the British Monk who inspired the Carolingian renaissance that would some day flower in the great medieval schools and universities of Europe, had been master of the Cathedral school at York. As a youth there, his own teachers had included at least one Irish peregrinus, Colchu, to whom the famous disciple would address a reverential letter in 790. Further, Alcuin brought several Irish scholars from York to Aachen to aid his enterprise as head of the "royal academy." Charlemagne extended this practice, replacing Italian scholars with these wandering "Egyptians" as Latins called them. Even Alcuin took notice of the Irish invasion, and he was himself succeeded in 796, when he became Abbot of Tours, by an Irishman, Clement the Scot.

Politically, Charlemagne's empire did not survive him, but the educational and ecclesiastical reforms he instituted with Alcuin's help became a lasting part of European civilization. Alcuin himself as Abbot of the proto-monastery of France continued the work of reform for many years. Another Irish monk, John Scotus Eriugena (810-877) gained the support of Charlemagne's grandson, Charles the Bald, and assumed direction of the palace school at Laon. A great scholar and original thinker, Eriugena's philosophy became suspect of heresy two centuries later, mainly because of the strong mystical under-currents he had absorbed from his Celtic forebears as well as the intellectual mysticism he found in the Greek Fathers. Such notions were not well received in the heady atmosphere of the early thirteeth century. Eriugena's most important contribution to learning in the ninth century, however, lay in his introduction of the writings of Dionysios the Areopagite to the Latin West, as well as hitherto-unknown works of St. Maximus the Confessor and St. Gregory of Nyssa.

62

The Hint of an Explanation

As with Arthur's achievement, that of the Celtic monks was taken up into the brighter future of the Middle Ages and the Renaissance. Celtic monasticism, like "Camelot," was gone by then, having accomplished its mission. The illustrious monasteries had been either destroyed by the Vikings or taken over by the Benedictines. Both achievements were more, not less, significant for all that, for in each case, the real victory was absorbed wholesale into the movement of western civilization. Perhaps it would be truer to say that they are the story of western civilization, still providing lessons for those of us concerned about the dimming of the light once more. Arthur, Ninian, Patrick and Alcuin remain beacons shining in the night of history, guiding us forward in hope.

Roberto Vacca maintained that the crisis of western civilization now in its early stages will require a host of such widespread "conservers" of civilization and catalysts of a future renaissance even if we escape a conflagration such as that envisioned by Walter Miller in A Canticle for Leibowitz. The new monks "would have to conserve knowledge, and the memory of the ways in which certain things are done, if we assume (rightly, as I think) that the very concept of culture implies both knowing and doing (savoire faire)."5/Cultural conservation in the future as in the past must therefore include not only science and history, but also literature, art, crafts and music.

The Celtic monastery was ideally suited for such a conservative task because its engagement in culture was as profound as its detachment from the institutional structures of Church and State in the late Roman Empire. Seeking a lifestyle of simple wants and needs, the monastics accepted poverty, scarcity and adversity-even to the point of revelling in them. Their motivation was unusually pure and strong, however, just as the compass of their cultural appreciation was unusually large. To fathom the profound capacity of Celtic monasteries to conserve the richest and rarest gems of classical culture, we need to explore the spirituality that inspired them—we may thus be more able to estimate our own chances of successfully emulating them.

Varieties of Celtic Spirituality

Celtic spirituality, like all spirituality, is basically a category comprising a multitude of different spiritualities which in concrete terms are distinguished by many factors—personalities, situations, even geography. Welsh and Breton approaches to life differ from Irish and Scottish attitudes no less today than a thousand years ago. Perhaps more so. Yet there are common elements today as there were among the ancient Celtic spiritualities. The major factors we will be considering here as clues toward our own future possibilities are, first, the Celtic temperament—its vision of life as well as its "character" and, second, the structure and function of the Celtic monastic settlements of the early medieval period, in some respects the final product of what can be called the classical civilization of the Celts.

The Celtic World

The ancient Greeks called them Keltoi. To the Romans they were Galli, the Gauls, a disparate family of peoples who had, it is believed, come from the lands north of the Alps and south of the Danube, an area including parts of Germany, Austria and Switzerland. According to ancient accounts, the Celts were fond of boasting, drinking and gifts, being vastly generous. A hardy people, they were known for their valor in war, their use of horses, chariots and a tendency to go into battle stark naked. They loved beauty in nature and art, developing superb forms of design and decoration, music and, wary of written words, a rich oral tradition, preserved by a class of poet-musicians known as bards. Deeply religious, even mystical, the Celts also had a priestly class who came to be known as druids, whose sway over Celtic life was almost total.

About 1000 BC, the Celts began to expand from their original homeland in every direction. By the fifth century BC, they had reached Asia Minor, Britain and Italy, where they sacked Rome in 390. By Caesar's time, Celtic tribes occupied most of northeastern Europe. There two major branches of Celtic language and culture eventually emerged, Goidelic or Gaelic— that of the Scots and Picts of Ireland, Scotland and Man—and Brythonic—the language and customs of the Celts of Britain, Cornwall and, later, Brittany. Although Latin was spoken by the Romanized Celts of Imperial Britain, the language of their ancestors was preserved by the peasants and hill people who also held onto the old ways during the centuries of occupation.

A Matter of Temper

From their first appearance in the annals of world history, the character of the Celts manifested not only definite but remarkably constant components. Concerning this tendency, Professor Proinsias MacCana points out that "while the popular notion of them as reflected in modern literature has undoubtedly been coloured by eighteenth- and nineteenth-century romanticism with its susceptibility to mist, magic and melancholy, it certainly did not originate there. In fact, many of the attributes which it ascribes to the Celts— eloquence, lyric genius, volatile temperament, prodigality, reckless bravery, ebullience, contentiousness, and so on—have a much longer lineage, appearing in the accounts of classical authors of two thousand years ago."6/

All the observers have seemed to note the same cleavage in the Celtic soul—the life-loving, boisterous, expansive attitude of the true extravert, as well as its "shadow"—a dreamy, melancholy air, an introverted gaze on realities beyond this visible world with all its beauty. This polarity has found expression in every phase of Celtic life, particularly in art, music and literature.

The Celtic Monastery

The wholesale conversion of the insular Celts to Christianity in the fourth and fifth centuries owed much to their heroic and romantic temperament. Christ was immediately recognized as "the Chief of Chiefs," yet embodied the wisdom and beauty of the invisibly pervasive Godhead the druids had intuited in oak groves and battlegrounds. Celtic monasticism was a natural outgrowth of such a deeply lyrical spirit, a development similar to but in important respects very different from its counterparts elsewhere.

Similarly, the Celtic monastic communities differed from each other over the centuries of their existence and from place to place, among them the double monastery presided over by St. Brigid, St. Colum's famous settlement on Iona, and its daughter monastery founded by St. Aidan at Lindisfarne. Nevertheless, they can be recognized from Iceland to Italy as members of a single family.

Typically, the Celtic monastery was designed for sufficiency, protection and privacy, as can still be seen from the ruins of Clonmacnois and Nendrum, particularly good specimens among the hundreds in Ireland. Enclosed by a circular stone or earthen wall, and sometimes two or three concentric walls, the buildings were distinguished by their functions—prayer, meditation, instruction, reading, writing, crafts, storage, eating and so on.

Worship and eating were done in common, like much of the ordinary labor. But privacy was generously protected. Each monk had a separate hut, a circular stone cell with a thatch or wooden roof, arranged, as McNeill notes, "in an irregular circle around that of the abbot...(which) was larger than the others and prominently placed at the top of a knoll."7/ Agriculture was carried out on a small scale in the form of gardens and limited fields often within the enclosure itself. Pigs, cattle, fowl and sheep were raised for meat, milk, eggs, wool and leather. A cemetery was usually located within the enclosure near the church. Later the tombs of sainted members of the community—and there were many—became the object of pilgrimage and devotion. Kings and nobles were often buried there as well.

In many enclosures there are still found both ruined and intact roundtowers. Built after the beginning of the terrible Viking raids in the eighth and ninth centuries, these tall stone structures were primarily designed for protection. During peaceful interludes, they served as belfry and storage chamber.

Social Service

Even more than their continental counterparts, the Celtic monasteries exercised a variety of social functions in addition to providing a milieu for a life of prayer and meditation. Hospitality was a major service in a country lacking towns and inns. Children were frequently fostered there, either as orphans or in hopes of an education. Since ancient Ireland had no prisons, sometimes persons convicted of or sought for crimes were "imprisoned" at monasteries as well. There alone they might find sanctuary from vengeful victims or their relatives.

Monastic barns provided storage and safe-keeping for their own grain and that of nearby farms after harvest and in times of peril. Similarly, monasteries occasionally served as banks, keeping treasures such as brooches and other ornaments and utensils along with their own books, art objects and valuable liturgical vessels. This was no doubt one major reason for the devastating Viking raids and even attacks by Irish warlords that eventually brought an end to the great monastic era.

Monastic Personnel

Not all the inhabitants of the settlement were celibate—many were not even monks in the strict sense. Lay monks, married and single, were present, and sometimes even abbots were married. Work was carried out by the whole monastic community, according to appropriate skills—farming, animal husbandry, fence-making, grinding, weaving, cooking and teaching, among others. There were maintenance men as well—masons, smiths, carpenters and boatbuilders. Metalworkers and jewelers plied their crafts. The great number of hand-lettered and beautifully illuminated manuscripts at larger monasteries must have required a sizable library staff—editors, vellum- and parchment-makers and copy ists. The school required teachers and administrators. There may even have been a kind of militia and a sergeant-at-arms.

Undoubtedly, many of these tasks could have been performed by a limited number of individuals possessing multiple skills, but a successful monastery like Clonmacnois would have required as many as two or three hundred persons of both sexes. For this reason, as Hughes and Hamlin observe, "Once set up, the monastery was economically an almost self-sufficient unit. It maintained people who did no manual work, the administrators, scholars, teachers, ascetics, but its manaig (monks) supplied the essential farm-labor force, for their land was monastic land and they paid a heavy rent in produce on it. It also had a regular income from fees for baptism and burial."8/ Students also paid tuition in kind, and the monks engaged in petty barter with surrounding farms for goods they did not produce themselves.

Lessons from the Celtic Past

In the literature of the Dark Ages, Ireland was usually described as a rich as well as beautiful land, "flowing with milk and honey." Yet it was a land without coinage, in which such commerce as existed was conducted by trade and barter. There was neither army nor navy, no great cities and no centralized government. Value was reckoned in terms of beauty and excellence, valor and holiness. Friendship and clan solidarity counted more than gold and silver. The giving of gifts was one of the chief social transactions.

Social organization was minimal, if strong, being based mainly on kinship ties and proximity. Housing was simple, even primitive. Roundtowers are the oldest large structures extant, along with simple chapels and a scattering of corbelled "bee-hive" hermits' cells. The ordinary living center was the homestead, whether a poor croft or a family or clan-based settlement similar to the Roman villa on which they were perhaps modeled. These contained as many as five hundred persons in the huge extended family.

By modern standards, such a society is primitive, even barbaric. Yet it was precisely in such a decentralized but highly sophisticated, even aristocratic society that the life of the mind and spirit flourished in a splendor of richness unrivalled perhaps since the glory of Pericles' Greece. We stand to learn much from them.

Sufficiency and Survival

As if in response to Vacca's suggestion, what could be called Celtic monastic settlements have begun to appear again in the British Isles, Ireland and America. In Latin America, communidades de base have much in common with these northern spiritual cooperatives. Such a contemporary "Celtic" community, unlike many religious as well as secular institutions, sects and cults, is decentralized, non-authoritarian, informal and open. It is structured, however. Art, crafts, music, literature and (often) common prayer blend with shared work and resources to produce a kind of extended family group. Laypersons of both genders, married as well as single, religious sisters, brothers and priests may all belong and participate on various levels of involvement. Some members have jobs outside the group, or family responsibilities. Others work at home. Children and pets are welcome.

The settlement is more likely to be located in a rural area than in a city, although nothing prevents the establishment of a cooperative in an inner-city neighborhood. Several attempts have been made along this line. Like the ancient Celtic monastery, however, spirituality and adequate living space require a measure of detachment and privacy for individuals and families or couples which urban limitations tend to inhibit or preclude.

Among very disparate communities that seem to embody at least some elements of the Celtic approach, I would mention several: the Iona Community, founded by Presbyterians in 1938 to restore and perpetuate the ancient center; Lothlorian in Galloway—also in Scotland and near the protomonastic site of Britain, St. Ninian's Candida Casa; the Findhorn community on the Grampian coast near Elgin; and the Alternative Technology Centre near Machynlleth, Powys, Wales.

Several American communities warrant mention in this respect—the famed Bruderhof movement in New England; the Farm, a huge cooperative venture in Summertown, Tennessee; William Irwin Thompson's Lindisfarne Association in Crestone, Colorado; and David Spangler's Lorian near Madison, Wisconsin.

Perhaps far more than Roberto Vacca could have foreseen, the seeds of a new Renaissance have already been sown in the twilit years of imperial technological civilization. The most common element shared by these ventures and the Celtic monasteries is, I submit, a radical commitment to holism and symbiosis—intrapersonal and inter-personal integration and a positive interaction with the natural environment.

Leadership

Celtic myth and legend are rife with figures harkening back to the dim beginnings of Ireland's legendary past. Real personages were no doubt remembered and all but deified by later bards, much as Arthur was in later days—Cuchulain, Fionn mac Cumhaill, Deirdre, Diarmid and others. True heroes existed of the calibre of the aged King Brian Boru, whose brutal murder by retreating Danes deprived him of witnessing their final overthrow. Later biographers of the saints embroidered and enlarged upon their true accomplishments and character, borrowing in many instances heroic features from the Celtic past. But even when reduced to normal perspective, these men and women present outstanding examples of heroism and exploit.

Today, as in the fifth century, as well as in the twelfth, fourteenth, sixteenth and nineteenth—when the Celtic past was summoned again for inspiration, even in Plantagenet costume and Victorian sensibility, we scan the horizon of the past for leaders and heroes. Which is to say, we are sorely aware of the dearth of contemporary leadership—clear vision, real honesty, constancy and a robust pursuit of ideals worth achieving and sacrificing for, in contrast to bigger profits, greater security, more devastating weapons and tighter control over our own and other people's lives.

Celebration

From the earliest times, the Celts were renowned for their exuberance in celebrating life—its tragedies as well as its triumphs. Social boasting was an art form and virtually a social requirement on great occasions—a feature attributed even to the great saints, whose accomplished curses were as feared as much their powerful blessings were sought.9/

Music was typically the chosen medium for celebrating the exploits of heroes and clans. The bards recited their epics to the accompaniment of the harp or the lyre-like cruit (the Welsh crwth). Satires, panegyrics, elegies and laments were formal modes of social observation as well as entertainment. The world is undeniably richer for the wealth of melodies contributed to the folk music of every land where Irish missionaries and laborers migrated.

Our world longs for celebration today as it surely will in the future—not merely the ability to laugh and revel, but the equally important and complementary ability to lament well. To remember in song and story the sorrows as well as the joys of life. Folk music has traditionally fulfilled this need for most people. I think that in an authentic spirituality for the future, there will be a large place as well as need for the bard and harper. Each of us in our own way becomes such a singer of songs and teller of tales, but not while our dependence on the electronic media for entertainment renders us silent and passive, or at most enthusiastic devotees of someone else's genius.

Liquid Spirits

Celtic celebration has perhaps always turned on drink as well as song. Ale, mead, beer and even brandy were all known and loved by the ancients. Today, alcoholism remains one of the sadder residues of customs torn from their appropriate context. But the abuse of drink should not blind us to the real and symbolic function of inebriation as part of a genuinely heroic culture. William James reminded us that wine is mysticism of the poor, providing an entry into, not an escape from, other realms of awareness. And one of the most charming images of Greek as well as Celtic tradition is that of Socrates or Silenus, the sage who utters his wisest sayings when under the liberating influence of the little god of wine.

What we will need in the realm of celebrative consumption in the future is not a proliferation of adolescent smokers or "Animal House" antics nor the spread of cocktail lounges. Rather, I would hope to see a return to the mead house, the village inn, or just the local pub—which in Celtic countries is a meeting place for festal exchange and merry-making as well as the high business of politics and religion.

Creative Imagination

Exaggeration, hyperbole and the imaginative reconstruction of the world are powers of the Celtic soul that also have potential value for us Flatlanders now and in the future. Reality was never humdrum for the Celt. Possessed of a sense of presences unseen, the Celt feels involved in and perhaps drawn to an Otherworld whose occasional manifestations here are experienced as ghosts, spirits and halflings such as those masterfully catalogued in Peter Haining's The Leprechaun's Kingdom.10/

A psychiatrist might dismiss this as vestiges of primitive mentality, a form of collective—and regressive—primary process thinking not at all conducive to survival in the present world much less any Coming Dark Age. On the contrary, I believe that the power to envision alternative realities, the adamant refusal to declare our accounts with Reality prematurely closed, as William James cautioned us, better disposes us to survive in hard as well as easy times.

Symbiosis

Environmental factors have always played a greater role in spirituality than religious authorities were wont to admit. Perhaps nowhere was this more the case than in the Celtic islands. The fierce, wind-lashed sea, the rolling mists, the green hills, steep cliffs and craggy, heather-clad mountains, the forests, moors and bogs, the mild, rainy climate—all fashioned the Celtic temperament as they dictated the form of its dwellings.

Surely, one of the reasons why architecture never attained monumental proportions in Celtic lands is the Celt's love of the land itself. Except for the roundtowers, Celtic buildings remained far closer to the earth in spirit and practice than in any other advanced civilization. A truly symbiotic relationship developed out of their intimacy with nature.

Particularly in Ireland, the monastic architectural style was simple, efficient, modest and decentralized. As a whole, the buildings and fences must have seemed as much a part of the landscape as their ruins do today. Fields were small and cultivation followed the natural contours of the land. Animals grazed more or less freely. Even boats were simple—the typical curragh being a frame covered with hides. Yet so skillfully were they made that it is likely that peregrine monks sailed in them as far as America, a feat commonly ascribed to both Madoc ab Owain Gwynedd and St. Brendan the Navigator and demonstrated in our own time by the voyage of a small, skin-covered boat called The Brendan.

The Celtic Legacy

The Celts, and particularly the monks themselves, came and set up their earthly dwellings and after a while departed, having left almost as little trace on the land as they did on the sea—a lesson in ecological management we could well imitate today. Even the inscriptions they left anonymously behind on standing stones and high crosses were simple, concise, and almost invisible against the natural ground. Having set their hearts on a transcendent goal, they apparently felt little need to leave memorials behind, except as markers pointing the way they had gone.

Their gift to future generations, in addition to the priceless artworks they created and the learning they preserved, was in truth the land itself—undisturbed, peaceful, fertile. But the beacon of their passage, and our invitation to follow, remains pre-eminently the symbol not of death and disappearance, but of final triumph, the great carved stone crosses which once dotted the valleys in the hundreds and many of which stand to this day.

FIVE

Hope in the Wilderness

For some time, beacons have been appearing which seem to herald a reawakening of Celtic spirituality. On the level of myth and story, the pre-reflexive matrix of the imagination which grounds every spirituality, ancient and medieval Celtic influences have already shown their influence on a new generation of youngsters attuned, as we have seen, to wizards, dragons, dungeons and heroic exploits.

J.R.R. Tolkien extensively plundered Irish and Welsh mythology for his still-popular trilogy, The Lord of the Rings. More recent writers have capitalized on his somewhat subtle borrowing. Katherine Kurtz has invented a fictitious but undeniably Celtic world in her fascinating adventure trilogies The Chronicles of the Derenyi and The Legends of Camber of Culdi. Evangeline Walton has successfully novelized the medieval Welsh epic, the Four Branches of the Mabinogi, as a series of adventure tales, Prince of Annwn, The Children of Llyr, The Song of Rhiannon and The Island of the Mighty. (Scholars may prefer Patrick Ford's superb translation, The Mabinogi and other Medieval Welsh Tales.1/)

Another popular and richly Celtic fantasy is the "Riddle of Stars" trilogy by Patricia McKillip—The Riddlemaster of Hed, Heir of Wind and Fire and Harpist in the Wind, with their shape-shifters, wizards, harps and ghosts. Leon Uris' sweeping Trinity continues to be a best-seller along with his and his wife Jill's Ireland: A Terrible Beauty and the calendars based on it. Fr. Andrew Greeley has contributed a small library of books: May the Wind Be Ever at Your Back; Nora, Maeve and Sibi; The Magic Cup; The Irish Americans: The Run to Money and Power and That Most Distressful Nation: The Taming of the American Irish. In 1980, the London stage experienced a sensational Celtic invasion with The Romans in Britain, which addressed the tragic and volatile Ulster question with a reprise of the conquest of Britain in the first century. Brian Friel's plays about contemporary Ireland continue to draw enthusiastic audiences on both sides of the Atlantic.

In the world of music and the fine arts, singer and harper Mary O'Hara has enchanted thousands of Americans in her personal appearances and recordings. Similarly, groups such as the Chieftains, the Boys of the Lough, Planxty and Ar Log now rival the Clancy Brothers. Breton harper Alan Stivell is acquiring an American following as devoted as his European fans. Treasures of Early Irish Art, a magnificent exhibition of metal and graphic arts from 1500 BC to 1500 AD, successfully toured many American cities not long ago, attracting thousands of spectators from New York to San Francisco. (A beautifully illustrated book on the exhibit is available from the Metropolitan Museum of Art in New York.) Within the past three years, a half-dozen new editions of plates from the Book of Kells and other illuminated Celtic manuscripts have also been published. In all, twentieth-century America seems to have been triumphantly invaded by a horde of ancient Celts armed with pen, brush, harp and hammer.

In print and pigment, a revival of the Celtic spirit may look promising. But in terms of a contemporary equivalent of a monastic settlement such as those called for by Roberto Vacca, are there any grounds for expecting to find something along these lines in today's world—groups of men and women committed to a life-style integrating contemplation, art, literature, crafts, music and dedicated to the preservation of the deepest values of sacred and secular culture?

Despite the inevitable demise of the commune craze of the late 'sixties, many cooperative societies and intentional communities continue to flourish. At least some of them offer reason to hope for a human future, if on a relatively small scale. A useful Guide to Cooperative Alternatives 2/ provides ample testimony as

well as resources concerning that promise. It identifies
dozens of groups under sections such as Family Life and
Relationships, Energy and Environment, Communications
and Networking, Politics, Education, Culture, and Self
and Spirit. Celtic monasteries, however, are not listed
among them. Following a different impulse, I recently
chose to begin searching for contemporary examples of
Celtic spirit (by whatever name it calls itself) in the
southwestern desert—partly in preparation for a later
voyage of rediscovery to Ireland and the British Isles.
Only one of the centers I eventually visited is listed in
the Guide. None of them are exactly orthodox.

First, why the desert?

Crucible of the Spirit

At spiritually critical moments in human history, many
who would one day emerge as the leaders and founders
of new liberation movements have typically withdrawn
first to a "desert place." There, bearing within
themselves the deepest hopes and ideals of their people
and the seeds of a future of promise, they undergo a
profound transformation. In the wilderness their com-
forting shell of social custom and religious convention
is gradually, inescapably and painfully dismantled,
ultimately revealing to them the spiritual values
underlying the encrusted formalities. Truth, obscured
by centuries, perhaps, of disputed questions and
volumes of commentary, finally stands forth in the
clear light of human simplicity. Unstinting love is
unleashed by the force of compassion. Action is
channeled by a sharpened sense of justice and the acute
awareness of injustice. At last, the mystic process
finished, at least in its initial phase, the exiles return
from the desert in order to manifest to their
contemporaries the meaning and objective of their
great journey and to begin the next stage of the
process. The prophet appears.

If prophets are being prepared in our time, I would expect to find them in the desert. The desert seems always to have been the crucible of spiritual leadership. It need not be the barren wasteland of Palestine or the red mesas of Arizona. The Celtic monks' diseart was any silent place "far from the madding crowd" where it was possible to hear again the distant accents of a divine summons—a mountain top, an island, a secluded grove such as that beloved by St. John of the Cross, the sea, even a jail cell.

But as the divine logic of salvation unfolded in concrete human experience, it was in fact the actual wastelands that attracted spiritual pioneers—or, rather, to which they were expelled: "And Jesus, full of the Holy Spirit, returned from the Jordan, and was led by the Spirit into the desert for forty days, being tempted by the devil" (Lk 4:12). Mark wrote, more forcefully, "The Spirit immediately drove him out into the wilderness" (1:13), using a word literally meaning "to cast out" or "hurl."

Salvation in the Wilderness

Centuries earlier, Abraham had similarly been compelled to abandon the fertile crescent of ancient Mesopotamia to seek his destiny and that of an infinite multitude of physical and spiritual descendants in the deserts of Palestine and Egypt (Gen. 12:1-9). Moses fled into the wilderness to escape vengeance and there was formed by God to lead his people out of slavery (Ex. 2:15-4:31). The Israelites returned to the desert, where for forty years, God fashioned them into a Chosen People (Ex. 13:17-18).

Midbar and Arabah

Throughout the Hebrew scriptures, the desert wilderness (midbar) or empty plain (arabah) appears as the proving ground of the spirit—a place of refuge where visions come in the night and the voice of God is heard, as in the stories of David, Elijah and Elisha. (See 1 Sam. 23ff., 1 Kings 17-2 Kings 2:12-9). It was, for instance, in a cave in the desert (midbar) that Elijah finally heard the "still, small voice" of God following the tornado, the earthquake and the volcano, and after which he renewed his mission to Israel.

Isaiah sang his songs of the desert as had David before him, including the triumphant exhortation "A voice cries: In the wilderness (midbar), prepare the way of the Lord: make straight in the desert (arabah) a highway for our God" (Is. 40:3). This theme was taken up, of course, by John the Baptist, himself a desert dweller (Mt. 3:1-3), setting the tone for the eremiticism of both Jesus and his followers as well as announcing Christ's mission.

The Greek word for desert, eremos, appears frequently and importantly in the New Testament. The charter for the first desert hermits in the third century is found in Jesus' invitation to his disciples, "Come away by yourselves into a desert place (eremos) and rest awhile" (Mk. 6:31). Jesus himself often spent long periods of prayer alone in the desert, and urged his followers to imitate him (see Mt. 14:13, Lk 4:42, 5:16, 9:10, John 1:23 and 11:54).

Philip's encounter with the eunuch of Candace occurs on a desert road near Gaza—an event of importance to the early Church (Acts 8:26). After his conversion, Paul withdrew for three years into the desert of Arabia, a name which literally means "wilderness" (Gal. 1:17-18). In the Book of Revelation, the persecuted Church, in the form of the Woman clothed with the sun, "fled into the wilderness (eremos) where she had a place prepared by God (Rev. 12:6; cf. also 12:14 and 17:3). Perhaps the most condensed and provocative allusion to the spiritual fecundity of the desert forms Luke's conclusion to the infancy narrative: "And the child grew and became strong in spirit, and he was in the wilderness (eremos) until the day of his manifestation to Israel" (Lk.1:80).

Spirit in the Desert

The desert tradition remained strong in Christian spirituality, as it had in mystical and radical Judaism among the Essenes, the Therapeutae, Zealots and other sectarians. One day it would surface in great power in militant Islam. For Muhammad, too, received his summons to convert his people in the wilderness of Arabia.3/

In Christianity, over the centuries mystics and prophets from St. Antony to Charles de Foucauld have sought the living presence of God in the real desert, and countless others, like the Celtic monks, in the disearts of seclusion, called, aptly, "retreats." The spiritual theology of St. John of the Cross as well as the Spiritual Exercises of St. Ignatius of Loyola are deeply imbued with the spirit of the desert. Francis of Assisi actually traveled to the Egyptian desert to convert the sultan. And now, as then, we can still reckon with assurance that in the desert is being prepared the salvation of the world.

Fire on the Mountain: Sedona

My first stop in a remarkable journey into the great American deserts of the Southwest was to visit the Carmelite hermitage of the Spiritual Life Institute at Sedona, Arizona. For years, I had heard of these mystical "outlaws" who had traveled in search of solitude as far as the forests of Nova Scotia. By chance, I had met their founder and spiritual director, Fr. William McNamara, O.C.D., at a vocations conference in 1980. A bearded preacher in the ancient brown habit of the Carmelites, who trace their lineage back to the prophet Elijah, McNamara combines the eloquence and imagination of his Celtic forebears with the wisdom and daring of his great Spanish predecessors, Teresa of Avila and John of the Cross.

I was received with warmth and enthusiasm by the hermits, some of whom were clothed in their "work habit," a scapular-like tunic pulled over ordinary working togs. Several were hoeing in the communal vegetable garden, which was being prepared for spring planting. Although I arrived on the day normally spent in quiet solitude, the youthful group broke their routine readily to spend a few hours with me.

"Nada," the title of the more official-sounding Spiritual Life Institute hermitage, is located in central Arizona, just south of Sedona in one of the most breathtakingly magnificent regions of the Southwest. Chosen as a site because of its remoteness, the area has, ironically, become increasingly popular as a retirement haven. Now, like the monks of Miller's Canticle for Leibowitz and the hermits of Carmel a thousand years before, these contemplatives find themselves being slowly surrounded by a suburban housing project.

A Thirst for Life

A decade before hippie communes achieved notoriety in the mass media, the hermitage at Sedona was founded by McNamara and a small group of supporters following a visit to Pope John XXIII in 1960—several years before the Vatican Council would convene. But the Pope's mandate was the same in both cases: a renewal of the contemporary Church. The old patriarch richly blessed McNamara's dream of a truly contemplative adventure in modern monasticism.

Within a few years an old ranch became available, and by hard work and what money they could earn, the pioneer hermits slowly transformed it into a monastic environment, preserving its desert features. The old stone buildings became the basis of individual "cells," now named for the groups' heroes and heroines: Joan of Arc, Dag Hammarskjold, Gandhi, e.e. cummings. New structures were added—a beautiful library and kiva-like chapel. The ranch was christened Nada—Spanish for "nothing," a mystical motif in the Carmelite spirituality of St. John of the Cross and the great mystical tradition of Christianity as a whole.

Within a few years, the number of members and retreatants began to outgrow the Sedona Center. Having visited Nova Scotia giving retreats and talks, Fr.

McNamara found there the ideal location for another hermitage—an old hunting lodge near Kentville, set in a wonderful forest wilderness, "uncrowded, unpolluted, remote." With the barest minimum of equipment and resources, the transmigrated hermits adapted their new site to ancient ends, building a chapel with their own hands. Encouraged by the bishop of Yarmouth, the settlement became Nova Nada—"New Nothing."

Like St. Brigid's monastery at Kildare and other monastic exceptions in the ancient Church, the SLI hermitages are mixed—female and male, clergy and lay, and like a budding Taize, ecumenically open. One young aspirant at Nada was a Mennonite. While not strictly canonical, all regular members of the Institute observe the traditional monastic vows of poverty, chastity and obedience. McNamara reflects, "A mixed community is much more conducive to holiness. The men tend to be more manly and the women more womanly—a human condition to be highly prized these days."4/

Also like the Celtic settlements, each member lives much of the time in a separate hermitage. Common work, worship, meals and recreation are carefully integrated into the eremitical way of life, however. The members typically spend two days a week and sometimes entire weeks in complete solitude. But they are anything but idle. "We pray, read, study, enjoy the outdoors, and concentrate on individual creative projects: composing and playing music...writing poetry or prose for Desert Call (SLI's quarterly), choreographing dances for an annual Fall Festival...and creating arts and crafts that range from needlework and carving to collages of driftwood and wildflowers."5/

McNamara adds, wisely, "Creativity is an important part of the monastic life." It was the hermits' integration of art, crafts, literature and music with traditional solitude and prayer that reminded me strongly of the great Celtic centers that produced the

Books of Kells, Durrow and Lindisfarne, as well as immortal treasures in stone, wood and metal.

In addition to these contemplative activities, the monks also spend one full day and two half-days in manual labor. They grow their own vegetables and flowers, cut their own firewood—nearly twenty cords a year—bake their own bread, do their own building and repairs, and personally answer every letter received. Saturdays are devoted to domestic chores and preparation for the Sunday festival—a day of holy leisure "when we break the ordinary pattern of our daily existence all day long and carefully waste the day by praying, playing and enjoying true Sabbath rest."6/ On the first Sunday of the month, friends and neighbors join the hermits and retreatants for their midday Eucharistic festival. "Outsiders" are also welcome on that day for visits and tours. Men and women who select the hermitages for retreats have been known to stay for days, weeks or months.

Apostolic work has begun to take other members besides Fr. McNamara more frequently into the world, the "City of Man" where they share their message of serious playfulness and festal realism to anyone longing to hear a promising word. But retreats, conferences and lectures mean increasing demands on the hermits' physical and spiritual resources. The spectre of "apostolic burn-out" still lurks at the edge of engagement.

Thus, the earthly heart of both the Sedona and Kentville hermitages remains the real desert, in the Celtic sense of a remote place of solitude and communion. SLI writings frequently cite Hosea 2:14—"I will espouse you and lead you into the desert. There I will speak to your heart." Yet for all their eremitical fervor, McNamara and his co-laborers have written eloquently about the mystical and celebrative dimensions of life available to everyone, wherever they may live. The true hermits' cell, as St. Catherine of Siena ceaselessly repeated, is the cell of self-knowledge. But the discovery of the hidden depths within and among us and the One who can be found in-dwelling there seems to require an explicit experience of active contemplation in the wilds of the desert, a visible reminder of the balanced life any civilization needs to preserve its soul. It is this witness that the mystic hermits of Nada and Nova Nada have come to embody.

Arcosanti: A City from the Future

If the Carmelite hermits have espoused a simple life-style which embodies symbiotic principles hardly seen since the Dark Ages, a few miles south of Sedona there is a project underway which raises symbiosis to an exponential degree. As a beacon of hope for a human future, it would not be inaccurate to call Arcosanti a Celtic settlement. But for that appellation to make sense, some explanation is required.

Arcosanti is a small city being built on the side of a canyon about fifty miles south of Sedona, just off Interstate 17 near Cordes Junction. Initially, the project appears to differ in every respect from the voluntary simplicity, poverty and nature-love of the hermits of Nada. But on closer examination, the differences seem more quantitative and superficial.

First glimpsed from the road several miles away across the high desert, Arcosanti resembles an airport under construction or possibly a concrete circus—grey vaults and terraced domes perch on a seemingly disordered heap amid volcanic boulders and cactus on the edge of a deep arroyo. Only a few trees relieve the stark tension of randomly scattered geometric solids under a uniform turquoise sky.

My journey along this rutted dirt road to a barren construction site in central Arizona began almost ten years ago in Chicago. Paolo Soleri, the great Italian architect, was exhibiting models of his "arcologies" at the new Museum of Contemporary Art. Two other Dominican friars interested in art joined me in what was to be a profoundly unsettling preview of the future.

Walking among these huge designs for mammoth city-structures to be built over canyons, on the sea, in space, in the arctic or the desert was an experience I could not easily forget.

"Arcology" is a neologism of Soleri's for architecture-and-ecology. His vision of cities as aesthetic environments where the social and natural dimensions of life are blended to create a truly humane and ecologically sound habitat is revolutionary and—to many critics—completely impracticable. Arcosanti (another Soleri neologism combining the first with the Italian words for "before things") exists as a developing disproof of the criticism. Recently, it has been featured on CBS' 60 Minutes, in the Futurist 7/ and Science Digest.8/

Evolutionary Perspectives

Soleri was born in Turin, Italy, in 1919. There, he graduated with a doctorate in architecture from the Torino Polytechnico, receiving highest honors. After World War II, he came to America to study under Frank Lloyd Wright, whose school, Taliesin (named for the sixth-century Celtic bard) was located near Phoenix. One of Wright's most brilliant pupils, Soleri soon found himself clashing with the master's monumental ego and departed before finishing his studies.

In 1955, Soleri took up residence in the desert six miles from Taliesin. He supported himself and his family by creating the now-famous bronze and ceramic bells, the sale of which is still a major source of revenue for the Cosanti Foundation. Cosanti—the name of Soleri's foundry, studio and home—has also been the headquarters for the Arcosanti project, which was begun in 1971. But like the Celtic monks and the hermits of Sedona, the suburbs have now encircled Soleri's desert refuge and new studios have been readied at Arcosanti.

Soleri's revolutionary approach to urban planning owes much to his reading of Teilhard de Chardin, whose writings come as close as anything to an official spiritual theory behind Arcology. The centenary of Teilhard's birth, 1981, coincided with the tenth anniversary of the founding of Arcosanti. An enormous festival was celebrated there during the autumnal equinox in September. But Soleri has gone far beyond Teilhard's projection of an evolutionary symbiosis in the realm of the biosphere-noosphere, particularly the city.

According to Peter Blake, director of the architecture department of the Catholic University of America, in his foreword to Soleri's magnum opus, Arcology: The City in the Image of Man, "What I think he is trying to say is this: there is an inherent logic in the structure and nature of organisms that have grown on this planet. Any architecture, any urban design, and any social order that violates that structure and nature is destructive of itself and of us. Any architecture, urban design, or social order that is based upon organic principles is valid and will prove its own validity."9/

Soleri's approach to urban design thus recognized the need for ecological balance and integration on every level of organic and spiritual interaction. His immense arcologies are envisioned as symbiotic, three-dimensional structures, rising vertically as well as extending horizontally. Thus, large numbers of people could live on a relatively small area, but without the pressure of overwhelming density that usually results in modern cities. At Arcosanti, for instance, 5000 people will occupy approximately 13.2 acres of land. The chief building will rise some twenty-five stories, however.

The important factor in concentrating people in a livable habitat, as Teilhard foresaw, is miniaturization, our rapidly developing ability to condense information and energy into increasingly smaller spaces, such as microcircuitry and computer chips, but without reducing human scale. Other devastating aspects of modern urban life have also been designed out of arcologies: "the robotization of man, the blight of the environment, the slavery of the car, the starvation of culture, all scourges of our Western success story."10/

Soleri has incorporated further important "low-tech" developments into his designs, such as passive solar heating, greenhouse effects, air flow, heat sinks and storage. These and other features of his radical approach warrant additional discussion. But here, I would rather dwell for a moment on less evident but, I am sure, equally important spiritual aspects of arcology.

Spirit, Concrete and Steel

Once immersed in the vaulting arches and domed apses of Arcosanti, the vast <u>charm</u> of the place began to affect me. But the material environment itself was not the major factor. Rather, the infectious hospitality, friendliness and quiet enthusiasm of the staff first began to impress me and other visitors. Later at Cosanti, where I was granted a long interview by the director of Arcosanti events, Fred Halgedahl, this impression was strengthened. The music of the ever-present bells at both sites also contributed to the pleasantness of the situation, as did the evidence of an on-going humanization of the older establishment, where Soleri and his family have resided and worked for over twenty years. It is difficult to evoke warmth out of poured concrete and reinforcing steel, but it obviously can be done. Amid the low domes and sunken dwellings, I would have been less startled to have suddenly come upon Bilbo Baggins than Yoda or R2-D2.

Arcosanti, like Cosanti, is being built by volunteer labor of a special kind. Over 2000 people have paid an average of $350 to help build the city in the desert during the five-week seminars held several times a year over the past decade. Most are architectural students, artists or humanists. Even priests occasionally turn up. These young people, including the forty permanent staff members, live on or near the site in a special camp.

Arcosanti is thus an <u>educational</u> adventure of a unique character, especially since it is not funded by public or private agencies. Government grants from the now hard-pressed National Foundation for the Arts have, however, helped defray the expense of bringing artists and musicians from around the nation to Arcosanti for concerts and exhibitions, which are an important part of the Arcology program. Each year, thousands of people migrate to the wilderness to celebrate and enjoy themselves in the midst of the slowly emerging ecometropolis.

Although not a religious believer in any traditional sense of the phrase, Soleri is nevertheless keenly sensitive to the spiritual dimension of his work and the needs of his co-workers as well as the thousands of people who will one day live at Arcosanti. (He hopes to see the project completed by the turn of the century.) Soleri even speaks of integrating a monastery into the city. Further, he is alert to the theological significance of his theories, no doubt a legacy from Teilhard. He writes, "Since I am convinced now that religious systems are powerful attempts to predict the future, what the theological effort is, is the establishment of those operational 'constraints' that will best force spirit out of matter. Therefore, in a not too-long thread of rationalization, it appears that ecological dynamism is a theological unfolding of the future. At present, for this unfolding, sainthood and aesthetogenesis are the most direct and powerful ways. They are ever so slowly constructing the immanent sacredness that is symbolized in its potential by the simulated god of the religious tradition."11/

A Celtic monastery? Not, of course, in the literal sense. But I am inclined to think that Brigid and Colum Cille would be far more at home among the young artists and architects of Arcosanti than among the seminarians and postulants of most urbanized religious institutions. Similarly, while the Spiritual Life Institute, now moving its desert retreat into the deep forest of the Rocky Mountains near Crestone, Colorado, has not enjoyed official recognition by canonical authorities, surely these contemplatives, like their Celtic forebears, embody the age-old Christian tradition of desert spirituality in a far more authentic fashion than more institutionally acceptable monks and friars of the great metropolitan centers where they congregate. In the wilderness are still found signs hopeful for the salvation of the earth....

SIX

New Age Spirituality

The comparatively brief span of recorded history in humankind's perhaps four-million-year journey is rife with periods of profound change as one era passed and another began. In the West alone, we can follow eye-witness accounts of the end of the Bronze Age with the advent of iron, the collapse of the Roman Empire and the beginning of nation-states, the decline of feudalism and the rise of cities and a mercantile economy, the decline of chivalry and the emergence of mechanized warfare, the destruction of catholic Christianity with the Protestant Reformation, the industrial revolution and the end of handcrafts and cottage industries, the electronic age and the end of mechanization, the atomic age and now, the possible end of civilization....

These examples are themselves but moments of fluctuation in a much larger rhythm of change that has encompassed three great shifts in human culture—from hunting and gathering to an agrarian economy, from that to an urban-industrial economy, and from that to a "post-industrial" society—whatever that may turn out to be. Each major and minor transition period has been marked by a felt breakdown in custom, institutions, values and goals as a new way of life was slowly born out of the ashes of the previous epoch. Since different sectors of society inevitably occupy different stages of cultural development and have different capacities for adaptation, the process of change can never be smooth. Rather, it is a time of anxiety, distress and confusion, partially because our sense of security—what John Dewey called "certainty"—is pinned down by routine, and partially because the formation of new customs, institutions, value systems and objectives is at least initially an _implicit_ process, that is, not wholly conscious.

Diremption

Our era is undoubtedly unique in the rapidity and thoroughness of the felt shift of cultural values, structures and standards. Such a rapid transformation can only be experienced as a kind of violence, and since we are not at all sure what the brave new world we are so quickly entering will be like, it is also a period of vast and unprecedented insecurity if not downright terror. Many of our most cherished institutions, beliefs and customs seem either to be already crumbling or seriously threatened. It is not without reason that "historians of the future" refer to the present transition period as a "Dark Age" or an "Age of Chaos."

Among recent writers who have explored the meaning of this transformation, perhaps none have probed both the immense scope and profundity of the challenge we face as did E. F. Schumacher. He also suggested an effective strategy for coping with social change. Whether or not we follow his advice, it is worth noting that his suggestions do in fact constitute a _model_, that is, an explanatory representation of a complex phenomenon pared, as it were, to its essential structures and functions, miniaturized but basically incomplete.

Any adequate model for a possible future must, in fact, include every aspect of human significance: ideas, values, beliefs, goals and norms. In addition, some sense of meaningful continuity with the past must be preserved and a way out of our current predicament must be indicated. Such a model becomes, in effect, a _spirituality_ when it is translated into particular, concrete terms for both individual persons and groups. For spirituality, as we have been using the term, means the total way of life deliberately adopted by a person or a group of persons which crystallizes the meaning and purpose of life and provides a plan of action for realizing goals and values. In this sense, Schumacher was a spiritual writer.

Partial Views

The industrial age has had its philosophical critics, among them the most profound minds of the era—from the brooding Kierkegaard to Heidegger, Jaspers and Sartre. Marcuse, Hannah Arendt and other European intellectuals have wrestled with problems of meaning and value in the wake of Auschwitz and Hiroshima. In America, James, Hocking and Dewey attempted a more constructive critique of industrial civilization. Many other thinkers have scanned the horizon of history and sounded the depths of social transformation in search of the meaning of what we have gained and lost in the relatively short era since the dawning of the industrial revolution.

Among the philosophical prophets of post-industrial society, few have searched so deeply into the past as well as attempted to anticipate the future in a critically responsible manner as Marshall McLuhan1/and Jacques Ellul.2/ The former, a professor of language, devoted his immense skills to evaluating the impact of electronic media. The latter, a professor of law and theology, has consistently excoriated the totalitarianism of la technique—the ideology of technical expertise. For all their brilliance—and in my estimation, neither has been surpassed with regard to their understanding of two powerful social forces—neither has provided an encompassing vision of the human dilemma facing the world as a whole.

Buckminster Fuller, possibly the greatest engineering genius of our times, has written extensively and optimistically about constructively designing the future through further developments of technology.3/ In this, he represents the antithesis to Jacques Ellul's position, and his views are not without merit. But Fuller has never developed a comprehensive and coherent world view that could be considered a genuine philosophical system. Similarly, while the books of Barbara Ward and Rene Dubos, she an outstanding economist, he a laureate microbiologist and medical pathologist, are philosophically profound as well as scientifically sound, they did not attempt to present an encompassing vision of the meaning of human experience which we call a philosophy of life.4/

The visions of these unusually gifted and remarkable men and women are far from being one-sided, narrow interpretations of life. On the contrary, their lucidity, humanity and wisdom have offered hope to millions of concerned people throughout the world. But as might be expected, being partial accounts of a vastly complex situation, these interpretations and proposals often clash like enemy patrols encountering each other by night. And although there are still plenty of philosophical systems, few if any seem to have much relevance to the rapidly changing world situation as we have been considering it. The current of fashion in professional philosophy has, if anything, mirrored the fragmentation and specialized detachment which have so vitiated contemporary life—from the disintegration of medicine into isolated compartments unintelligible outside their own precincts to the deterioration of cities, the breakdown of the economy and, indeed, the social system itself. Such catabolic phases are, I suppose, natural enough, especially in the throes of vast change. The tendency of all large systems is to devolve into smaller units—an illustration of the entropic function of process. But there is a proportionate need, especially in the realm of human concerns, for some form of comprehension in order to render this fractionalization itself meaningful.

The Amateurs' Hour

Ironically, the most penetrating and self-consciously philosophical attempts to provide a foundation for assessment and redirection of western culture seems to have come from amateur philosophers. "Amateur" of course means "lover." E. F. Schumacher was an amateur philosopher in this sense—although the phrase is redundant, since philosopher means "lover of wisdom."

It was indeed to wisdom that Schumacher called upon the West to return, sensing that this tradition-hallowed goal of human searching had been too-nearly displaced by technical "know-how"—even, I might add, in philosophy. Like his elder professional colleagues of a generation before, Hocking, Heidegger, Gilson and Maritain, Schumacher believed that the root of our troubles was in fact a metaphysical disorientation and that the true remedy for the pervasive malaise of our time lay in recovering our ultimate bearings, not in solving problems as they arise by ever more stunning feats of technological legerdemain.

Toward a New Summation

Schumacher's career well prepared him to grasp the implications of the environmental disaster our industrial civilization had set in motion. An industrial economist, he was among the first internationally recognized authorities to sound the tocsin. Further, he was able to propose an overall solution to many of the interconnected aspects of our global problems, one which he set out in fairly simple terms despite its extensive ramifications. He also carried through his theoretical proposals in the form of concrete programs, living to see them succeed where many other plans had failed. Finally, and by no means least, in the last book published while he was alive, as well as in his extensive lectures, Schumacher was able to articulate a nascent philosophical system which bridged the gulf created in the nineteenth century between traditional western thought and the modern world. His work and his philosophy were sides of one coin, and, as it turned out, a very surprising coin.

For Schumacher was not only a man possessed of keen philosophical insights and a classical appreciation for what has been revered as "wisdom." He was also endowed with acute spiritual sensitivities. In fact, his philosophical scheme, which he did not live to complete, clearly inclined toward a theological resolution, but one always attuned to the demands and possibilities of real people living in a concrete world.

A Man Called Fritz

E. F. Schumacher—"Fritz" to his friends—was a native of Germany. He came to Oxford in 1930 as a Rhodes scholar to study economics. Except for brief periods of teaching and advisory work abroad, he lived in England until his death in 1977.

In his early career, Schumacher worked as a businessman, farm laborer and journalist, positions which earned him first-hand acquaintance with small-scale or what he was later to call "appropriate" technology. After four years of service with the British Control Commission in Germany after World War II, he served as chief economic advisor to the British National Coal Board for two decades, gaining an intimate knowledge of large-scale technology as well as the advantages of decentralized administration. He next became president of the Soil Association, director of the Scott Bader Commonwealth Co., and in 1965 founded the Intermediate Technology Group with the help of a group of friends similarly concerned about the place of technology in the economic development of Third World nations. As George McRobie, one of his associates, points out in the introduction to Good Work, a posthumous edition of lectures and essays, "Today, there are more than twenty similar groups operating in as many countries, and the concept has been taken up by U.N. agencies, governments, and voluntary organizations throughout the world. It is now recognized as being every bit as relevant to the rich countries as to the poor."5/

Expert on problems of rural development, Schumacher served as an advisor to the governments of several

Third World nations, for which he was later decorated, becoming a Commander of the British Empire. In the mid-seventies, following the publication of Small is Beautiful, he toured the United States lecturing to over 60,000 persons. His visit climaxed with a presidential audience with Jimmy Carter. Schumacher died on Sept. 4, 1977, in Switzerland, at the age of 66.

Philosophy and Sufficiency

Small is Beautiful, Schumacher's first and largest book, catapulted him into international prominence. It was basically a collection of essays and talks concerning the dilemmas confronting the creation of a humane economics. In his next book, A Guide for the Perplexed, he articulated the philosophical concerns close under the surface of the earlier work but which had received only passing attention. The title of this book, significantly, is taken from a philosophical work by the great Jewish thinker and mystic of twelfth century Cairo, Moses Maimonides.6/ Schumacher also made explicit in his second book that the real basis of both his philosophy and his practical programs was a profoundly Christian, indeed a traditional and theological vision of life. In Good Work, the third, posthumous book, we discover in several of Schumacher's U.S. lectures further dimensions of his moral, metaphysical and theological world view, although much less systematically organized and presented.

As a traditionalist, Schumacher repudiated the dismemberment of the classical philosophical corpus in the so-called modern era, first by Descartes, then by Kant and his successors in the dominant philosophical establishment throughout the nineteenth and twentieth centuries. Arguing against the still-prevailing fashion, he wrote, "All traditional philosophy is an attempt to create an orderly system of ideas by which to live and to interpret the world."7/ He continued, "The classical-Christian culture of the late Middle Ages supplied man with a very complete and astonishingly coherent interpretation of signs, i.e., a system of vital ideas giving a most detailed picture of man, the universe, and man's place in the universe. This system, however, has been shattered and fragmented, and the result is bewilderment and estrangement...."8/

Schumacher believed that the modern preoccupation with hard data and quick results, as if establishing facts were all that mattered, has prevented the development of an effectively comprehensive world view for most of us, resulting not only in alienation from both nature and society, but the wholesale destruction of both on an unprecedented level. Before the modern era can reclaim its "center" and regain a coherent vision of life, it will therefore be necessary to overcome several major philosophical misprisions of the late nineteenth century that have endured up to the present in various forms. The first of these ultimately destructive ideas is that of universal evolution, which reduces the vastly variegated cosmos into a mechanical process of pointless change. Allied to it is the so-called Darwinian idea of competitive "natural selection" or the "survival of the fittest," which in the form of Social Darwinism continues to vitiate Western society. Similarly, both "scientific" and Marxist materialism relegate higher life functions to the status of by-products of mindless, physical interactions, thus depriving humanity even further of dignity, nobility and spirituality. Schumacher also rejected the crude Freudianism which reduced human behavior to the vestigial spasms of frustrated infantile sexuality. In the same vein, he excoriated both relativism and positivism which in similar ways deny any absolute standards of truth and morality, maintaining that only empirically demonstrable, factually-based knowledge is valid, if never certain, and that morality is mere conventional utilitarianism.

Against these underlying assumptions of the modern worldview, Schumacher opposed what he conceived to be the classical tenets of Christian philosophy. He maintained, first, the existence of different levels of being manifesting different grades of significance—the principle of "hierarchical order." Schumacher was too careful a scientist to deny the evidence of biological evolution; he refused to condone elevating that fact to the status of a universal, reductive principle, however. Similarly, against attempts to fashion a single-valued, reductionist theory of knowledge, he defended the inescapable necessity of thinking in terms of logical opposites, what might be called the principle of paradox. As a practical corollary, he maintained a distinction between convergent and divergent problems in life, the first admitting of "solutions" in both the ordinary and scientific senses, but the second requiring a real reconciliation of opposites—a function of wisdom, not science. He ascribed to the power of love the ultimate ability to effect such reconciliation in the world of life-problems, the principle of unification.

Schumacher did not devote much attention to a demonstration of the superiority of this classical philosophical approach in his first book. But in A Guide for the Perplexed, he spelled it out in detail. It is not possible here to present an adequate summary of this interesting, challenging book. It is worth noting, however, that in elaborating a careful philosophical system, Schumacher never departed from his intense concern for the social and natural health of the world, nor indeed for the spiritual anxiety which lay at the heart of civilization's woes.

The Christian Foundation

Justice and peace were never far from Schumacher's thoughts. He was particularly concerned with the dehumanizing power of industrial society, and especially of large-scale technology. No foe of technology as such, he insisted, however, that because of the power inherent in technology, its application should be as fully appropriate as possible for the particular environments where it was to be applied. Thus, he considered nuclear energy, for instance, to constitute a serious threat, given the damage it inescapably wreaks upon life wherever it is used. "No degree of prosperity," he wrote, "could justify the accumulation of large amounts of highly toxic substances which nobody knows how to make 'safe' and which remain an incalculable danger to the whole of creation for historical and even geological ages. To do such a thing is a transgression against life itself, a transgression infinitely more serious than any other crime ever perpetrated by man. The idea that a civilization could sustain itself on the basis of such a transgression is an ethical, spiritual, and metaphysical monstrosity. It means conducting the economic affairs of man as if people really did not matter at all."9/

Schumacher was especially concerned with economic plight of the poor—poor nations as well as poor people. Here and elsewhere, he unabashedly disclosed the Christian ethical underpinning of his words and work. For instance, he thus recast the Beatitudes, which he saw, along with the rest of the Sermon on the Mount, as "pretty precise instructions on how to construct an outlook that could lead to an economics of survival."10/

"We are poor, not demigods.

We have plenty to be sorrowful about, and are not emerging into a golden age.

We need a gentle approach, a non-violent spirit, and 'small is beautiful.'

We must concern ourselves with justice and see right prevail.

—And all this, only this, can enable us to become peacemakers."11/

In all his works, Schumacher frequently referred to the Gospels and to the example and teachings of the saints, such as Francis of Assisi, Augustine and Thomas Aquinas. He pointed to the papal encyclicals as sources of wisdom and right, especially regarding the sacredness of work and the dangers of merciless industrialism. He cited Christian philosophers as teachers for our own era—particularly Etienne Gilson and Jacques Maritain. But Schumacher was neither reactionary nor narrow. He also cited from the works of Ouspensky and other non-orthodox savants. He was fond of introducing elements of oriental wisdom into his argument, having experienced it first hand during his extensive travels and work in the East. It is clear, in short, that the real force behind Schumacher's approach to both economic and philosophical problem was a profound and personal spirituality.

A Spiritual Guide

If Schumacher correctly identified the root of the disease of contemporary western civilization not only to be a metaphysical disorientation, but also its inevitable correlative in the practical order, a profound spiritual impoverishment, the answer he proposed was not merely philosophical. It was a program for spiritual renewal. Moreover, he was not only a spiritual reformer, but indeed an excellent specimen of the mystic in action, striving to rectify the course of history. This is clearly evident in three major aspects of his teaching—his reliance on the great mystics, his use of philosophical studies of mysticism, and his own incorporation of the major tenets of the classic mystical outlook on life.

First, Schumacher displayed a surprisingly wide knowledge of the spiritual classics of humankind, both eastern and western. He cited ancient Buddhist texts as well as the Bible, and found support in the words of Patanjali, the Yoga sage, the Cloud of Unknowing, St. John of the Cross, and the Philokalia.12/ Although chiefly relying on the great classics, Schumacher did not limit himself to them, citing as instances of mystical illumination and communication at higher levels of reality the experiences of Edgar Cayce and Therese Neumann.13/

Philosophically, in addition to his reliance on the great mystic sages of the West, Augustine and Thomas

Aquinas, Schumacher also cited Plotinus and Pascal and drew on the studies of W. T. Stace and Maurice Nicoll. Ouspensky figures in his argument frequently, and behind Ouspensky (and indeed Nicoll) stands the enigmatic Gurdjieff, a contemporary of undeniable power.

Finally, it can be safely concluded, I am convinced, that Schumacher was at least something of a mystic himself insofar as the central teachings of his philosophy, noted above, correspond to the fundamental axioms of the mystical worldview.14/ Briefly stated, these central tenets are as follows:

1) Unity—All is one. Beyond the undeniably manifold differences among things, everything in the universe is interrelated on a variety of levels. Connections are real in thought and action. In a religious sense, this unity is founded on the unity of God.

2) Paradox—"the path to the One is through the reconciliation of opposites." This, the hermetic principle of classical antiquity, called Enantiodromia by the Greeks, has come down to us as the coincidentia oppositorum. It was, for instance, the mainstay of the Christian metaphysics of the famed mystic of the fifteenth century, Cardinal Nicolas of Cusa.

3) Love—opposition is overcome not by thought alone or even chiefly, but by the will. The perfection of willing is to love, to intend and act out of good will toward all.

These elements are clearly stated in Small is Beautiful.15/ But they permeate Schumacher's thought in all his talks and writings. They are not static principles, moreover, but elements in a dialectic. The universe they describe is dynamic. The unity of all-in-God and God-in-all, which is a moral and spiritual unity in its final realization, is both a goal to be achieved by actual reconciliation as well as fact which makes reconciliation possible. For Schumacher, love is the highest expression of unity and also the motive and means of reconciliation.

Schumacher's Abiding Message

Schumacher's Christian humanism, as an economic proposal, directly counters the policies and practices of the industrial state apotheosized by nineteenth-century moguls and economists and incarnated today in the economic programs of politicians such as Ronald Reagan and Margaret Thatcher.

The tragedy in both England and America is not that these leaders will bring about increased economic hardships in attempting to redress the manifest excesses of over-centralized social-welfarism. Rather, it exists in the unequal burden of suffering thrust on the shoulders of the poor, as Schumacher clearly saw. It also exists in a regression to an outdated concept of private enterprise whose inevitable excesses created the opposite reaction of state socialism. Schumacher's "economics as if people mattered" represents an alternative to both extremes—large-scale private enterprise and national socialism, each of which still perpetuates inequities and subsists too largely on the strength of institutionalized greed and envy, which, again, Schumacher saw as the demonic fires driving the engines of industrial civilization.

Schumacher called the West to a Middle Way, a way of non-violence and humanity, of Buddhist compassion and Christian concern. He was too wise to think he might turn the historical tide alone, but his faith and deep concern for others fueled his optimism: "I certainly never feel discouraged," he said. "I can't myself raise the winds that might blow us, or this ship, into a better world. But I can at least put up the sail so that, when the wind comes, I can catch it."16/

Symbiotic Spiritualities

A spirituality such as that envisioned by Schumacher capable of guiding the world's peoples into a humanly possible future must have, I think, four distinguishing characteristics. It must be person-centered, holistic, social and ecological, that is, creation-centered. Ways of life that lack one or other of these hallmarks can perhaps lead to a possible future and may well do so for many people throughout the world. Whether or not such a future will be recognizably human, much less spiritual, that is, open to and transmitting the life of God, is another question. Let us take a brief look at each characteristic.

1) Person-centered approaches: Schumacher identified the rot at the core of industrial society by subtitling his major book "economics as if people mattered." In fact, for the past century and more, factories, business, industry, politics, economics and even religions have been manifestly run as if people did not matter first and foremost. What does matter in an essentially commericialized economy are increased profits, power and unlimited growth. In this respect, industrial societies, whether capitalistic or socialistic (as Poland is now witnessing) simply perpetuate the worst features of feudalism, colonialism and imperialism.

Any proposal for a humanly possible future must, in contrast, begin with the common good, the welfare of persons, and not with benefits to pressure groups, syndicates, cartels, corporations, unions, lobbies and the like. Ordinary human beings, both singly and collectively, must come first. The rest will follow in due order.

2) Holistic emphasis: The welfaring of each person and by extension that of the whole of humankind entails the possibility of integration and development to the fullest degree attainable. Such a process of growth necessarily pertains to the total human person—body, mind and spirit.

First of all and most fundamentally, food, housing, clothing, hygiene, sexual expression, recreational opportunities and even furnishings are all elements of human bodily wholeness, which is to say, health. Thus, all must be constructively integrated into a life-affirming "style" or way of living. Such a healthy synthesis does not occur spontaneously nor without effort. But achieving bodily integrity now and in the future must be considered a basic right and opportunity for all, if not an actual obligation. Further, whatever interferes with the exercise of that right is by nature unjust. Thus, persons have a right to clean air and water, food free from contaminants and additives, an environment free from industrial pollutants and radioactive wastes, commercialization and exploitation.

Second, mental integrity is no less a human birthright. The Buddhist exhortation to right-mindfulness is echoed by St. Paul's injunctions to "be transformed by the renewal of your mind"17/ and "to be renewed in the spirit of your mind."18/ Mental health requires discipline as well as freedom from psychological coercion by government and business as well as cults and sects of all kinds. The contemplative dimension of life, so alien to an industrial society, can be and must be cultivated for a full and satisfying life on earth and, indeed, as humankind reaches forth to the stars.

Third, the pre-eminent domain of spiritual integrity is the social realm itself, where bodily and mental health is manifest in the interplay among persons of different temperaments, dispositions, persuasions and intentions. All the excitement and adventure of life reaches its culmination in forms of social and worldly engagement: music, art, literature, science, worship, recreation and work. Here, the God of our future is revealed as Omega drawing us onwards as well as the God of the present within us (and our neighbor and the world-process itself) guiding us ahead. Out of the past, God as Alpha urges us on and reminds us of our destination through the pages of scripture and the collective history of the human family.

3) Socially Constructive Endeavor: Only a life-way undertaken and consciously pursued as if people mat-

tered, indeed as if civilization matters, can properly be considered a spirituality for a possible future. If a single word could characterize the most necessary element in such a spirituality, I would submit the word "social." Almost every facet of the possible life-patterns we are envisioning reflects this fundamental reality and value— which, I hasten to add, has been sadly neglected in the spiritualities of the past. Admittedly there were promptings to attend to the needs of the poor, to engage in missionary activity, to be self-sacrificing, especially in favor of religious institutions, always in the context of individual "perfection," one's own and that of the "souls" one hoped to save. But the fundamental attitude conveyed was in fact one of distrust of the social dimension of human experience in favor of a "God-and-me" approach. At best, social action was peripheral to the spiritual projects, an "over-flow" of contemplative charity.

4) Ecological Creativity: Finally, a spirituality for a humanly possible future will necessarily take the world of nature seriously, "as if creation mattered." After over a century of Calvinistic pessimism, an attitude is surfacing in contemporary spirituality that depends less on images of redemption with roots in the banking world of old Europe and more on those of salvation, with their roots in the art and creativity of ancient Hebrew culture. Primordially, Biblical writers envisioned God poetically, as a divine potter rather than a war-lord, judge or king.

A creation-centered approach, often identified with its most recent exponent, the Dominican preacher and writer, Matthew Fox, in fact underlies the perennial spirituality of the whole Judeo-Christian tradition. It is manifest in the "Buddhist" work ethic of Schumacher and the Earth-centered teachings of the late Dr. Kit Pedler, who bade us, for the sake of human survival, to "put earth first." As an attitude distinct from the world-denying, exploitative, socially negligent spirit of the nineteenth century, a creation-centered approach is pos-

itive, world-affirming, value- rather than profit-
oriented, friendly, simple and...earthy.

Novus Ordo Saeculorum

We are indeed living, as Fr. Bill Callahan has said, in a
world on the brink of a nuclear holocaust, or, in the
words of one of President Reagan's chief advisors,
Eugene Rostow, "in a pre-war world." Envisioning an
alternative to such potent darkness may seem almost
glib in the present world context, but if alternatives do
not exist, at least in our imagination, we are as good as
dead already.

There are, in fact, many alternatives which incorporate
in some degree the four characteristics explained
above. We have considered several already. In addition,
there are New Age groups, intentional associations
including "base communities" modeled on Latin American developments, even new forms of religious life.19/

Some so-called New Age groups, seminars, programs and
literature seem to be the old occult-fringe elements
under a novel and promising label—spiritualism, esoteric
religion, "psychic arts," theosophy, Tarot readings and
the like. Gnosticism redivivus seems to be the major
philosophical undercurrent of such enterprises. Also
parading under the New Age banner are popular movements espousing biofeedback, holistic health, herbalism,
metabolic therapy, bioenergetics, iridology, health foods,
colonic irrigation, aerobic dancing, solar energy, wind
power, hair-protein analysis, and a variety of other
preoccupations which basically have in common a departure from or repudiation of conventional practices—
medical, therapeutic, dietary, exercise and so on. In this
regard, "New Age" means in effect "alternative," and
what it is alternative to seems to be mainstream western
culture in general and particularly industrial society.

But "New Age" is not just an umbrella for the old
occultism or countercultural attitudes toward health.

Nor it is simply synonomous with the orthodox and profoundly Christian commitment of the Celtic monasteries, with their gospel values and voluntary simplicity. This is especially important with regard to assessing hybrid groups such as the Findhorn Community in northern Scotland and William Irwin Thompson's Lindisfarne Association in southern Colorado. Both represent remarkable achievements in the material as well as spiritual orders. But despite their interest in and profession of Celtic mysticism, their penchant for the esoteric, occult and heterodox weakens their claim to spiritual kinship with the likes of St. Colum Cille and Aidan. If New Age spiritualities are to be Celtic in inspiration and expression, it will be found in their embodiment of the ancient monks' love of God, closeness to nature, their delight in art, literature and song, their loyalty to the Christian ideal of service and simplicity of life, not in esotericism and discordance. It will be found no less in their ability to integrate a passionate commitment to humankind's most deeply cherished values with the best of what is truly "new" in the age to come.

Signs of Hope: A Surprise Factor

Contenders other than those which claim a real or imagined Celtic connection may just as well embody the elements of the equally unselfconsciously Celtic spirituality of early Christian Britain and Ireland. We have investigated some contemporary examples, such as the Carmelite monastery near Sedona, Arizona, and Paolo Soleri's dream-project fifty miles south of there. Here I want to pause to view a development on the spiritual horizon which quite unexpectedly fulfills many of the criteria of New Age and Celtic spirituality. More than that, it is whimsical, strenuous and even fun.

The Society for Creative Anachronism

Throughout the United States and Canada, more than 5000 high school and college age youths, young adults and few Middle Agers like myself deliberately (if

somewhat haphazardly) inhabit a medieval world spanning the sixth to the sixteenth centuries. Another 5000
participate in various ways without formal membership.
Begun by a group of science-fiction enthusiasts in 1966,
the Society for Creative Anachronism (SCA) is now
localized into eight kingdoms and a host of lesser
principalities, duchies, shires and the like. The network
is linked by national and regional newsletters as well as
a variety of events from minor revels to full-scale
"wars."

The involvement of thousands of bright, creative, dedicated, exuberant young people in a movement which
extols medieval social structures, values, ceremonies and
emblems, costumes, weapons, arts, food and music obviously indicates a deeper significance than mere re-
creation. First of all, if somewhat negatively, SCA
represents, I think, a repudiation of the modern era in
the form of a deliberate "regression" to an epoch more
coherent, more humane, and more fulfilling than ours.
Not that SCA members literally attempt to recreate the
Middle Ages. Like the novels of Katherine Kurtz and the
countless games of "Dungeons and Dragons" around the
country, SCA's world is as mythological as the universe
of Star Wars. As such, secondly, their medieval world is
in fact a mirror of this era, not that of a millenium ago.
Third, and most positively, SCA does not represent a
gesture of desperate disappointment in the future.
Rather, it is a sacrament of hope that a future can be
brought into existence which is not alien to the hearty,
boisterous but fundamentally humane values of the western tradition. SCA is a paean to justice, revelry and
gallantry.

It can be legitimately objected, I grant, that much—
perhaps too much—of SCA's energies are directed to
weaponry, wars, battle practice and mayhem, even if
the weapons are padded rattan and there are stringent
safeguards against personal injury. But SCA's jousts,
tournaments and skirmishes are nonetheless a protest
against the inhumanity of modern warfare. If there

were ever a subtle pacifism, it is precisely in this humane warrior cult, which is far more eloquent in its repudiation of nuclear weapons than the grotesqueries of much street theater. Even as a release for pent-up aggressiveness, the controlled but strenuous frays of these contemporary knights and commoners are far more effective and less dangerous that the equally ritualized slaughter of the football or hockey fields.

Even granting the occasionally bellicose character of ancient Celtic monasticism, how can any of this be taken as evidence of spiritual values? Lip service is indeed paid to religion and the Church. But the presence of ersatz monks, bishops, abbots, friars, priests and nuns, while ostensibly Catholic, does not in itself testify to a factual spirituality.

Here again, I suggest that the importance of SCA's creation of an anachronistic medieval world, with all its religious panoply, is primarily and richly symbolic and must be interpreted as an indirect commentary on the current religious situation. The spirituality of the Middle Ages was not merely hierarchical and monastic. More importantly, it was pervasive, natural and holistic, affecting every aspect of life without artificial stress. It is to religion as a vital part of life that the religiosity of SCA pays genuine homage. SCA is also holistic in the total physical, mental, emotional and even spiritual involvement it encourages of its members. As a whole, the society is also personalistic enough so as to require the creation of a new persona of each member, including an appropriate name. (Titles must be earned.) Here, too, we are dealing as much with implicit social criticism as self-indulgent whimsy.

Overall, SCA happily demonstrates that the development of spiritualities for a humanly possible future need not be a grim affair of non-conventional technological options and political activism. A wide variety of manifestations are possible, each as valid an incarnation of the essential characteristics of symbiosis as any other. As a model for alternative lifestyles, such an anachronistic pastime is thus far more important than it might first appear. It also reminds us that perhaps the most crucially human attribute needed for a successful venture through the Coming Dark Age is what got us through the first one and was so brilliantly exhibited in Celtic spirituality—creative imagination.

Beyond Narcissism

In sum, any spirituality for the future must, I believe, be compassionate, ecological, egalitarian, generous, inclusive, but above all (or, rather underlying all), social. Cooperatives, coalitions and basic communities must replace the largely unworkable structures comprised of the so-called nuclear family, the market-place and government, especially with its monstrous off-sprout, the "military-industrial complex." For individ-ualism has increasingly little to say to a world overburdened with problems and challenges that cry out for social solutions and responses. Environmental deterioration, the oppression of minority groups, widespread and increasing poverty, the spectre of global famine, brushfire wars and the real possibility of nuclear war, overcrowded and inadequate prisons, escalating crime rates, the commercialization of entertainment and sports, the felt loss of ethnic, traditional and family roots, the loss of transcendence—all are essentially social issues that bear mightily on everyone's spirituality.

Because of the intensely communitarian character of such a spirituality, it will also require a dimension of privacy and creative solitude, however. Such a retreat into the deeper recesses of self-knowledge will not be a capitulation to individualism, however, for it can no longer be merely an escape from social reality into a world of idiosyncratic fantasy, if that had in fact ever been the case. Far more, it will not represent a rejection of the human world with its problems and promises. Rather, periodic and regular withdrawal into contemplative silence must be undertaken with the social dimension at heart and in mind, as a re-creation of personal and communal energies, a refreshing of the sources of action in the depths of the spirit.

Contemplative withdrawal allows for the necessary distancing from the collective structures, forces and institutions which so powerfully bear down upon human consciousness so that they can be recognized clearly for what they are, how they operate and what they mean. Paradoxically, this process of social disengagement for the sake of re-engagement occurs only by indirection. It is only by pursuing contemplation for its own sake that it can accomplish its essentially social function.

The egolessness of true spiritual development is no more a suppression of personality than it is a rejection of society. Real illumination is part of a growth process which overcomes the heightened self-consciousness of adolescence by going beyond it. C. G. Jung called this process "individuation," which is as good a term as any. But Jung also recognized the presence and operation of collective forms of conscious and subconscious forces, and he clearly saw the emergence of new depths of social awareness as the climax of individuation.

A New Kind of Consciousness

Perhaps the most ecstatic of all human experiences is the mind-expanding discovery that at the ground-level of all consciousness there is not a solitary "I" forever locked in a prison of self-awareness, but a mutual "We" which forms the basis for transcendence itself. Thus, beyond the relatedness of "I-Thou" encounters, even the mystical experience of God, there is a further dimension of life and experience that is radically social. William Ernest Hocking, the American religious philosopher, called it "con-subjectivity." Its unifying "We-Thou" encounter with the Spirit of the living God is the highest form of mystical experience. It unites us into a communal, organic society, a body of sharing, suitably and perfectly symbolized in the ecstatic meal we call Holy Communion. For Christians, the Eucharist is the social sacrament par excellence, and the eschatological sign of the "heavenly banquet," the beatifying vision which is simultaneously a total experience of God's presence in immediate directness and clarity and a felt participation in the wholeness of the human family.

Traditional images such as the "Wedding Feast of the Lamb" fail in some measure to convey the intense communal nature of our collective union with God because of the cultural distance between the twentieth century and virtually the entire previous history of the human race. For a technologically oriented society, other images may be more useful. Among them, the network bids fair to become of the most powerful and fruitful.

Systems of the Spirit

The dynamic, cybernetic character of the network makes it an apt symbol not merely of future human relationships, but also of the atom, the central nervous system, the solar system, the galaxy and perhaps even of the universe itself. In a social and spiritual sense, networks are voluntary or "intentional" associations of persons often distant from each other because of social or geographical factors. They exist for information exchange, to consolidate research, economics or action as well as to provide a real sense of personal commitment and solidarity. Networks may be primarily informational or supportive, they can even be therapeutic or "merely" serve to enhance friendship and personal development.

As a form of potential consubjectivity, networks are likely to succeed both individualism and isolated groups as the primary agency of personal effectiveness on the world scene in the future. Many, including playful groups such as the Society for Creative Anachronism, already have. In this, they are reminiscent of the early Christian churches, the families or paruchia of Celtic monasteries in the Dark Ages, the mendicant orders of the medieval period, the early Jesuits and similar groups. In the political sphere, similar examples might include the

Freemasons, the Rosicrucian Brotherhoods, the revolutionary cells of late eighteenth-century Boston and Paris as well as those of twentieth-century communists and terrorists groups such as the Irish Republican Army, the Palestinian Liberation Organization, the Red Brigade and other "popular fronts."

Such "dark" sides of social networking should remind us of the destructive potential in all organization. Well-disciplined, tightly bound bands of assassins have, after all, existed in both the West and the East in times past. Furthermore, contemporary terrorist groups operating throughout the world at this moment seem to have more in common than strategy, as Claire Sterling has argued persuasively in her important book The Terror Network. The alternative to a humane and open global society of the future may well be a vicious, semi-hidden tyranny of power-crazed misfits armed with nuclear weapons.

Whether benevolent or destructive, what such associations have in common besides their computers, dedicated workers and amazing resources is a shared vision, a sense of solidarity, effective lines of communication and a high level of active participation. These are necessary qualities for all social action and indeed of survival. They can and must be developed on a wide scale by anyone hoping to contribute creatively to the eventual success of a truly humane world, a spiritually vital New Age.

Having examined the groundwork for a humanly possible future, the next part of this book will investigate in greater detail some of the key areas of contemporary life in the light of some of the prognostications we have reviewed as well as the illuminating lessons of the Celtic past. Only a few of the crucial issues facing us could be addressed in a single book. But these forays into the possible are not isolated excursions; they have their own ramifications and, if successful, will point out a host of related areas ripe for spiritual questing.

SECTION TWO:

MATTERS OF LIFE AND DEATH

...in Christian asceticism detachment is for a new kind of involvement, for joy in creation unspoiled by possessiveness either of the creature or of oneself, because one has found God in all creatures and all creatures in him.

—Gerald W. Hughes, S.J.
In Search of a Way 1/

SEVEN

Project Earth

A global paradigm shift occurred on a massive scale at Christmastime in 1968. As a greeting to the people of Earth, the astronauts aboard Apollo 8 had prepared a surprise —Frank Borman's reading of the opening passages of Genesis. Then he described the earth as seen from space. For many of us below, like Borman, and, later, Edgar Mitchell, "Buzz" Aldrin and other space voyagers, the sight of the planet, so radiantly blue against the black velvet emptiness of space, came as an awakening, a true enlightenment.

The globe hung there like a fragile Christmas tree ornament—vulnerable as well as exquisitely beautiful. For centuries, its inhabitants had known that they lived upon a sphere whirling through the night. But now, people whose perception of the planet had been limited to the apparently flat surface of land and sea viewed their Earth "out there"—even lonely in its majestic loveliness. And it became startingly evident that the fate of the azure globe with its vast seas and teeming cities, its mountains, forests and deserts, its animal life and precious atmosphere, was a system of interacting human and natural systems, a single, integral process of processes.

Humankind was one, and the Earth was also one. For the first time in human experience, we had acquired the perspective of distance, and with that the possibility of real intimacy, a new reverence and love for our home.

Throughout the world, it seems, wherever the message of Apollo 8 was heard or its photographs seen, a new kind of earth consciousness was born. Among the consequences of our new awareness was a heightened ecological sensitivity. Earth Day, April 22, 1970, became a watershed event for a new impulse toward conservation. Action groups sprang up like wildflowers after a spring rain. Campaigns were mounted to clean up rivers, the air, the landscape. Polluters were identified, vilified and fined. Lists of endangered plant and animal species were drawn up. Songs were composed, poems written. And, for a time, the situation improved. Even the Great Lakes showed signs of revivification. Chicago's air became cleaner than it had been in two decades. The snail darter was spared.

All that seems long ago and far away. A new mood of "economic realism" has swept away the enthusiasm of the young ecologists. Air and water pollution standards are being lowered. Herds of wild burros and porpoises are being mercilessly slaughtered. Agricultural policies are reverting to pre-Dust Bowl days. Oil spills multiply in the wake of newly opened fields for exploration and exploitation.

The success of the space shuttle has done little if anything to rekindle the dying sense of Apollo 8's enthusiasm for the good earth. It is not a time, it appears, to remind politicians and government officials that unless we drastically and quickly change our priorities concerning the earth and its fragile, interconnecting ecosystems, we may well live to see the wholesale destruction of this, our only home. We are like passengers on a ship headed for shoals who, in our greed and panic, can only urge the stokers to add more fuel to already overheated engines.

The Misshaping of Things to Come

"If present trends continue, the world in 2000 will be more crowded, more polluted, less stable ecologically, and more vulnerable to disruption than the world we live in now. Serious stresses, involving population, resources, and environment are clearly visible ahead. Despite greater material output, the world's peoples will be poorer in many ways than they are today."

These are the opening words of Entering the Twenty-First Century, the Global 2000 Report to the President commissioned in 1977 by President Carter. Prepared by the Council on Environmental Quality and the Department of State, this important report only emphasized what worldwatchers had been predicting for decades. In his sobering 1971 account of the future, The Coming Dark Age, Roberto Vacca had already identified the fundamental causes of the coming global crisis: "(1) industrial: the available deposits of raw materials in the world are being exhausted; (2) agricultural: the mechanization of agriculture cannot go on increasing at its present pace, nor will agricultural production suffice to satisfy the hunger of the world; (3) environmental: among the direct results of increasing pollution is an increase in mortality."1/

Even if steps were taken to clean up the environment, such efforts would now be too little and too late. A major breakdown of world systems is inevitable, Vacca believed, for two main reasons: "(a) the population explosion involves a large and unceasing increase in the extension of human settlements that will rob the cultivable surface of the earth still further and (b) increasing industrial pollution worsens the total problem of pollution even though reforms reduce some of its local and individual offenses."2/

Similar and even earlier warnings came from other individuals and groups—The Club of Rome, The Worldwatch Institute, even the United Nations itself in a decade-long series of conferences still going on, amplified by books and speeches by scientists and economists such as Barbara Ward, Rene Dubos, Rachel Carson, Margaret Mead, Buckminster Fuller, Barry Commoner, Paul and Anne Ehrlich and E. F. Schumacher, to name only a few. For a while, we listened.

Earth, Air, Fire and Water

Current writers carrying on the campaign for a livable earth such as Lester Brown and Wendell Berry remind us that the entire planet depends as a livable habitat upon the health of four major systems: fisheries, forests, grasslands and croplands. Not only food, but all human life support comes from these sources. Garrett Hardin and William Ophuls remind us that, in the spirit of the "commons" of past centuries—public pasture-lands—we must now consider as "commons" the components of the planet as a whole: airsheds, watersheds, the land itself, oceans, the upper atmosphere, biological cycles and the biosphere—that thin layer on the surface of the planet where, and where alone, living organisms exist.3/

The immediate and long-term threats to the integrity of these systems are also far fewer in principle than might seem apparent: pollution, over-use of the land, over-grazing, over-fishing and deforestation. The reasons for excessive exploitation and pollution are manifold. Vacca's twin sources seem to be common to all of them, however: over-population and industrial over-production. As a group, over-population, pollution, exploitation and their inevitable result, waste, are today's "four horsemen of the Apocalypse." In its own way, each affects the four biological systems on which human life depends.

Population Expansion

Behind most of the severe problems facing earth's biological capacity to sustain life is the exponential growth of population on the planet as a whole, but especially in under-developed countries. From 1950 to 1975, world population almost doubled, from 2.5 billion people to 4 billion. Barring some kind of terrible calamity, it will increase as much again by the turn of the century.

A world which cannot feed its present population will have to double its food production even to maintain the existing situation of scarcity, much less abundance. Its ability to do so is very doubtful. By 2030, the world population is expected to reach 10 billion, and by the year 3000, 30 billion, the absolute maximum number of persons the planet can provide for even at maximum productivity.

As the Global 2000 Report noted, of the 100 million people added to the earth's population every year, 90% are born in the poorest countries, where human misery is already assuming tragic proportions. Even if world food production increased by 90% by the turn of the century, as the Report hopefully predicts, the expected doubling of food prices in the same period will nullify that gain for the poor. As it is, the amount of arable land which can be brought under cultivation is about 4%, which means that multiplying food production capacity will depend on increasing yield by means of added fertilizers, using more pesticides, and the extension of electricity and fuel supplies to remote regions. The fact that world oil production will reach a final peak by 1990 casts great doubt on the use of these technological means, since all of them are based on a petroleum economy.

Pollution

All living things produce waste; every virus, every cell, every plant and animal. Some of these waste products, the residue of metabolic and catabolic life processes, are toxic to the organisms which produce them as well as to others. As we commonly speak of the pollution problem, however, we are referring to the toxic or hazardous waste products of human, technological systems. Two factors compound the seriousness of human wastes: numbers and machinery. The enormous population expansion of the past fifty years resulted in so great a multiplication of wastes that natural and human-made disposal systems cannot adequately absorb or recycle them. Second, the specifically artificial waste products of our technological civilization are not capable of being absorbed by natural processes. As a result, they accumulate until a crisis point is reached.

These crises, such as the Love Canal tragedy in 1978 and the severe mercury poisoning in Japan which had cost over 1000 lives by 1981, will inevitably increase as the high technological pace of contemporary civilization accelerates and spreads to the less developed countries. Perhaps the most immediately threatening pollution problems are toxic chemicals already added to the soil and seas by industry, and the hazards of nuclear accidents as well as fallout connected with power plants and military operations. Air and water pollution are likely to be more long-range but perhaps even more destructive problems in years ahead.

Wastes and Shortages

In each of the major ecological systems we shall explore, the wasteful attitude of the earth's inhabitants is all too manifest. This is not merely the "conspicuous consumption" of the rich and powerful nations which consume three-fourths of the world's resources although comprising only one-fourth of its population. The poorest of the poor are also responsible for the wholesale destruction of their only source of life and livelihood in the future: the environment itself, which in their desperation and ignorance they devour beyond replenishment. Whether rich or poor, satisfying immediate needs and wants without regard for tomorrow spells disaster for all in the lean years ahead.

Mother Earth: The Nurturer

The first and most obvious system of life support is the land itself, if it is not ultimately the most important nor the most extensive. We live primarily on air, and the sea is our greatest source of protein. But we recognize the earth as our mother through whom Our Father gives us our daily bread.

One of the most serious concerns of ecologists is the increasing worldwide loss of croplands, grasslands and forests to eventual desert, a process called desertification. Not all abandoned land becomes submerged under dunes, of course, but the advance of "wastelands" throughout the most fertile areas is cause for alarm.

The Worldwatch Institute publication on cropland loss indicates three major causes of abandonment besides desertification which are especially serious in industrial nations: urbanization, energy production and transportation. The cancer-like expansion of cities, which is expected to more than double between now and the year 2000, tends to encroach upon the richest farm-lands, both in developed and less developed countries. By the turn of the century, cities themselves will have consumed the food-producing land of the equivalent of 84 million people. Energy demands, with the resulting construction of dams, mines, power plants, refineries and oil fields, as well as strip mining, have doomed more millions of acres of prime farmland. Related to energy is the automobile, which in the form of streets, highways, parking lots and service stations, as well as the urban sprawl of such cities as Los Angeles and Houston which are a direct result of the automobile-transporation system, has continually eaten away at prime lands as well.

Nevertheless, the major factor in cropland abandonment seems to be desertification. One-third of the planet's land surface is naturally arid or semi-arid; 630 million people live in these zones, 78 million of them on land almost useless because of human wastage. Fully one-half of the earth's deserts cannot support human life. Year by year, these desert regions relentlessly expand into croplands, imperilling food production everywhere. In Africa, the Sahara has been expanding both northward and southward for decades. In the north alone, more than 650,000 square kilometers of once-arable land have been lost to the desert in fifty years. In the north, 100,000 hectares of range and cropland are lost to the desert each year. (In the metric system, a hectare is equal to 2.47 acres.) Other regions of the earth threatened by desertification include large sections of the Middle East, western Asia, northwestern India, Australia and the Americas, where areas of Argentina, Mexico, Brazil,

Chile and the southwestern portions of the United States are becoming desert.

Desertification results from erosion of croplands and rangelands by wind and water, dune formation, vegetation change and salt or alkaline encrustation. Soil erosion is perhaps the major cause, itself the result of inappropriate methods of plowing as well as the uprooting of windbreaks. In Italy, more than two million hectares of land have been thus lost in the past decade.

With erosion comes the loss of topsoil, the thin layer of rich earth which alone can grow vegetation. Over most of the earth's croplands and rangelands, topsoil is only inches deep and once lost cannot be renewed for centuries, if ever. (A temporary remedy can be found in the use of fertilizers, but such artificial means actually accelerate the process of thinning and depletion.) In the farm state of Iowa, 200 million tons of topsoil are lost every year because of inadequate farming methods. Wisconsin also suffers severe losses, and the situation is worse in Europe. Waterlogging and salt/alkali encrustation further devastate croplands throughout the world, being a serious problem in the Soviet Union, China, Egypt, Argentina, India, Pakistan, Mexico and the United States. Salinification and alkalinization are usually the product of improper irrigation techniques, particularly inadequate drainage.

As a consequence of human mismanagement, world land productivity, rather than increasing, is falling off— slightly in the United States, France and China, but greatly in the Soviet Union, Egypt, Africa and Latin America. Together with losses of land to erosion and desertification, such reverses can mean only one thing in the face of unceasing population expansion: famine on what will likely be a world-wide level within twenty years.

There are possible solutions to these problems, all of them falling under the category of conservation: the introduction of regional land management programs, especially in less developed countries; the reduction of herd size and over-grazing; improving farming methods with appropriate technologies; educational programs and improving grain reserve facilities.4/ The only alternative will be increased malnutrition, famine, serious under-employment of agricultural persons, migrations, deepening poverty and depths of human desperation never before seen on earth.

Deforestation

More than 20% of the earth's land surface is covered by forests dense enough to be considered "closed." Another 12% is open woodlands. The importance of forests cannot be underestimated as a factor in providing food, fuel, building material and protection for animal and plant species. The global temperature also depends on trees, which reduce carbon dioxide and produce oxygen. The moisture content of the air also functions as a forest-related phenomenon. It is for these among other reasons that the rapid disappearance of forests throughout the world has become a grave concern to scientists.

Although 42% of the world's tropical forests are still wooded, between 25 and 50 million acres are lost each year. The U.S. Interagency Task Force on Tropical Forests now projects that within fifty years the world's tropics will be denuded of trees, with the following effects: wild fluctuations of surface temperatures, a sharp rise in the carbon dioxide content of the atmosphere, and the extinction of over a million species of animals and plants, 20% of the total number in the world.

Since 1970, Thailand has lost one-third of its forests, the Ivory Coast and Costa Rica a fourth, Southeast Asia and Latin America two-thirds of their original forests, and Africa one-half. Haiti's woodlands will be depleted completely by 1985, those of the Philippines by 2000. While Asia, Africa and Latin America will face extra-ordinary shortages of trees within a few years, Europe, North America and the Soviet Union will fare better. In recent years, however, only China and South Korea have shown net gains in forests. The worldwide tree shortage will also be felt in the developed nations, however, which still import some lumber. More important by far will be the loss to pharmacy, for more than one-third of all drugs manufactured in the United States are obtained from tropical plants.

Remedies are of course possible. These include the expert management of existing forestlands; reforestation on an unprecedented level; the introduction of re-plenishment systems such as coppicing—allowing trees to produce new growth from stumps; substituting other materials for wood when possible; the development of alternative methods of cooking fuel, such as solar energy and biogas; and extensive recycling, especially of paper products. The most urgent development in Third World countries should be the formation of cooperative com-munity action and education programs.

The Breath of Life

The most pervasive, powerful and necessary element in the biosphere is, of course, the air itself. While a "shortage" of air is not a real possibility, pollution and the resulting shortage of breathable air has become a pressing issue. Throughout the world, the introduction of pollutants into the atmosphere has already produced highly destructive effects, from the acid rains which kill plant and animal life in lakes and rivers from Minnesota to Sweden and dissolve priceless monuments of art and architecture throughout Europe to the fumes of steel mills and paint factories which eat away the lungs of the American poor. A rising concentration of carbon dioxide in the air has been measured on moun-taintops in New Mexico and the plains of the Antarctic; there is no place to escape.

The saturation of the atmosphere with carbon dioxide is possibly the most threatening feature of worldwide air pollution. Caused by the combustion of petrochemicals, especially coal, by industry, and by the burning of wood for fuel throughout the world, the mount of carbon dioxide in the air has increased from a preindustrial level of less than 290 parts per million to about 330 parts per million today. By the year 2000, the level will have increased another 30%. According to the National Academy of Sciences, it will take one thousand years to dissipate the carbon dioxide already accumulated in the atmosphere.

The eventual effect of increasing carbon dioxide will be a rise in the mean temperature of the earth's atmosphere, which will affect weather patterns all over the world. In fact, it already has. A meeting of an international society of meteorologists in Geneva predicted in March, 1981, that the temperature will rise one degree centigrade by the year 2000 because of excess carbon dioxide. This alone will produce devastating effects on agriculture and fishing, altering the jet stream, rainfall patterns and the Gulf Stream. In itself, the rise in temperature will not melt the polar icecaps, which would require a rise of four degrees. Taken together with the effects of further combustion, deforestation and desertification, however, it is very likely that the mean temperature will rise more than four degrees, inaugurating a rapid deglaciation of West Antarctica and the North Polar region.

The sudden addition of water to the earth's seas from the poles would cause an elevation of sea level of some five meters—enough to flood most of the coastal regions of the world, including some of the world's most populous cities. The imperative to develop alternative sources of energy and to restore the world's forests, grasslands and croplands is thus urgently serious.

To Build a Fire

One-third of the world's population uses wood as fuel for both cooking and warmth. In poorer countries, 90% of the population so depend on wood, spending as much as a fourth of their yearly income on firewood. On the average, each person burns as much as a ton of wood per year, not only helping to deplete the world's wood supply, but adding to the carbon dioxide in the atmosphere. By the year 2000, demand for firewood will exceed supply by 25%.

The loss of available wood from deforestation will, in the absense of strong conservation measures, inevitably result in soaring prices, scarcity, the conversion of animal manures to use as fuel—thus impoverishing the soil even further; greater deforestation and desertification and an increase of poaching practices and other forms of law-breaking. In terms of wood shortage, the worst problems will exist in developing countries, where prices have already soared as much as 300% in two or three years: India, Africa, the Andean countries, Central America, the Caribbean and the Far East.

Alternatives do exist but are difficult to initiate where shortages have not already become acute. These include many of the remedies for deforestation, for the two problems are closely related: use of solar energy, the introduction of biogas and even petroleum-fueled appliances, and the creation of more hydroelectric power plants—even despite the devastation such dams could wreak on farmlands. But planting and replanting of trees remains the essential component of any workable plan to preserve wood for fuel and other purposes.

Not a Drop to Drink

Water, next to air, is the most vital of all natural resources for living creatures. It is also the second most abundant, covering 71% of the earth's surface. But only 3% of that water is fresh, and only one-third of that is available for drinking. Another one-third is frozen, and the other lies underground. Less than 1% is found in lakes, streams and rivers.

As with other natural resources, the threats to water as a resource are pollution and shortage. "Pure" water exists only in laboratories. Naturally, water is a mixture of many elements beside oxygen and hydrogen.

Gases such as dissolved nitrogen are always present, as are metals such as iron, calcium and magnesium, which make water "hard." Other metals which might be present include selenium, arsenic, chromium, lead, cyanide, copper, nickel, mercury and barium—some of which are toxic. "Artificial" and usually beneficial additives found at least in the U.S. include chlorine and flouride. Real pollution exists in the form of industrial wastes such as vinyl chloride and poly-chlorinated byphenyls (PCBs), pesticides such as DDT and dieldrin, and various radioactive compounds which have seeped into groundwater. In addition, earth's water systems have been found to contain "oil, chemical effluents, lethal gases, radioactive wastes, junk metal, trace elements, organic wastes from humans and animals, automobile exhaust products...detergents and other wastes...."5/

The U.S. Coast Guard estimates that there are 10,000 oil spills in our own navigable waters each year. A million tons of oil seep into the seas from ships and wells, as do several million tons of crude oil products such as waste crankcase oil. From 1946 to 1970, 114,500 barrels of radioactive wastes were routinely dropped into the oceans. Needless to add, fish, mammals and birds have been increasingly poisoned by such pollutants, and through them, increasing numbers of human persons. For most of the peoples of the world depend on the sea for their protein.

Water shortages have already begun to appear in this country as well as abroad for a variety of reasons. By 2000, a critical situation could exist in many western and southern states, and recent droughts have adversely affected even New England states. There, over 200 communities could be short of drinking water by 1990. In the world as a whole, 1.5 billion people already lack safe drinking water and the situation is worsening. Demand is expected to double, moreover, by the end of this century.

In addition to pollution and shortages, the plight of the oceans has been exacerbated by overfishing, which has seriously depleted some of the world's richest fishing areas, including vast stretches of the northwestern and northeastern Atlantic. As stocks dwindle and catches decline, prices will climb, further worsening the condition of the poor in particular. Species of animals such as the whale will face extinction, and serious malnutrution will affect possibly the majority of humankind.

Remedies and solutions are possible here as in other areas of the worldwide ecological crisis. Most of them are reducible to a single theme with many variations: conservation and replenishment, together with alternative methods of producing food and fuel. The major factor to be added is the collective will to implement the necessary and sometimes unpopular policies necessary for Planet Earth to continue as a viable habitat for its passengers.

Conclusions

The awesome sight of the world hanging in space gave humankind the opportunity to envision the problems of the world as a whole, perhaps the major paradigm shift of this century in our ways of viewing reality. No longer is it possible to consider hunger or water shortages or clean air as local problems. John Donne was right: there are no human islands. We are all part of the main.

What was an opportunity in the late 'sixties has become a mandate for the 'eighties. In the United States, however, we may one day look back to the elections of 1980 as a tragic turning point in the natural history of Planet Earth. It is now clear that instead of continuing, accelerating and expanding the conservationist policies of previous administrations, the Reagan administration largely turned its back on environmental protection. In fact, policy was placed in the hands of powerful and wealthy interests diametrically opposed to the programs urged not only by the Council on Environmental Quality but of the United Nations conferences on planetary resources, the Worldwatch Institute and every conservationist association in this country.

The slow work of years of conservation can be reversed in months. In 1981, for the first time in five years, the Environmental Quality Index of the National Wildlife Federation showed no signs of improvement. The quality of water, wildlife, soil and living space actually declined. Not only here, but throughout the world, the crisis has begun in earnest. As an element in a spirituality for a livable future, a "new asceticism" now requires commitment and support for persons and groups pledged to protecting the environment. It likewise requires personal involvement in conservation practices at the everyday level of ordinary life, that is, adopting a lifestyle more in harmony—symbiosis—with all the living systems of our home, the earth.

EIGHT

Dissipating Energies

Severe depletion of natural resources on a worldwide scale looms ahead in our planetary future whether or not both rich and poor nations adopt effective conservationist policies. The difference will amount to whether we will suffer a sudden, catastrophic shock when the wells run dry, or, rather, gradually reduce our drain on reserves to prolong their utility until new sources of energy can be found. Ultimately, we will have to turn to the original source of all energy on earth—the sun. Wisdom suggests that we begin that conversion immediately, for all conventional sources of energy are not only finite, but in relatively short supply. Even the sun will die, of course, and when that happens, the earth will also die. That, however, need not be the end of the human race. For not all energy is physical. Even physical energy is surprisingly more mysterious than might at first glance seem evident.

Energy Famine

So serious is the coming global energy shortage that the United Nations sponsored a special Conference on New and Renewable Sources of Energy at Nairobi in August, 1981. Almost 4000 representatives from 123 nations attended. Third World delegates, whose perception of the scope of the situation probably exceeded that of those from highly industrialized nations, repeatedly urged the wealthy nations to help them finance new energy programs. The representatives from the Rich Nations, which consume the vast majority of the world's energy resources, would make only tentative and paltry bids to provide such assistance. Ironically, these same overdeveloped nations stand to lose most by a worldwide collapse of energy sources. Yet the deepest issue is not social justice or even the survival of industrial society. Rather, the survival of civilization itself is the crisis at hand.

By definition, a crisis is a turning point, a moment of danger or suspense, the outcome of which is serious and often unpredictable. Since a permanent crisis is all but a meaningless notion, it would be wiser to refer to worsening energy shortages as a global problem. For it is a difficult challenge hurled before humankind as a whole. Resolving this problem will demand appropriate decisions on both the individual and collective levels in the very near future. The real energy crisis thus involves how and when we decide to use the remaining available resources while developing new ones.

How we as a nation and a planetary people face up to the problem of growing energy shortages will determine the quality of life for many generations to come. Further, resolving the multiple problems connected with energy production, distribution and consumption will necessarily affect every aspect of life for some time to come. Thus, addressing the critical issue of dissipating energies must be considered a supremely spiritual challenge for a humanly possible future. No spirituality adequate to the needs of the present or the future may neglect it.

Energy and Entropy

Like life itself, energy is almost indefinable. We speak of nuclear energy, electrical energy, chemical and biological energy, even mental and spiritual energy. There is energy in stars and electrons, in worms and waterfalls. What energy "is" can be best described, perhaps, in terms of what it does. It makes things go. All the dynamism, thrust, movement and activity in the universe are the effect, indeed the manifestation, of energy.

Basically, energy is the capacity to do work, the power to make things happen, to move or to stop moving. It is not a single phenomenon, but a multiform expression of the dynamic character of reality, manifesting itself differently on different levels. Thus, nuclear energy and mental energy represent different capacities of reality and are not effectively measurable in equally applicable terms. Mental energy, for instance, particularly the brilliant insights of Albert Einstein, made possible the development of atomic energy—whether for good or ill. Which is more powerful?

It is therefore not misleading to speak of qualitatively higher forms of energy in contrast to quantitatively higher levels. A failure to appreciate this important fact has led to some serious blunders in recent discussions of the meaning of energy in terms of human values. One of the most awkward and persistent involves the tricky concept of entropy and the so-called Laws of Thermodynamics formulated in the late nineteenth century.

Negative Energy

Human and animal fatigue, like the "wear and tear" of life itself, testify to the character of "entropy"—a word coined by Rudolf Clausius in 1868. It means, in literal Greek, "toward (the) transformation." Energy means "toward (the) work." Entropy thus refers to the amount of energy spent in bringing about any kind of change and which as a result becomes unavailable for further use. It is not an absolute value, but a relative factor used in comparing energy levels before and after temporal and spatial changes. And that's all. Entropy is not a thing, like anti-matter, but an abstraction, a measurement of loss.

A lot of philosophical confusion has resulted from treating entropy as if it were concretely real, some kind of force, for instance. This is a good example of what Whitehead called "the fallacy of misplaced concreteness." Similarly, the Laws of Thermodynamics only describe the various relationships existing in the universe between matter and energy, perceiving the full significance of which led to the insights and equations behind the atomic bomb. The First Law states that the amount of matter and energy in the universe is constant. Neither can be created or destroyed, but each can be transformed into the other. All transformations in fact involve such matter-energy interactions. The Second Law of Thermodynamics points out that every such transaction entails some "loss" of energy, that is, the energy required to convert matter into energy or vice versa is rendered unavailable for further use in the system, usually being radiated away as heat. Entropy represents that loss.

"Lost" energy radiated out as heat (or light) becomes appallingly evident in a nuclear explosion. But it is not present in the operations of the cells in our bodies, merely less abundant than in the violently efficient transformations of fissionable materials.

The "Heat Death" of the Universe

Implications of the Second Law of Thermodynamics were recognized and dramatically promulgated by Sir James Jeans and other articulate scientists at the beginning of this century. Since the fusion transformations in the sun and other stars inexorably result in energy loss in the form of heat radiation (sunlight) they realized that it is only a matter of time—if immense eons of it—until the sun burns out. All stars will eventually radiate away their mass as energy, sometimes violently in the form of supernovae, sometimes quietly. New stars may be formed from the debris of stellar explosions, but ultimately the finite character of the material universe and its apparently steady explosion mean that they, too, will die.

At that inconceivably remote moment in cosmic history, a steady state of absolute equilibrium will have been reached. Every molecule in the universe will have attained its maximum distance from every other molecule. No more movement will ever occur. Time will cease. Light will not exist. The universe will have assumed an eternal condition of absolute darkness, coldness and immobility.

This is what James and others meant by the "heat death" of the universe.

Of course, it might not happen that way. But the dreary picture still seems to represent the strongest likelihood. For there is no compelling physical evidence to warrant believing in the creation of new matter or energy ex nihilo. Thus, the physical destiny of the universe as the consequence of entropy seems to be inescapable and absolute rest. Not unexpectedly, widespread gloom and even despair followed the publication of these bleak visions of the future. For among other things, they imply the total cessation of all life. Or seem to.

Hope for the Flowers

Without intelligent life in the universe, the "heat death" envisioned by Jeans would occur without any observers present even to lament it. It would thus be a totally meaningless event. But it is well to bear in mind that there are factors other than matter and energy in the universe which make a difference. It is also important to distinguish clearly between the heat death of the universe and regression to a steady state of absolute disorder, a view which many writers automatically espouse.

To begin with, it is evident that energy is not merely dissipated away into lower and lower levels of material immobility, but is also concentrated on increasingly higher levels of complexity in organisms of various kinds. In his important book The Quest for Gaia, the late Dr. Kit Pedler referred to this process as a "solar drive chain." He also called it, more poetically, "the flow of life in the earth organism. The circulation in the body of a Goddess."1/

Pedler showed how, ultimately, we "eat" sunlight. Solar radiation, the basis of almost all energy transactions on earth, continually bathes the planet. About 30% is reflected back into space or dispersed in the upper atmosphere. Another 47% is absorbed and reflected upwards by the land, oceans and vegetation. Only about 23% is converted by various chemical and biological cycles into different forms. Plants, for instance, "capture" solar energy and store it in their leaves as carbohydrates. Animals store it in their tissue as protein and fat, and human beings in artificial structures of all kinds. But animals and human beings do not directly convert solar energy; they acquire it indirectly by consuming plant and animal tissue as well as some minerals and metals.

This "stored sunlight" is used for work—various kinds of movement. And on a large scale, despite inevitable losses to entropy by heat radiation, chemical and biological energy is <u>concentrated</u> when more complex organisms feed on simpler ones. Bacteria ingest chemicals and other bacteria. Protozoans eat chemicals, bacteria and other protozoans. Insects and other tiny animals eat all three plus each other. All of the above can also become parasitical upon higher organisms. And thus we scale the food chain upwards until we come to omnivores like human beings that eat almost anything.

The ancient Upanishads traced the food chain upwards even farther: "As many beasts nourish a man, thus does every man nourish the Devas." William Irwin Thompson comments upon this passage, "The cosmic food-chain is an energy symbiosis, from the plants that feed off the sun to the devas and asuras (divine beings) that feed off the astral emanations of collective human thought."2/ The "gods" thus derive energy from human thoughts and prayers.

While we may not subscribe to such a mythopoeic view of divine-human relations, what is important in regard to the exponentially higher and lower aspects of the food chain is the concentration of energy in progressively more complex and intelligent life forms. A bird eats hundreds of berries and insects before becoming a feline snack. A cow must eat fifteen pounds of hay to obtain the same benefit, proportionately, as human beings get from a large steak. Happily, human beings can—and should—eat different and better foods than beef. But how many prayers does it take to nourish a deva?

Fortunately for cows, humans and perhaps devas, the transition from one to another level of order entails a shift in our concepts of measurement. We cannot assess the value of Don Giovanni in terms of the weight of sauerbraten Mozart consumed while composing it. But neither can we consider the contents of Einstein's garbage cans merely a concession to entropy.

Energy and Disorder

Like entropy, chaos is a relative concept, but not the same one, contrary to the views of some writers. If the universe ultimately thins out into a tenuous film of matter too weak to sustain any kind of energy transaction, the resulting equilibrium will not constitute absolute chaos, but absolute order, the most symmetrical of all possible patterns. Energy transformations are only possible, in fact, because of relative imbalances in systems, and, in that sense, disorder. One sector of the universe contains more matter and energy than another, and the natural "flow" from the greater to the lesser concentration makes work possible.

Creation, then, is an on-going process, in the sense that different kinds and levels of emergent order reduce the relative disorder in the universe. Such transactions not only increase the overall entropy of the universe, but imply a kind of ordering principle even in entropy itself. Further, it is important to recognize than an increase of entropy on a lower level may bespeak a concentration of energy on a higher level or order. The universe is evolving "upwards" in terms of complexity and power, but differentially. Operations of increasing order involve the realization of new kinds and degrees of complexity and intelligence. In this regard, a deva serves to represent intermediate levels of living energy forms between human beings and God.

Among the implications of such a view of the relationship existing between matter and energy, and its possible connection with life and spirit, both human and divine, is the qualification that while conservation is at least as important as consumption of energy, it is not an absolute value. Losses of available energy must be reckoned as cost factors against the gains made on conceivably higher levels and forms of organization as well as against future demands for energy. Nevertheless, as we can see from an analysis of the growing shortage of energy resources, conservation will have to play an increasingly important part in all areas of life, both in the sense that wiser use must be made of existing supplies and that alternatives to conventional energy resources must be developed.

The Crunch

The industrialized and developing nations of the world derive their energy from four "conventional" sources which represent different forms of "stored" sunlight. Together with wood, which is used as fuel throughout most of the world, these constitute a pentagon of diminishing potential. They are, in descending order of current usefulness, oil and natural gas—the fossil fuels, hydrokinetic energy, and nuclear energy.

These are by no means the only areas of critical shortage, as we shall see. They represent only part of the global depletion of materials essential for industrial development and operation. The ultimate reason for this depletion should not be hard to identify. Entropic loss inevitably dooms all such resources to final exhaustion. But entropy is not the prime agency in the global energy crunch. Rather, exploitation without regard to coming shortages is a sufficient explanation. Our primary fault is greed, not finitude. The same dynamic is tragically evident in the improvident extinction of whales by the whaling industry, which is dooming itself along with the majestic beasts it destroys.

Conventional Sources

Beginning in the nineteenth century, after millions of years of slow development from decaying organic materials, oil has been pumped from the ground in ever increasing amounts. It quickly succeeded coal as the major fuel of the industrial societies of the northern hemisphere. Presently, petrochemical combustion supplies about half of America's energy. Comparatively recently, however, it has become painfully clear that known world reserves of oil will be depleted by the end of the century—even before that if drastic conservation measures are not quickly adopted. Further, the cost of oil, and its nearest chemical neighbor, natural gas, which provides another 25% of U.S. energy requirements, will continue to rise as the fields are played out one by one. The developing nations of the world have cause to view this situation with even more concern than the industrial giants. For their possible advancement in the near future hangs in great measure on their access to oil, unless they can develop effective alternatives.

Coal, which supplies about 18% of our energy, remains fairly abundant, especially in the U.S., the Soviet Union and China. At present rates of usage, supplies could last well over two thousand years. However, the expected return to coal as a major energy resource could exhaust these reserves in just over a century. Mining it, moreover, threatens to be one of the most ecologically destructive calamities of the twentieth century. Further, coal is a relatively inefficient and highly polluting source of energy when burned.

Water remains abundant, of course. The use of hydroelectric generators to supply energy, at present about 3% of the total in this country, will undoubtedly increase in the future. Nuclear power, the youngest of the conventional resources, presently supplies about 4%

of our energy needs. But because of the financial cost of building and maintaining reactors, together with the environmental and health hazards of accidents and the disposal of waste products, it is doubtful that we shall see a major increase in the use of nuclear energy. (In 1980, almost 4000 nuclear accidents occurred in America's five dozen reactors—an increase of some 65% over the previous year, memorable for the Three Mile Island incident.)

Oil, gas and coal also produce a variety of health and environmental hazards as by-products of their use, including air, water and thermal pollution as well as increasing amounts of carbon dioxide in the atmosphere. But even if such problems as well as rising costs did not becloud continued reliance on these conventional resources, they would still be inadequate to satisfy expected demands in the next twenty years no matter how much we increase their efficiency. For with the exception of water, their supplies are diminishing.

Heavy Metal

Nor are conventional fuels the only resources in short supply. At the present rate of consumption, world reserves of gold are expected to play out in about 10 years, mercury in 13, silver in 15, tin in 16, zinc in 20, lead in 24 and copper in 30. Aluminum, platinum, chromium, asbestos, high grade phosphorus and nickel are also scarce and expected to be depleted by 2050. The reason is that worldwide demand for these metals is increasing exponentially, faster in some cases than population itself. As industrialization of developing nations increases, these rates can be expected to escalate even further. As a result, costs will also soar. In the last 30 years, the price of lead has risen 300%. In 20 years, mercury has increased in cost by 500%.

Coping

Almost every study of energy resources views these projections with grave concern, even while differing about details. It is also clear that even wholesale conversion to alternative energy sources cannot reverse the process of depletion nor appreciably alleviate the resource drain. Conservation alone, even if so strictly enforced as to necessitate a static industrial situation, could only retard the inevitable process of exhaustion. Technological innovations may reduce some of the drain on critically short resources. For instance, the new technology of micro-electronics is conservationist in so far as the main ingredient of its basic component, the microchip, is one of the most abundant of all natural materials—silicon. Miniaturization will also reduce some of the drain on scarce resources. But such developments can never halt the overall depletion of world resources.

The only workable course toward an energy-sufficient future for even a minority of the world's peoples is a combination of all these measures. But the greatest of these is conservation. Without it, all conventional energy resources together with all feasible alternatives will not be able to meet demands which are expected to multiply by sixteen times with the next century. Hence, as Stobaugh and Yergin comment in the Harvard study Energy Future, "Among the unconventional sources of energy, conservation presents itself as the most immediate opportunity. It should be regarded as a largely untapped source of energy. Indeed, conservation—not coal or nuclear energy—is the major alternative to imported oil."3/ Only with the addition of strong conservationist programs can solar power, wind power, the power from tides and ocean currents, geo-thermal power (i.e. subterranean heat) and biogas, especially methane from organic wastes and sewage, effectively supplement conventional sources and permit a reduction of oil imports.

Personal Energy Conservation

At first glance, it might appear that individual conservation efforts can only negligibly alleviate the overall energy crunch since industry accounts for at least 40% of the total demand, transportation another 25%, while residential use accounts for only 19% and "other" uses 16%. Nevertheless, as Stobaugh and Yergin point out, "the decentralized character of energy systems means that decisions to conserve, unlike decisions to produce energy, have to be made by millions and millions of often poorly informed people."4/

Yet individual persons, especially if well-informed, can and, we can hope, will make a considerable difference in meeting the series of energy crises that lie ahead. It is imperative, first, to support programs and groups as well as political leaders who promote policies of conservation. Second, choosing not to support wasteful uses of energy, including industries which pollute, multinational corporations which exhaust natural resources, fuel-guzzling automobiles and the industries which make them, unnecessary appliances, over-heating and over-cooling homes and offices, etc., when multiplied hundreds of millions of times, can contribute enormously to energy savings.

As an element in a personal spiritual lifestyle, a conscientious effort at conservation of natural resources is not only a way of rectifying our disordered relations with nature. It is also a real contribution to social justice.

Energy Justice

Economic or social justice may be considered to be the equitable distribution of goods and services among the peoples of the world. The major energy issue in this regard, as the delegates to the U.N. Nairobi conference learned, concerns the inequitable divisions among the rich and poor nations of the earth. America is not the only "rich man" in this scenario, nor are Third World countries the only "Lazarus." But since Americans have for a century enjoyed the highest standard of living in the world, becoming a model other nations have emulated, it is appropriate to look at our energy use in comparison with the world as a whole.

United Nations per capita energy consumption statistics indicate that for 1976, the average U.S. citizen accounted for the equivalent of 11,554 kilograms of coal, while the average world citizen used only 2,069 kg. Per capita use in Nigeria, for instance, was 94 kg. English and Soviet citizens consumed the equivalent of 5,264 kg a piece.

It is also important to take into account, however, that America has for a century been the greatest energy producer in the world and is overall still the most productive nation on earth. Further, as Gerard K. O'Neill observes, world development is rapidly overtaking us. In 1881, America consumed 20 times the world average of energy resources. That figure had increased tenfold by 1981. But the world use in the same period had multiplied 30 times. In 2081, at present rates of growth, America will have increased its energy requirements another 6 times, but the world rate will have by then reached America's 1981 level. Thus, the disparity between America and the rest of the world has actually decreased by a factor of 6 during the past century and is still declining.5/

This should not blind us to the glaring inequalities of distribution throughout the world, to the immense waste of energy resources, or to the strain increased industialization will place on reserves. If, as expected, the world's energy demands in fact quadruple by the end of this century, a massive economic breakdown is inevitable. Even at present rates of development, by 2000, 80% of the world's estimated 6.5 billion inhabitants will be living in dire poverty. Today's greed portends misery and starvation for most of the world's peoples tomorrow. The solution is present to hand, however, if we only have the will to care.

Omega

As Henri Bergson perhaps first realized at the turn of the century, an increase of "dead" matter, and thus of entropy, is the inevitable residue of collecting and concentrating some energy on higher levels of cosmic order. But if the gods "eat" human thoughts, what is to prevent human thoughts from becoming divine? It is an ancient Christian belief that through, not despite, the material nature of human existence we are able as a race to become divinized. This belief lies at the heart of all the sacraments and pre-eminently the Eucharistic liturgy. Such mystical insights also formed the basis of the "great work" of material transformation that absorbed the alchemists of the Middle Ages and the Renaissance. They have appeared in our own time on a more poetic and more scientific footing in the writings of Teilhard de Chardin.

This great Jesuit visionary, mystic and scientist, the centenary of whose birth was celebrated in 1981, followed more in the footsteps of Gregory Nazianzen than those of Charles Darwin. He held that at some distant point in cosmic history, the collective consciousness of humankind would effectively "graduate" from its material setting and attain the final liberty of God's children. Far from being a revival of gnosticism, which in its ancient intellectual conceit disdained matter, Teilhard's vision was authentically Christian and fundamentally humane. For he believed in the transformation of matter, not its abolition.

In the Christian mysteries, belief in the resurrection of the body safeguards the dignity of material creation. It does not deny our lasting relationship with the material universe—even one possibly dispersed in an almost infinite film of gas molecules—but it more fundamentally affirms our ultimate independence from matter. Such an achievement, as Teilhard clearly realized, remains remote in the human future, an

Omega Point toward which we aim. It may cast its radiance back through time to beckon us forward, but presently, it lies beyond our grasp. However, our way toward that ultimate point of transformation, at which the universe itself may be altered, can be accelerated. As has been taught by many Christian mystics, it can be hastened by fulfilling our divine mandate to be the stewards of the natural world as well as heralds of a new social order, a realm of truth, justice, love and peace. Spiritually, this is the only adequate response to present and future energy crises, which are in turn revealed to be but a phase, if a truly critical one, in our learning process as apprentices in creativity.

NINE

The Spirituality of Food

"I have learned the secret of facing plenty and hunger, abundance and want. I can do all things in him who strengthens me."

—Philippians 4:12

From a holistic perspective, spirituality is more a how than a what. It is the way in which we organize or integrate our pattern of life as a whole, including the primary systems that constitute human experience on a day-to-day basis. Among the various areas of body-mind-spirit interaction with the world, food occupies a place of cardinal importance, taking into consideration only the amount of time and money we devote to its cultivation, distribution, preparation, consumption and the elimination of its wastes. As a result, whether we are aware of it or not (and I tend to think we generally are not), food expresses more distinctly than any other human concern the quality of life, the spirituality of a person or a people. For food represents our closest tie with nature, society and the Creator God.

Guts and Glory

A moment of shattering enlightenment occurs in Joseph Heller's brilliant Catch-22 when Lt. Yossarian discovers "Snowdon's secret" as he fumbles to help the mortally stricken flyer. Opening the youth's bullet-riddled flight-suit, he suddenly understands what it means to say "man is made of matter."

No ordinary human experience conveys this simple truth in all its humiliating earthiness or its exhilarating transcendence as does eating. The cultivation or catch, cooking, serving and consuming of food and drink is, next to breathing, the most common human experience.

It has also been an often sadly neglected one in conventional spirituality, except for injunctions against gluttony and drunkenness. Even the disposal of waste is spiritually significant. As the hero of A Thousand Clowns recognized, the quality of our garbage is an index to the quality of our life. Some years ago, a national magazine featured profiles of celebrities based, in fact, on the content analysis of their garbage cans. On a far more serious level, the disposal of human waste products, both garbage and sewage, has become a monumental and disturbing problem in the United States and other zones of the affluent world. We are running out of room in which to dump our refuse.

The Human Dimension of Food

There are three distinct but related functions which food, like most other elements of our lifestyle, performs in daily life. There are the physiological, the psychological and the spiritual or celebrative, which encompasses aesthetic, moral and religious dimensions. From a holistic point of view, none of these functions should conflict with each other. Rather, they are complementary. The psychological function or dimension adds to the physiological, and the spiritual adds to the psychological. Here, too, grace does not destroy what is natural, but builds on it and completes it at a higher level of integration. Nevertheless, the psychological and spiritual functions of food can temporarily supersede the physiological purpose.

The primary intention of eating food is, obviously, physical nutrition— the assimilation of the necessary proteins, carbohydrates, fats, vitamins, minerals, trace elements, water, fiber and other chemical substances involved in sustaining and developing life. Humankind has never remained content with mere nutrition, however. From the earliest times, the symbolic and celebrative dimensions of eating and all the connected activities surrounding food have grown into the most important aspects of human culture, next only to sex— if that.

Religiously, food symbolized life itself to ancient and "primitive" peoples. Because of that, food came to represent the primordial human connection with creation—the world of nature. Both food and drink were placed in graves and later in tombs as an aid to the dead in their journey to the next world. It was inconceivable that life could continue in any form without them. Food sacrifices were perhaps the earliest of human religious acts, based on the awareness that our dependence upon food is in turn a dependence upon forces far beyond our control. By offering their most valuable possession, food itself—whether the first fruits of the harvest or the choice parts of the hunt—the ancients not only recognized their indebtedness to the Creator but hoped to assure continued divine benevolence and protection.

Anthropologists such as Margaret Mead and Claude Levi-Strauss have observed that the ceremonial aspects of food are a clue to a people's deepest understanding of themselves and their relation to the cosmos, other people, and the Holy. By converting natural substances—plants and animals—into edible form, especially by cooking, human beings change the very condition of the world. The passage lies from the realm of disorder and decay by way of cooking to the realm of human utility, of order and culture. Food is thus the primary medium of socialization and cooking is a metaphor for the whole social enterprise. This transforming process is simultaneously natural, social and cosmic, moreover, as Levi-Strauss wrote with regard to the food practices of Amazonian tribes: "Culinary operations (are viewed) as mediatory activities between heaven and earth, life and death, nature and society."[1]/

Soul Food

Even among technologized Americans, the cutting and eating of a wedding cake, like the eating and drinking in holy communion of the Christian eucharistic meal, transcend the needs and limitations of nutrition. Neither the cake nor the communion wafers are intended primarily to nourish our bodies, but rather to feed our souls. In both cases, food is the manifest sign of social bondedness. Eating and drinking in common effects what it signifies, moreover; it enacts community and as such is sacramental.

Similarly, ritually passing the peace-pipe among Native Americans, or its contemporary equivalent—the "joint", is more important physiologically and psychologically than the effects of inhaling the smoke. A toast is important not because of its alcoholic content (although perhaps necessary in some regards), but because of the sentiment expressed: "To your health" or "Long life."

Tension can arise, however, when the psychological and spiritual symbolism breaks down, when, for instance, the mythic significance of ceremonial rites is lost. Likewise, if the biological foundation of these activities shifts dramatically or outweighs the sacramental significance, conflict can result. It was in large measure for reasons such as these that the Catholic liturgical reform movement which began fifty years ago led directly to the Second Vatican Council. Significantly, just after the council, a decree was issued from Rome to the effect that bread used for communion should look like bread, feel like bread and taste like bread. For gradual "symbolification" of communion wafers, long since reduced to coin-shaped images, had in fact altered the appearance of the sacramental meal and therefore changed its significance.

It is important that real bread and real wine be used in eucharistic celebrations, but not—if possible—the everyday "bread" available in supermarkets, which may be a technological "wonder" but it is hardly recognizable as bread. Despite its "fortification" with vitamins, such stuff is generally even less nutritious than the microthin wafers stamped out in convent kitchens. Further, such travesty bread wipes out the ceremonial value of hand-made bread.

Ideally, the bread and wine of Eucharist would be made by the community from its own grain and grapes, a collective effort which also effects what it signifies, both in origin and result. It is worth mentioning in this regard that the custom of the bride and groom sharing the wedding cake, actually feeding each other, derives from the ancient practice of communicating each other with a special eucharistic bread at the wedding mass. As the ministers of the sacrament, and, as Cardinal Hume recently pointed out, the sole recipients of its graces, it is also fitting that they should administer communion not only to each other, but also to the congregation gather to witness the sacramental pledging of their covenant love. Matrimony symbolizes God's union with his people; the eucharist is the wedding cake of the Lamb.

Other examples could be multiplied: birthday cakes and anniversary cakes, which are primarily commemorative; eggnog and wassail bowls at Yuletide; Easter eggs; the Passover meal; the Japanese tea ceremony; old English "mayfly" on Mayday; even the ritual cannibalism practiced among certain peoples throughout history. For one ate the slain enemy's heart not to gain weight but acquire his courage.

On a more rudimentary level, simple gatherings of friends at the local pub or at a dinner party must be considered primarily to be symbolic functions rather than nutritional exercises. In some sense, the human way is to make every meal into an occasion of friendship and "grace." Thus, the nutritional aspect never wholly lacks the psychological and spiritual dimensions of food and eating, whether we honor them or not. By honoring them, however, it is also likely that we will enhance the nutritional aspects.

Spirituality and Food

Looking back over the Christian centuries, it is interesting to see how diet and spirituality were traditionally coordinated. Food was an integral part of the spiritual life, both positively—in its cultivation, preparation and consumption—and negatively, in the forms of abstinence and fasting. "Fish on Friday," rogation days, ember days and special days of fast and abstinence all but identified what it meant to be Catholic. Even today, as Mary Douglas has shown, immigrant Catholics from Ireland have clung to these patterns of behavior in order to preserve their identity in cities such as Liverpool and Manchester.

Catholicism was by no means unique in this respect. Food consciousness is, rather, a characteristic of all religions in their prime. Moreover, the more manifest the religious spirit, the greater is the care given to matters of diet. Generally, this involves the attempt to achieve simplicity, poverty and sufficiency. Red meat, spices, delicacies, waste and, often, alcohol, are forbidden or reduced as far as possible. For instance, when taken as a beverage, wine is customarily diluted with water.

Hindus, Buddhists, Jainists, even the ancient Greeks and Romans conscientiously integrated food into their religious lifeways—most often for symbolic purposes rather than for nutritional or economic reasons. Jewish kosher restrictions, based in large measure on ancient tribal customs, are perhaps the best known examples of dietary laws. Islamic customs are themselves largely based on such Jewish practices, unlike those of Christianity.

And today, while the affluent West has all but eliminated food asceticism such as fasting and abstinence, ramadan—the month of fasting—is observed even more strenuously in many Islamic nations. Food restrictions are similarly practiced among cults and sects such as the "Hare Krishna" movement, Sikhism, Zen Buddhism and "neo-paganism." Several conservative Christian groups have adopted similar attitudes, sometimes espousing a vegetarian regimen. Among these bodies, Seventh Day Adventists are outstanding in their practice of meatless diet and abstinence from all forms of drugs, including those found in alcohol, coffee, tea and cigarettes. Mormons are similarly sensitive to the place of food and drink in their lives. But as a whole, Christianity, perhaps paramount among world religions, has seemingly lost consciousness of the connections between food and spirituality, a propensity even in the eucharistic meal, but startingly present in the meals of monasteries and convents as well. Protestants have fared even more badly in this regard than Catholics, Orthodox Christians perhaps better than either. (The use of unleavened versus leavened bread for the Eucharist still separates official Catholic and Orthodox practice, but the difference now seems slight to most Western Christians.)

The connection between food and spirituality thus poses a series of interrelated problems and possibilities as we face an ever more uncertain future. It is an area worth considering in some detail.

Aliens in an Alien Land

Contemporary alienation from nature, from creation in terms of a religious sense of life, manifests itself clearly in urban attitudes toward food. My father, who was reared on a ranch in New Mexico, tells a favorite joke about the city boy who discovered a pile of empty milk cartons and shouts, "I've found a cow's nest!" One of the most shaking events in my own life, and a milestone on the road to eventual if moderate vegetarianism, occurred while accompanying a group of high school filmmakers to a slaughterhouse. Watching the terrified eyes of the pigs as they were prodded toward execution, hearing their squeals of fear, was for me only the beginning of a journey into the mystery of food, and through that into the deeper mystery of death and life.

Learning that a beloved calf or piglet, a duck, rabbit or other farm animal has been slaughtered for Sunday dinner is often a farm child's first dramatic encounter with the reality of loss and sacrifice. And, as Robert

Ferrar Capon has urged, it is proper to speak of sacrifice in such instances.2/ But in countries like our own, such experiences are increasingly denied the young—not to mention visits to slaughterhouses. To several million American youngsters, moreover, milk does come from a box or a machine, not from an animal. Fruit and vegetables also appear magically in supermarket bins or, more likely, in tin cans, or frozen boxes. Wheat, oats and barley come in paper or plastic bags. And the unused portions of all of these disappear, equally without trace or question, into garbage disposal units, trash compactors, or merely the great cans which are ritually emptied into huge, noisy trucks which appear and disappear more or less routinely on our streets and alleys. (Unless there has been a collectors' strike, in which case mountains of plastic bags begin piling up on every street corner.)

Thus, we live for the most part in isolation from and ignorance of the origin and end of the food chain which sustains us day by day. Small wonder that in this society "junk food" could become a national passion, and "fast food" a necessity, while throughout the vast Third World constant and often death-dealing hunger already stalks the majority of earth's peoples.

Food and the Future

Unless drastic reform measures are undertaken by all sectors of our society—business, government and consumers alike—the immediate future will only magnify the errors of the recent past in regard to food. For despite the survival of "health food" consciousness and an effort to return to the land on the part of a few determined souls, the eco-political movement of the late 'sixties has been largely co-opted and disarmed by business and governmental interests. Fast-food franchises and junk foods are proliferating everywhere.

Such trends point to a future of food trouble but one we can prepare for now by altering our thinking and behavior constructively. In general, we can expect to see increased hunger and scarcity, meat shortages, further reliance on synthetic foods as well as the development of more positive alternatives.

1. Hunger and Scarcity:

A particularly threatening future looms ahead in the form of soaring food prices and almost certain famine on a world-wide scale within the next ten or twenty years, as the world food shortage spreads from Africa and Asia to Latin America and perhaps the Soviet Union, Europe and America. Such a probability presents a grim reminder that all spirituality is concerned with social issues as well as particular ones. Food above all is a sign of the unity of the human family, as well as its apparently incorrigible diversity.

Preventing wide-scale starvation is not merely a matter of producing more food or reducing the number of mouths to feed. Many nations now facing devastating food shortages have the ability to produce sufficient food, but lack the social and political will to do so. Government interest in such countries is more easily subverted to "defense" and impressive projects that require enormous expenditures of money and resources and thus create the illusion of progress. Likewise, the use of artificial fertilizers, pesticides and ever-larger and more complicated farming equipment, while increasing the profits of multi-national corporations, only decreases available food in the long run by driving up costs. Applying fertilizers temporarily increases land use. But the soil gradually loses its ability to restore itself through natural processes of renewal, thus increasing dependency on artificial nutrients. Pesticides similarly lose their effectiveness in time, requiring ever larger applications, more expense, and cause greater harm to the human as well as natural environment. Expensive farming equipment requires maintenance and parts, as well as fuel—none of which are readily available in poorer countries. All such technological "advancements" also reduce the need for human labor, thus creating increasing unemployment, poverty and the weight of human misery.

As E. F. Schumacher and others have argued, developing countries in particular require "appropriate" technologies which are labor intensive, providing more jobs for people. By using simpler machinery, hand implements and natural or organic fertilizers, letting land lie fallow and producing food crops rather than cash crops (coffee, sugar, etc.), world hunger could be alleviated in many areas.

2. Meat Shortages:

Even in the United States, meat will increasingly lose importance in the next two decades as the major item in the menu because of three related factors. First, it will become economically more and more expensive to produce cheap meat. Second, avoidable diseases such as colon cancer, hypertension and atherosclerosis are being more closely related to over-consumption of meat, especially beef. Obesity is also an effect of meat-addiction. Third, the higher costs of meat production will result in higher prices to the consumer as well as the producer.

3. Processed Foods:

The expense of meat will necessitate greater reliance on meat substitutes, many of them probably artificial. Thus, synthesized foods laden with additives will probably continue to proliferate, adding to overall food costs and health impairment.

4. Alternatives:

Conversely, ecologically sounder methods of producing and distributing food can help to alleviate the coming crisis to some extent. These include employing organic fertilization, pest and weed control, recycling, hydroponics or "soil-less agriculture," the development of family and community gardens, food cooperatives and farmer's markets. Such methods would have to be introduced on a vast and therefore improbable scale to be very effective, however. Some difference can be made by the negative and positive efforts of a new asceticism, on the other hand, at least a beginning. As individuals and groups, we may not be able to reverse the tide, but we don't have to drown in it.

Food Exploitation

Surely one of the major sources of the disastrous American diet is the food industry itself and its henchman, the advertising industry. Thanks to them, our choices among food products, like their very availability, are determined not on the basis of nutritional need or even desire, but on that of commercial expediency, that is, profit. For instance, refined flour, which is more a health hazard than a food, and other worthless and even "junk" foods—those loaded with useless sugar and fat— are merchandised, bought and consumed with equal mindlessness solely because they are identified with status, speed or some other extrinsic factor.

"Exploitation" is not a bad word, since it merely means "to turn something to economic account." But it also means "to take unfair advantage of." From the dawn of civilization, human beings have exploited nature in order to make full use of "the fruits of the earth" in sustaining life and promoting growth. But from the same time, people have as surely taken unfair advantage of each other in order to profit from the production, distribution and preparation of food.

Today the food industry represents one of the largest and most powerfully exploitative institutions in the world—in both senses of the word. The earth has been exploited with increasing violence and ruthlessness as modern technology has streamlined agriculture and animal husbandry. The result: depletion of the soil, higher prices, widespread hunger and food laden with the residues of artificial fertilizers, pesticides, antibiotics, coloring, flavoring, preservatives and other chemical additives. Small farms have been rendered economically moribund by merciless competition on the part of agri-corporations. The result: increasing unemployment, greater alienation from the land, and the disappearance of a valuable way of life from our society. Commercially processed as well as "junk" foods have increasingly displaced home-prepared and home-grown fruits, vegetables and dairy products from our diet. The result: since the turn of the century, the quality of food eaten by the American public has steadily declined, and with it, our health.

Over-Nutrition and Under-Nutrition

Malnutrition cuts two ways. In 1976, researchers from the Worldwatch Institute reported that the middle-class American diet, what they called "over-nutrition," was as dangerous to health and even to life as was under-nutrition. Moreover, our "affluent diet," consisting mainly of animal proteins and fats, refined flour and sugar, and processed foods is spreading over the world—into Japan, Western Europe and even the Soviet Union. And with it go the diseases of the rich: coronary and heart disease, diabetes, diverticulosis and colon cancer chief among others. Deficiency diseases such as beri-beri are on the rise. Just the loss of fiber from our diet because of the demand for "refined" ingredients has resulted in an increase in constipation, obesity and diseases of the lower intestine, including bowel cancer. The vast growth of laxative manufacturers and their mushrooming profits over the past several decades stand as a tribute to our food folly.

In the whole area of food production and consumption, America and most of the rest of the world are firmly in the velvet grip of a steely-handed and vast commercial empire. It is also a powerful one. Attempts to prohibit the sale of junk foods in school cafeterias are met with lawsuits alleging restraint of trade. Home economics classes are subsidized by giant flour corporations whose profits arise from denaturing wheat and opposing grain reserves. Even hospitals persist in serving worthless gelatine desserts to the sick.

Food and the New Asceticism

Actively anticipating the future of food in order to prepare for probable scarcity and increased artificiality will require attitudes that can be described as elements of a true spiritual discipline. Unlearning bad food habits and acquiring more positive approaches will involve the entire range of human interests—bodily, mental, emotional and religious. Such a new food ethic will, moreover, reflect social as well as particular implications for each of us, and on both nutritional and symbolic as well as economic levels of concern. While new in some respects, a contemporary spirituality of food will also embody some of the early ascetical practices of the Christian people.

Fads and Fascism

In turning toward roads of possible action with regard to food, nutrition, and the world situation, it is vitally important from a spiritual standpoint to avoid two initial pitfalls: bandwagons and guilt-trips. As with most components of contemporary spirituality—health, exercise, ecological concern, and others—it is easy to adopt the most obvious or appealing trends as the only solution to our problems and the sole means of development. Some food fads, such as the notorious "Zen" macrobiotic diet or the liquid protein craze have proved to be lethal blind-alleys. The use of food as a personal or political tool to gain attention, to control people or to punish them is no less perverse, a manifestation of spiritual malnutrition.

"Food fascism"—a totalitarian, severe and absolutist approach to the world of nutrition—is by no means the least of our problems. But it only represents the extreme opposite, I think, of the mindless attitude that shrinks from questioning, challenging or changing our national foodways. An authentic spirituality of food will require, it is true, the application of the ascetical principle—detachment for the sake of reattachment. But nutrition alone cannot determine our whole attitude toward food, nor can economic or political considerations. The symbolic, psychological and spiritual aspects of food must be allowed their play for overall fitness. Food for the body must be balanced by food for the mind and body.

Food Attitudes as Spiritual Indicators

Again, how we deal with food, our chief link with nature, other people and God, is an important manifestation of psychological and spiritual wholeness or health.   An impairment of our food relationships points to deeper disturbances. St. Catherine of Siena suffered spiritually and psychologically as well as physically because of her long inability to eat normally.   The many references to food, eating and drinking in The Dialogue are not accidental. But apparently, Catherine had converted the ordinary desire to eat and drink so completely into a craving for the Eucharist and for ministry ("devouring souls" as she put it) that she was unable to eat "real" food. Similarly, "drinking the blood of Christ" totally replaced her ability to drink "real" wine.

Such disturbances need not be destructive, although they undoubtedly take their toll. Catherine died at 33. A more anguished state of mind, both psychological and spiritual, was incisively portrayed in William Blatty's The Exorcist. The hero, a priest tormented by religious doubt, recites in a moment of existential estrangement an entire litany of revulsions beginning significantly, with "The need to rend food with the teeth and then defecate."3/

Horror at natural functions such as eating, digestion and elimination evinces a deep tension between matter and spirit presaging further disintegration—incipient insanity, possibly, or perhaps the advent of the dark night of the soul. Anorexia nervosa, the self-starvation syndrome that appears to be increasing afflicting adolescent women as a reflection of their internalized, destructive social self-image is only the opposite extreme from compulsive over-eating, which many adopt as a way of coping with anxiety or stress.

In terms of individual, particular experience, such problems with food and eating reflect, I believe, a growing awareness of the devastating inequality of food distribution as well as malnutrition among both rich and poor nations of the earth. The United States and other affluent, industrialized nations are compulsive "over-eaters," while some "starving" nations, it can be shown, actually have the capacity to feed their teeming populations, but refuse to do so for a variety of reasons—economic, political and social. Individual experience is often a microcosm of much larger processes.

Fasting and Abstinence

For Catholics the world over a few years ago, these words virtually summarized what "mortification" or self-denial meant. Such food asceticism was largely a negative approach to meat, which was traditionally and somewhat accurately associated with prosperity, festivity and luxury. The poor and oppressed simply cannot afford meat. Since medical research has increasing shown that heavy reliance upon meat in our diet is also harmful to our health, such relative abstinence could be a blessing in disguise, if we take care to balance our diet accordingly.

Fasting, as a form of sensory deprivation, also has a "deautomatizing" effect. It awakens us concretely to dimensions of life we are likely to take for granted: the flavors and textures of food and drink, our relation to the earth, our dependence upon others, our addictions and preferences. Periodic fasting also purifies our physiological systems, breaking down and utilizing stored fat reserves and eliminating various minor toxins we have absorbed with our food. Psychologically, fasting alters our perceptions of the universe—from the way we see food itself to a possibly heightened perception of natural and social beauty and an increased sensitivity to God's presence throughout. Fasting clears the mind for prayer and thinking.

Fasting is a reminder that we are made of matter and yet that we are not wholly determined by our material dimension. It reminds us, moreover, that we are obligated to organize and direct our material embodiedness and environmental situation, to exert control, lest we do in fact lose our spiritual freedom to the dominating forces of the material realm.

In the future, fasting as a discipline will play a greater role in environmental spirituality for all these reasons, and not least for the symbolic function of relating us to billions of people on this planet who cannot eat a full meal ever in their lives. The ascetical principle involves both a negative and a positive dimension, however. Complete detachment from food on a periodic basis or for special reasons, private or social, ought to lead to reattachment on a more developed level of awareness and involvement. The social correlative of a new consciousness of creation in all its beauty, power and goodness is, therefore, a recommitment to working for a more just society for all, especially those who hunger and thirst for food and drink as well as for righteousness.

Abstinence Makes the Heart Grow Fonder

Abstinence is a less drastic form of food asceticism. It means, simply, periodically or permanently avoiding certain types of food and drink. Vegetarians, ex-alcoholics, orthodox Jews, Muslims and Seventh Day Adventists all display some form of characteristic abstinence. Such group identification is a psychological and social function of abstinence. Physically preserving health may require abstinence in the case of food allergies or conditions such as diabetes, hypertension and alcoholism. Spiritually, abstinence has been recommended for many reasons: as a sign of penitence, discipline (i.e. toughening), or dedication, including reverence for sacred animals and plants. Abstinence can even be a legitimate prelude to indulgence in so far as it sharpens our tastes and appetites. Satiation in fact dulls our sensitivities, and even the wise hedonist occasionally practices self-denial in order to heighten later appreciation.

In view of a future of relative scarcity, it is likely that food will become more expensive and our diets harder to manage. Abstinence can also help prepare us for that—whether going without favorite items or just going without. More positively, abstinence can direct us toward a new appreciation of neglected or unknown foods by helping us break accustomed patterns. Like fasting, abstinence helps us maintain a measure of voluntary control over our involvement in the social process itself, permitting us to exercise that increasingly rare ability of discretion.

Some Practical Advice

Both fasting and abstinence can be dangerous for beginners, because they deal with one of the most important and powerful elements in human experience. A few suggestions about both might help avoid common pitfalls.

1. Don't fast longer than three days without medical advice unless you are already an experienced faster. Know your limits.

2. Don't fast if you are engaged in strenuous physical and mental activity, especially of an unusual type for you. Fast beforehand if you can, but demanding tasks require extra energy.

3. If you have a physical ailment such as ulcers, diabetes, hypoglycemia, anemia, etc., fast only under a doctor's care, if at all.

4. Pay careful attention to any unusual reactions, such as fainting spells, dizziness, blurred vision, nausea, heart flutter or insomnia. If trouble starts, go off your fast immediately.

5. Be quiet internally and externally during your fast. Conserve energy.

6. In coming off a fast, do it gradually, beginning with small quantities of simple, easily digestible foods and fluids.

7. When abstaining, especially on a permanent basis, make sure that you are not depriving yourself of essential nutrients. This is especially important for a strict vegetarian regime. (Diet for a Small Planet is indispensible reading in this regard.)4/

Nutrition Education

Among the various strategies for improving nutrition and health, perhaps the most basic is education, although it is likely to be postponed in favor of more immediate action. In either case, the ascetical principle will be important in learning how to overcome our food faults and to develop better attitudes and patterns of behavior.

Nutrition education does not require obtaining a degree in biochemistry. Many resources are presently available to the average person interested in improving food habits. Courses are available in community colleges, universities and adult education centers. In addition to books such as France Lappe's Diet for a Small Planet, Adelle Davis' Let's Eat Right to Keep Fit and especially Dr. Rudolf Ballentine's Diet and Nutrition, several recent publications from the Government Printing Office and other sources are easily available. These include the report of the Select Committee on Nutrition and Human Needs of the U.S. Senate, Eating in America,5/Food, a publication of the U.S. Dept. of Agriculture; Healthy People, the Surgeon General's Report on Health Promo-

162

tion and Disease Prevention; and Nutrition and Your Health from the departments of Agriculture and Health, Education and Welfare.6/

Particular Dietary Strategies

In developing a food asceticism based in part on ancient Christian practices, it will also be helpful or even necessary to consider the counsel of current nutritionists concerned with both individual and global health. The following guidelines are based on recommendations compiled from a variety of sources.

1. Increase consumption of fresh fruits, vegetables and whole grains such as brown rice, as well as potatoes, squash, barley, lentils, beans, etc. These foods are particularly good as sources of starch and fiber.

2. Decrease consumption of red meat and increase consumption of poultry and fish.

A properly balanced vegetarian diet, whether strict (no animal protein at all) or the so-called "lacto-ovarian" diet (allowing milk, cheese and eggs), can be at least as nutritious as the average meat-centered diet, provided that care is taken to obtain supplementary protein by proper dietary balancing. Thus, whether a person's motive is religious, health, moral or economic (or a combination of these three), there is nothing to fear from partial or total meat abstinence.

Some vegetarians, taking a tip from St. Paul in I Cor. 8-10, will on occasion eat meat so as not to give offense to their host. The choice to eat meat, if made in full awareness of its meaning and place in life, can be no less spiritually fulfilling than the choice to abstain. The enormous waste of cereals in this country and elsewhere to provide unnecessary fattening for cattle does raise a moral issue on the social level, however. Our reliance on beef is a particular sign of insensitivity to the plight of the world's poor, besides being a threat to our own health. For economic, moral and health reasons, meats such as turkey, chicken, pork and especially fish are a wise choice.

3. Avoid too much fat, saturated fat and cholesterol.

The normal calorie intake for a person in our society should be about 2,500 per day. The recommended level of saturated fat, which now comprises about forty percent of the American diet, is 250 calories or less than 27 grams. Present consumption is estimated at about 400 calories per day or approximately 40 grams. Recommended allowances of cholesterol suggest about 300 milligrams per day, opposed to the 600 now typical.

Our high-fat diet has been associated with a variety of health problems, including cardio-vascular diseases, colon and breast cancer, obesity, and others. Many physicians are now reducing emphasis on a low-cholesterol diet, except where evident problems such as hypertension, atherosclerosis and high serum cholesterol levels require restriction. Behavior patterns pose a more serious threat of heart disease than does cholesterol, however. Thus, reducing cholesterol levels without altering self-destructive lifestyles could be seriously deceptive. Nevertheless, given the frantic, high-pressure style of life modern men and women are exposed to, and will continue to be for the forseeable future, it is still wise to reduce the amount of cholesterol in our diet whenever possible. This is also sound advice because foods high in cholesterol are usually high in calories and fat as well.

Meats high in fat/cholesterol include brains (raw), liver, shrimp, lobster, clams, halibut and tuna in oil. Moderate sources are lamb, veal, crab, beef, pork and dark turkey meat. Low levels are found in white turkey, chicken, Canadian bacon and salmon. Dairy products high in cholesterol include eggs, butter, whole milk, and cheeses such as cheddar. Moderate sources include cream cheese, ice cream and creamed cottage cheese. Low levels are found in yogurt, uncreamed cottage cheese and low-fat milk. Oils high in saturated fat include coconut, palm and cottonseed oils. Those low in saturated fat include peanut, soybean, olive, corn, sunflower and safflower oils.

4. Reduce sugar consumption from 24% to 15% of the total caloric intake.

Like salt, sugar is an "invisible" ingredient because we are so used to it in our diet. Our craving for sugar, which amounts to a national addiction, is an acquired taste, also like that for salt. In quantities, both are harmful to health.

Over-consumption of sugar in candy and processed foods is a leading factor in both tooth decay and obesity. Tooth decay alone accounts for billions of dollars in dental bills each year. Plaque-forming bacteria which collect on everyone's teeth secrete acids in the presence of sugar (and other carbohydrates) which attack tooth enamel and bone. Snacking between meals is therefore especially harmful. Further, a strong connection exists between obesity, which is directly attributable to a heavy sugar intake, and diabetes as well as heart disease. Hypoglycemia is also related to sugar intake. It also seems to be a factor in emotional problems such as chronic depression, as described by William Dufty in Sugar Blues.7/Even more problematically, sugar-added foods, because of their immediate and exaggerated appeal, push more nourishing foods out of the reach of both children and adults.

Restraining our probably decaying "sweet tooth" is thus good practice for the sake of health and economics. Considering the price of sugar and the destructive role sugar production plays in the economies of many under-developed countries, cutting back on sweets is also wise in terms of the household budget as well as world care.

Ordinarily, we get all the sugar we need in fruits and vegetables. The greatest source of unneeded sugar in our diet is processed foods. Although direct consumer use of sugar dropped 50% between 1910 and 1971, overall sugar consumption increased in this country at the same time from 76.4 pounds per person to 101.5 pounds. The "hidden" sugar added to manufactured foods quadrupled during those same years, more than making up for the decrease.

The biggest offenders include candies of all kinds, soft drinks, breakfast cereals, snack foods, ice cream and fruit drinks. Even various "granola" products contain far too much sugar to be truly natural.8/ Artificially sweetened breakfast "drinks" are a particularly poor substitute for fresh, frozen or even canned fruit juices.

In selecting foods and beverages for children, the wisest nutritional practice is to avoid whenever possible anything with sugar added. When sweetening is required for cooking or celebration foods, it is better to use honey, brown sugar, molasses and syrups, which are less refined and therefore more nourishing than white sugars. In terms of tooth decay and obesity, however, all sugars are suspect. The ascetical guideline here is to learn to appreciate the natural flavors of foods by reducing sugar as much as possible. Do not add sugar to drinks such as coffee and tea, cereals or fruits. Finally, read labels and try to avoid all products with added sugar.

5. Reduce salt consumption about half to three-quarters, or to about three grams a day.

Our bodies need a certain amount of salt, about a half a gram a day. We consume between six and eighteen grams a day, however. Too much salt, i.e., sodium in its various compounds, can be harmful to our health. It is especially dangerous with regard to hypertension (high blood pressure). Stroke is also often connected with a high sodium level in the bloodstream.

Like sugar, most of the salt we eat comes in commercially prepared foods. Sodium is perhaps the most common of all additives, whether included for "freshness" or flavor. Most often it is need for neither.

Our craving for salt is also an acquired taste. Babies in fact tend to cry when salt is first placed on their tongues. But soon they become habituated to it because of its inescapable presence. What amounts to a salt addiction is thus inevitable, at least to some extent. For as members of a consumer society, we are largely at the mercy of those who produce our food. In a 1974 report of the National Academy of Sciences, we read that "sodium intake is more and more determined by the food processors than by the individual."9/

Foods naturally high in sodium include milk products, meat, fish and eggs. Moderate amounts are found in vegetables, bread and cereals. Fruits and fats are low in sodium. In the artificially high category the following salted foods would be found: chipped beef, bacon, ham, bologna, corned beef, luncheon meats, sausage and salt pork; salted fish, such as anchovies, sardines, caviar and herring; peanut butter; flavorings such as catsup, vegetable salts, chili sauce, meat extracts, tenderizers, and salt substitutes; processed cheeses and spreads, Roquefort and Camembert cheese; olives, pickles or other vegetables salted or pickled in brine, such as sauerkraut; and snack foods, such as saltine crackers, potato chips, popcorn, pretzels and nuts.

Many of these are celebrative foods, some are only junk. Remember, however, that the salt of the earth could be killing you. The wisest procedure would be to halve the amount of salt you "normally" use. Do not add salt to foods already salted in freezing and canning. Avoid salted snack foods whenever possible and when shopping, avoid foods with high or unlisted salt content. Further, do not use a salt substitute without consulting a doctor. The ascetical principle applicable here is: learn to enjoy the natural flavor of unsalted foods.

6. Learn to eat wisely.

In addition to the above precautions, the following advice is common among nutritionists: 1) Eat breakfast every day. 2) Eat three or four meals a day, but do not eat or snack between meals. 3) Don't overeat; be moderate. 4) Drink alcohol only in moderation, if at all. 5) Try to maintain the proper weight for your age or size. 6) Get sufficient exercise.

To these suggestions, a final word of caution: avoid processed foods and especially junk foods whenever possible. Processed or manufactured foods, in addition to the other problems listed above, are very high in artificial additives. According to the McGovern Committee report, "There are more than 1,300 food additives currently approved for use as colors, flavors, preservatives, thickeners and other agents for controlling physical properties of foods."10/ Not all additives are harmful, some in fact are beneficial, such as vitamins, ascorbic acid, iodine, iron, potassium iodide and thiamine, which are considered nutrients. Most additives, however, are unnecessary and non-nutritious, being added only to enhance the commercial appeal of processed foods. Some are proving hazardous. The common preservatives BHA and BHT (butylated hydroxyanisole and butylated hydroxytoluene) and MSG (monosodium glutamate)—a "flavor enhancer"—are particularly suspect.

Perhaps the greatest fear expressed in regard to additives of all kinds in household products, including food, is that of contracting cancer. Although our understanding of this dread disease has grown enormously over the past several decades, we are still ignorant of its specific etiology, that is, how a particular person contracts it, or when. But among the forms of cancer, some appear to be clearly linked to contact with chemicals alien to the human organism. That is why it is wisest to avoid all additives even suspected of causing cancer.

Junk Food

Junk food can be described as "any food that relies on sugar and/or fat as its primary ingredients..."11/   Like processed foods, of which they are a sub-class, junk foods embody most of the food faults in all the injunctions mentioned before. The U.S. Senate Select Committee Report on nutrition observed in 1977 that fat and sugar, often referred to as "empty calories," in so far as they have little or no nutritional value in the forms frequently found, now comprise about 60% of total caloric intake. Such "over-nutrition"—along with excess salt intake, processed food additives and other dietary menaces—is now related to six out of ten leading causes of death in America.

The symbolic and celebrative aspects of eating, including recreational eating, excuse a certain amount of junk food, and they will continue to do so in the future. A wedding cake would qualify, after all, along with Christmas cookies. The excessive amount of empty calories in our systems suggests strongly, however, that the primary nutritional function of food can not be further subordinated to the artificial needs created by the food industry. Medical estimates place the number of children with tooth decay at 98%, and about a third of the population is either already toothless or well on the way.

More than 50% of the food that enters the American home is processed before it is purchased. We have clearly surrendered to commercial interests our right and ability to prepare our own food. It is no wonder that the majority of television advertisements are devoted to non-nutritive foods. Almost 70% of the total advertising time concerned with food promotes junk food. On weekends, the rate rises to 85%! 12/

So powerful are the giant corporations that manufacture processed and junk foods that they have been able to stymie congressional attempts to limit advertising on children's TV programs and to prevent the sale of such foods in school cafeterias. The only recourse at present seems to be education and individual action. Fortunately, food interest groups are forming around the nation. Such action-orientated associations aim at improving nutritional health not only in this country, but throughout the world. Among some of the more effective are Bread for the World, Food First and the Center for Science in the Public Interest.

Conclusion: Our Just Desserts

The future of food on Planet Earth can be different from the dire predictions of analysts, but only if a widespread movement for food justice and sanity gets underway soon. If it does not, calamity may ensue in short order, and the long-range portrait is grim indeed. Throughout the Bible, from Genesis' Garden to the Supper of the Lamb in the Book of Revelation, the mystery of food has been revealed to us as a mediation of God's presence in the presence of our fellow human beings. All food is thus sacramental, and in the Christian view of things, the greatest of the sacraments consists of shared food and drink. Food is a link in a chain that binds together the meaning and value of Creation itself. If sometimes a weak link, it is still our main link with the future.

TEN

Living Spaces

Among other stress-producing consequences of rapid population growth, the squeeze of crowding more than twice the world's present population into habitable spaces in the next fifty years may seem less serious than widespread famine and the exhaustion of natural resources. Spatial considerations nevertheless merit critical attention as we map a possible itinerary toward a future of relative harmony. For how living organisms, including humankind, deal with space is a fundamental determinant of all life processes, including provision for food, shelter and reproduction as well as survival itself. Our dealings with space no less influence and reflect our spiritualities, both personal and social, as well as architecture, urban planning, the space program and "simple" functions such as communicating and interpersonal relations.

Living Space

In his fascinating study of the human uses of space, The Hidden Dimension, anthropologist Edward T. Hall observes simply, "All animals have a minimum space requirement, without which survival is impossible."1/Space in this regard means the distance which separates as well as connects one organism and another. Symbiosis, therefore, can be taken to mean the mutually beneficial occupation of the same space by two or more dissimilar organisms.

Other possibilities exist. Fundmentally they are flight and fight. Halls calls the narrow zone separating flight distance from attack distance the "critical distance." For some large animals, this biological demilitarized zone is so precisely delineated that it can be measured even in centimeters.

We can thus first conceive of living space as an invisible bubble or sphere which surrounds the organism at a specified distance. This sphere is both fixed and flexible. For instance, an animal "stakes out" a definite territory for itself by its presence or activity, sometimes physically marking its boundaries. A mobile "sphere of influence" also accompanies the animal or especially a group of animals. A flock of geese, a herd of elephants or a school of fish thus has its own moving space in which each individual has its own determinate "personal" space, whether large or small.

Human Space

Human creatures are at once both more free and more restrained in their spatial existence than are other animals. The earliest remains of human culture indicate that space was utilized in both a biological and a symbolic fashion. In "primitive" societies, chiefs are still given more space to occupy and move in—ordinary people "keeping their distance" as a sign of respect and possibly of fear. Access is permitted, but only by express invitation or in a manner condoned by custom. Slaves and prisoners, on the other hand, are denied most if not all public space and have little private, personal space to themselves.

Encampments in which spatial distance were more implicit and informal historically gave way to tribal settlements and villages in which the importance of space was recognized more formally and explicitly. Urban civilization can almost be defined in structural terms as the way in which space became organized. The line from the Olduvai Gorge to Brazilia is as direct as that from a headman's hut to Versailles.

Making Room

Every aspect of human life is spatially organized—or disorganized, as the case may be—whether we advert to it or not. How we spatialize ourselves is, in effect, a psychological index of our personality and sanity as well as our cultural identification. Criminals and the insane may be characterized by a skewed sense of personal and social space. A saint, I am convinced, will also have a peculiar but nonetheless healthy sense of space. Jesus' remark that he had nowhere to lay his head and Francis of Assisi's claim that the whole world was his cloister both manifest the same remarkable and paradoxical awareness of total freedom and total poverty. Their personal space had expanded to include the whole world. But among those we call insane, which is to say "dis-integrated," this process has malfunctioned. Rather than ultimate expansiveness, mentally disturbed persons often experience terrible constraint, as if their personal space were being compressed about them or frozen into a rigid and alien system of compartments. Criminals, on the other hand, seem to conceive of space somewhat in the manner of Jesus and Francis, but from an inverted perspective. They, too, claim the world, not as an opportunity for love and service, but as a preserve for their particular benefit at others' expense.

Space and Spirit

By nature, spiritual development tends to overcome the limitations of space as well as time, continuing the process of transformation which began when human communities first transcended the relatively advanced social networks of their animal cousins. For only human beings use space creatively. I have often felt that the elements of telepathy and clairvoyance which link us in theological speculation with angelic beings who are completely free from spatial constraints are, in reality, vestiges of our animal ancestry. What is distinctively human is the invention of tools that overcome space— from the wheel to the telescope and microchip—and especially the inner attitude of presence experienced by mystics and saints that conveys a direct conviction of the unity of all in all. (It should be noted that in the mystical traditions of East and West, on attaining the higher reaches of the spiritual life, the nascent saint is often endowed with transcendent psychic abilities, including bi-location and psychokinesis—action at a distance.)

The Senses of Space

Our sense of space, whether liberating or confining, is not merely a function of our awareness of the size of the room or area we may happen to occupy. Spatial sensitivity is a complex, largely unconscious effect of combined visual, auditory, olfactory, tactile and kines-thetic sensations, all of which are previously condi-tioned and continually modified by specific cultural and personal values. Thus Japanese people have a vastly different sense of space from that of the Hopi Indians or Londoners.

Not only do the geographical features of a culture—island vs. continent, mountains vs. plains, lush vs. sparse—influence our sense of space, so do traditional styles of architecture, social class, economic back-ground and family size, among other factors. But in the final analysis, each one of us experiences space in a singular way as a reflection of our own history and personality.

Because people move, space is also a kinetic reality, not merely the dimensions of stationary location. Confinement in ancient prisons was particularly harm-ful because prisoners were shackled to walls and floors which greatly restricted physical mobility. Perhaps the worst instance of such brutalization was experienced by captured Africans chained to the bunks of the notorious slave ships of the eighteenth and nineteenth centuries. Born in the freest of environments, these people were suddenly confined to space as small as 1.1 to 8 square feet per person for weeks on end. It is astounding that any survived the psychological and physical stress.

Most of us live and move and have our being somewhere between the extremes of confinement in small spaces, with its attendant risk of claustrophobia, and exposure in wide-open spaces with the possibility of agoraphobia.

But contemporary women and men are more likely to be stressed by crowding, which can itself be lethal.

Crowding and Stress

After centuries of bewildered observation of the periodic and suicidal march to the sea of animals such as lemmings, rats and rabbits in various parts of the world, patient researchers finally discovered the biological factor that triggers off such deadly excursions. Among social animals in particular, crowding caused by rapid population growth eventually crosses a critical threshold. Thereafter, heightened anxiety, aggression, sickness, and, if the distress is not alleviated, depression and widespread death follow as a matter of course. The lemmings' death march is thus at least partially a population density check.

The desperately crowded situation of masses of poor people in Asia, Africa and the Americas shows a dramatic similarity. Eruptions of violence, widespread mental problems, and an accelerated mortality rate clearly demonstrate the need for effective social alleviation. Packing the poor into high-rise tenements has proved to be a disaster in urban planning. Even placing open spaces between the "projects" has not reduced the stresses of overcrowding—a lesson critics of Soleri's arcologies are quick to point out.

Body Space

Our primary sense of space depends upon the basic requirements of our body itself. A tight dress, loose shoes, door lintels that brush the top of our heads, all distress us perhaps mildly but really. A very tall or stout person will be highly distressed in a Volkswagen. Similarly, fantasies about being confined in a coffin present one of the common fears about death and premature burial.

A person's spatial "comfort zone" in fact varies from situation to situation. Perhaps the easiest way to determine your own personal body space, at least in our culture, is to extend your hands and feet as far up and out as you can, inscribing a kind of oval sphere around yourself. Consider that your basic space. It travels with you and grows or shrinks as you do, whether physically or psychologically. People who come within that sphere will affect you differently from those who remain outside, the reason why a ride on a crowded subway can be such an exhausting event, especially for a newcomer to the city.

Inner Space

Our sense of space is not limited to externals. Our "inner" perceptions are also organized in spatial terms. Memories, ideas and feelings seem to occupy certain areas of our head and trunk. In some respects this is fact true, as Wilder Penfield and other researchers have shown with electrical stimulation of the brain. Thus, when we speak of having someone's name "in the back of my mind" or "on the tip of my tongue," or someone's image "deep in my heart," we are not engaging in mere metaphor.

We are also vaguely aware of the placement of our internal organs, though we refer to them, as we do with respect to mental and emotional "states," in symbolic or metaphorical terms: butterflies in the stomach, a pain in the neck (or elsewhere), a "gut" reaction. Our whole sense of self as a socially functioning, conscious subject is also structured largely in spatial terms, even if we rarely reflect on that fact of personal experience. We speak, for instance, of a "close friend" or a "distant" relative, a "near miss" and a "far cry." It is also true that our minds can be as cluttered as our rooms or desks often are, that our emotions can be tangled or in as much a mess as our hair is.

From a spiritual as well as a psychological perspective, therefore, we can say that inner space is a reflection of our situation in outer space, particularly social space. Further, how we organize or reorganize outer space is a projection of inner organization and structure, if not necessarily in exact terms. Someone once quipped that a clean desk is the sign of a disordered mind. While an obvious exaggeration, the compulsive organizer who is uncomfortable if a paper clip is out of place evinces a precarious state of inner balance, most likely an abiding struggle to remain in constant control of an uncertain situation.

Acquired Characteristics

Our need to organize external reality is a function of mind—as the ancients said, sapientis est ordinare: "The mark of wisdom is order." The body is where we first bring order, genetically speaking, by adjusting to the demands of our parents when they began training us as infants. Left to ourselves, we would have engendered constant chaos in the environment, since humans lack most of the instinctual patterns of behavior found in insects, birds and other mammals. Humankind has externalized order in the forms of culture and gained by that evolutionary development an unparalleled range of freedom.

On the personal level, our habits or acquired patterns of bodily organization thus become the signs of our internalization of cultural norms and values, including manners and tacit ways of dealing with people in public. Ultimately, it gets down to a matter of style: how we express our particular awareness of our place in the scheme of things. Our style as a whole is an index of our total response to reality, a measure of our overall health, which is to say our spirituality as well as our sanity.

Disordered Spaces

Slovenly dress, an unkempt appearance, disregard for ordinary hygiene and social decorum are as eloquent as their opposites in terms of social communication. Such manifestations can indicate various degrees of social estrangement and mental disintegration as well as emotional disturbance. But they can also indicate a higher achievement of integration in some cases. Einstein's disdain for wearing socks, the careless attire and dissheveled appearance of the desert monks and saints such as Francis of Assisi, Benedict Joseph Labre and Caryll Houselander transcend ordinary cultural conventions.

The psychotic behavior of the insane, on the contrary, is a desperate effort to conserve psychic energy, a retreat from the social world back to the less structured world of infancy. Similarly, the litter and decay of slums and abandoned urban areas passively manifest a kind of collective insanity, a sense of alienation and forced disengagement from the commonweal. Its active expression, especially among the young, is vandalism—the deliberate if ultimately thoughtless destruction of an order perceived as oppressive.

Projections

Inner space is thus projected outwards, becoming visible and public as a form of communication, whether constructive and meaningful or destructive and chaotic. We derive and then reflect our own image, magnified, into our environment. Even our clothing and hair styles are manifestations of inner states as much as they are extensions of our skin. Our rooms and houses are projections of our personality in space. Architecture and urban design represent further extensions of cultural and personal identity into space. The Parthenon, Chartres Cathedral, the Eiffel Tower and the Transamerica Building are all forms of cultural communication, spiritual statements as eloquent as any monument or statue, book or painting.

Functionally, huts, houses, buildings and cities—even automobiles—are spatial projections of the human body, particularly the skin. It was not by accident that medieval artists and philosophers expressed the cosmos itself in such terms, whether the cosmic body of the zodiac or the celestial houses through which the heavenly bodies moved. Civic processes were also described in terms of body functions, the whole congeries of governed and government being called "the body politic." St. Paul employed the same image, but with a mystically literal intention, to describe the Church, and ultimately the human race as a whole, as the Body of Christ.

Scale

Spatially, a culture or nation with imperial designs or pretentions tends to express its self-perception in grandiose architectural and urban terms. Rome was the most monumental as well as the largest city of the ancient world. Every capital in the world since has tended to express its sense of self-importance in similar terms, as a brief tour of London, Washington or Buenos Aires will demonstrate. Size, or rather, scale, above all imparts a sense of power and dignity. Five hundred years ago, the collaborative genius of Raphael, Michelangelo, Bramonte, Bernini and others donated such a perfect sense of scale to St. Peter's in Rome, already the largest church in Christendom, that the visual, auditory and kinesthetic effect of the architecture dwarfs human ambition to the level of felt insignificance.

By contrast, cultures which do not value pomp and power do not evolve magnificent architecture except in isolated instances such as the gigantic oriental statues of the Buddha, which function in much the same manner as the scale of the Vatican. The Celtic lands of the Dark Ages, even those which had been occupied by the Romans, never ventured into heroic scale, their largest structures being the defensive roundtowers built against the Viking terror. The Celtic monks in particular seemed convinced well over a thousand years ago that "small is beautiful," avoiding bigness in every way except heroic generosity and courage. The intricate artwork of their illuminated manuscripts as well as the complex patterns in their metalwork and stone carvings strikingly illustrate the technique of miniaturization, which, according to Teilhard de Chardin, represents the most potent feature of evolutionary development.

When translated into architecture and technology, miniaturization makes possible the extraordinary concentration of energy necessary for accomplishments such as the space program and arcologies like Arcosanti. It also allows for the ultimate projections of the dwelling skin, the space suit and especially the space colony. The advent of micro-circuitry, the patterns of which so closely resemble Celtic designs, has now propelled our civilization to the threshold of a new epoch.

Space Settlements

In his exciting account of space exploration, Toward Distant Suns, Dr. T. A. Heppenheimer points out that "the interior layout of a space colony could resemble that of some old European villages. Nordlingen, in Bavaria, could be thought of as an Earth-side space colony; its shape, dimensions, and population are similar to those of the Stanford torus (a ring-shaped model). People have lived for centuries behind the medieval wall. Yet Nordlingen has a large church, parks, streets and mostly single-family houses."2/

If a developed space colony might well resemble a medieval town, the initial phase of the settlement would probably be best modeled on the pattern of the smaller, self-sufficient Celtic monastery, with its "staff" of skilled artisans, agricultural experts and scholars, all specially trained and motivated to endure sometimes severe deprivation and danger. For in the earlier phase of space colonization, smallness, sufficiency and spiritual wholeness will be necessary, rather than expansiveness, abundance and fragmentation. The situation will be dangerous and will require men and women of courage, high motivation and deep personal stability. The central position of the church or chapel at Nordlingen and the Celtic settlements should also remind future planners of the importance of providing a place for the cultivation and protection of inner spaces.

Several civilian associations have already begun working on designs for space stations and colonies which could integrate high technologies and human, spiritual dimensions of human experience. The first effort I knew of was author Ray Bradbury's Mankind One project in the early 'seventies. More recently, I have been impressed by the School for the Future program of Amicitia International, a group located at Stanford University. These young people and their professional mentors are engaged in studying, planning and promoting the peaceful civilian development of space as a resource for the whole planet. Membership is open to all.

Another non-profit educational association is the World Space Foundation of South Pasadena, California, which is presently concentrating on a solar sail project of tremendous promise and potential. In some respects, these fledgling organizations herald the advent of a second Renaissance glimmering on the dim horizon of whatever Dark Ages are coming. It is not difficult to detect among their members a reflection of the exploratory spirit of the Celtic monk-navigators or that curious, courageous Italian who sailed out of the Middle Ages into a truly new world.

Future Space

Whether dark or not, the coming age will differ from the present in many ways connected with our sense of space and spatial requirements, both particular and collective. As a consequence, a spirituality for a possible future will necessarily take space into account, in terms both of renunciation and development.

First of all, because there will inevitably be more people everywhere and, as a direct result, fewer resources to go around as well as a general condition of scarcity, we can assume that many of the spatial prerogatives we now enjoy will have to be jettisoned. This will be as true of the inhabitants of a space colony as for urban dwellers in the city of tomorrow.

Private space will increasingly diminish except for the very wealthy. Most of us will have to forego the luxury of the single-occupant automobile, taxis, private apartments, bathrooms, even graves. As we are crowded further together, it will be more important, therefore, to preserve and enhance personal privacy wherever possible.

Space Justice

The distribution of space as a private and social resource and requirement functions, as we have seen, as an index of social rank, even among animals. But among human beings, the major factors in the allocation of space are not mere bigness and meanness, much less intelligence. Too often, what counts is simply money and what money can buy: power and influence. The poor, aged, infirm and other minorities are too often cramped into tenements, slums and other prison-like institutions—retirement "homes," hospitals, dormitories, etc. where they are expected to live (and die) as quietly and obscurely as possible. But the poor, like the rich, need personal space: the possibility of privacy as well as room. We all need public space as well, but without private space, urban parks become junkyards and battlegrounds, the night haunts of mentally and socially deranged deperadoes.

The solitude of contemplative orders was preserved in crowded medieval monasteries housing more than seven hundred monks by providing each with a small cell for study and prayer, while eating, sleeping and manual labor were carried out in common. The Irish monks, pressured by pilgrims and the encroachment of towns, either fled deeper into their diseart or became peregrini, wandering like Davy Crockett toward ever newer horizons. In either case, solitude was held to be so valuable as to warrant fundamental changes in the very fabric of life.

Tomorrow, we may well see our teeming populations cleaving radically into distinctive and perhaps irreconcilably urban and rural lifestyles, the suburbs necessarily going the way of the dodo and the internal combustion engine. In cities like Paolo Soleri's arcologies or space colonies, providing for solitude and privacy will be even more urgent. But such provision cannot be a mere addition or luxury. In order to function constructively as a humane balancing factor, such spaces will have to be structurally integrated into "life support systems" as a whole. Except for Soleri's inclusion of a monastery at Arcosanti, however, we are presently far from even a promising start in that direction. Time is still on our side, fortunately—if only barely so.

The Soviet Cosmonaut Yuri Gagarin found neither God nor angels in the space he investigated as one of the first men to leave Planet Earth. He may well have missed heaven, not because he arrived at the wrong time or appeared at the wrong place, but simply because he was in the wrong space. The appropriate space for the whole person is not outer space, nor indeed inner space, but the space that is simultaneously both inner and outer. Pascal, who wrote of the mystical sphere whose periphery is nowhere and whose center is everywhere, might have understood. For he also realized that we could never look for God unless we had already found him—or, rather, we had let God find us.

ELEVEN

The City and the Future

At the dawn of human civilization stands the city, inextricably bound up with humanity's progress from a primitive hunter-gatherer culture to an agrarian and therefore civilized society. The earliest city was probably the biblical Jericho, perhaps the mother of all cities, established as long as 7,000 years ago. Archeological evidence exists for organized pre-urban settlements far older than Jericho.

Once the city had emerged, it came to be identified throughout subsequent history with civilization itself as the center of government, worship and trade. Even in Celtic Britain, where the few small towns that survived the departure of the Roman legions owed their very existence to foreigners, the concept of civitas endured to inspire national unity under Arthur and his successors. Derived from civis, "citizen," civitas was used by the Romans to refer to the whole body of citizens, the community. It designated, for instance, the independent Celtic tribes of Gaul and Britain. Urbs, from which we get "urban," "urbane," and "suburban," was the ordinary Latin word for Rome itself.

As humanity's past was bound up with the evolution of the city, the character of present civilization remains definitely urban. More than half the people in the world already live in cities, and millions more throughout the world continue to migrate there from the exhausted countryside. Tomorrow's world, too, will in effect be identified with the city, urbs et orbis, the center and focus of political, cultural, economic, educational and spiritual dimensions of the world's people. And as we address the fundamental problems and possibilities of the city of tomorrow, civilization itself may well hang in the balance, as the stakes for survival mount higher

184

and higher. Thus, the future of the city is a supremely spiritual concern, demanding serious thought, reflection and action. If we are to live together in a future symbiosis with our fellow human beings, we can be sure that with certain exceptions, it will be a civic harmony or none at all.

The Cross in the Circle

"The earliest known symbol for a city is an ancient Egyptian hieroglyph: a cross within a circle. The cross represents a central point where people, power and resources are concentrated. The circle suggests an enclosure, a boundary."1/ Significantly, the same symbol is also used for the earth itself in astronomical notation: urbs et orbis.

Not all ancient cultures envisioned the city as a circle, but all apparently recognized the identification of the city and the cosmos, as Mircea Eliade has amply demonstrated. Jones and Van Zandt tell us that "When the Chinese built a city they tried to reproduce what they thought was the plan of the universe. A city should be square in shape, because the earth was thought to be square. Its walls probably represented the mountains girdling the earth."2/ Similar patterns can be found among the Babylonians, Aztecs and Egyptians.

Spiritually, the city has had a checkered career. Nomadic and agrarian people tend to despise urbanity with its refinement, sophistication and inequalities. The Hebrews, as such a people, regarded all cities with suspicion, and it was by no means easy for David and his successors to consolidate royal power in Jerusalem. Eventually, however, with the building of Solomon's temple and the suppression of mountain sanctuaries and shrines, what had been a hated pagan citadel became the Holy City, the center of worship and national identity, as it remains to this time.

For Christians, Rome was similarly transformed from the capital of the Antichrist to the See of Peter, acquiring a sanctity exceeding even that of Jerusalem. By the Middle Ages, Jerusalem had also become a sacred city of Islam. (Mecca, too, had a parallel history for Muslims as Jerusalem and Rome had for Jews and Christians.) Muslim warriors often prevented pilgrims from visiting the sacred sites, while pirates and bandits made the long voyage there even more hazardous. But Rome was nearer, accessible and historically identified not only with the Vicar of Christ, but with the center of law and order as well as the Imperial glory of the classical era. Rome became again in Christianity what it had been for the ancient Romans, simply the City: Urbs.

Urban Ambivalence

Biblical writers frequently portrayed the human predicament as a tale of two cities, as Augustine did when he saw his beloved Rome fall to barbarian hordes: the City of God and the City of Man—or rather, the City of Satan. Jerusalem the Just and Babylon the Destroyer.3/ The earlier hostility toward cities in general had been replaced by an emergent love and even zeal for Jerusalem. Hatred was still directed at Babylon, however, where the Jews had been enslaved. Later, this antagonism was spiritualized, being addressed to the symbolic Babylon, any city which stood against the will of God and the welfare of his people, including Jerusalem itself in certain respects.4/

Jesus' own attitude toward the Holy City was mixed. In Luke's gospel, his whole mission is portrayed as an ascent to Jerusalem for the Passover.5/ He wept over the city in frustration and love.6/ For Jerusalem was hard of heart. She killed the prophets and would also kill him. Jesus was in fact executed outside the walls, as a final sign of repudiation by urban religiosity.7/

In the Book of Revelation, the Seer beholds a new, spiritualized Jerusalem coming down from heaven, a clean and holy city, indeed the kingdom of God, his Bride.8/ The "old" sinful Jerusalem had in fact been captured and largely destroyed by Roman legions in 70 AD and again in 135, after the futile revolt of Bar Kochba, when the Jews were dispersed and what was left of the city was resettled with pagans.

Split Definitives

Such mixed attitudes are hardly localized. When English colonists settled in "New" England, they brought with them a biblically based, largely political antagonism toward the city which, while one-sided to say the least, has nevertheless affected American attitudes right up to the present. For these staunch Puritans, every city was Babylon, especially Rome, the Scarlet Woman, the throne of the hated papal Antichrist. Virtue resided in the wilderness, the agrarian village and the farm.

Americans still tend to think mythically of the city as the den of vice and temptation, God's true dwelling being the country. The little chapel in the woods, rather than the urban cathedral, became the religious symbol of the appropriate house of worship. Even Thomas Jefferson, perhaps the most enlightened and humane of the Founding Fathers, described cities as "ulcers on the body politic." Such an attitude is not particularly Christian, more resembling the ancient Hebrew stance also affected by the colonial Puritans. It is an attitude fortunately changing. But over the centuries, it actually fostered what it denounced—through malign neglect, American cities have all too often been allowed to become centers of injustice, oppression, crime and poverty.

In this respect, the Reagan administration more than fulfilled its intention of returning to a former, simpler way of life by reversing decades of efforts at social renewal. As a result of withdrawing federal support from America's cities, we can expect to see an an acceleration of decay and increasing human misery. Schools and transportation systems are already faltering. Sanitation, communication and health services are simultaneously increasing in expense and declining in equality and number. Crime rates are soaring. Street gangs dominate entire areas by intimidation and terrorism. In many sections of urban America, not merely the aged, but few people at all will venture out of their homes after dark.

Flight to the City

Three hundred years ago, only a small fraction of the earth's population lived in cities, the vast majority working the land or living in fishing villages. In England, for instance, 42% of the population in 1770 were farm workers. By 1841, the number had declined to 22%. By 1975, only 3.2% still lived off the land, the equivalent figure for the United States being 4%. In 1600, London was already an enormous city, inhabited by about 200,000 persons. By 1750, that number had more than tripled. The metropolitan population of Greater London now is estimated at about 12 million people. With a population of 55 million, 78% of England's people live in cities, most perhaps in cities of more than 100,000 inhabitants. Fully one-fifth live in the Greater London area alone.

Tokyo with its 13,800,000 people is the largest urban center in the world. Between 1950 and 1970, it more than doubled in size. By 1977, five "greater" areas far exceeded ten million inhabitants each: New York City, Mexico City, Tokyo, Shanghai and Los Angeles. The total population of the New York metropolitan area, which extends across state lines, is estimated to be somewhere near 16 million persons.

But except for a few cities in the southern United States such as Houston and Atlanta, rapid urban expansion in the near future will undoubtedly occur in Third World countries, where population growth is already highest. As a result, with the addition of more job-hungry migrants from the country, the density, stress and misery of the majority of the world's peoples can be expected to increase proportionately. Already,

Africans and Latin Americans are receiving as much as 18% less food each year than they were a decade ago.

At the turn of the century there were only eleven cities in the world with more than one million inhabitants. As little as thirty years ago "the 'million' cities of the world were, with a few exceptions, located in the West. Now, most of them are in the developing countries, and some of them are doubling in size every ten years."9/ Shanghai now numbers over 10 million, Calcutta and Bombay 7 million and 6 million respectively, Seoul 7.5 million, Cairo 6 million, Jakarta 5 million, San Paolo 5.3 million, Teheran 4.4 million and Lagos over one million, to cite only a handful. By 1975, there were 130 cities of more than a million inhabitants, 31 of them in the United States. But according to current projections, there will be 273 such cities in the world by 1985.

Urban Crowding

The most immediate threat from rapid growth is not to the land or even to political stability, although both are seriously endangered. Rather, human health and welfare will be the primary victims. The threshold of over-saturation is explosively near in many great cities. More than likely, the first critical reaction will be a sudden, swift and uncontrollable onslaught of an epidemic of cholera or typhus. Augmented by wide-spread famine and despair, mortality rates will be extreme. Pestilence will follow and spread throughout the world, striking both rich and poor alike. Hospital space and medical supplies as well as personnel will not only be inadequate but inaccessible to the vast majority of persons. Cities will soon be filled with decomposing bodies too numerous to collect and bury, as in the calamitous fourteenth century.

The stress of overcrowding can wreak the same kind of destruction on the human race as a whole as it does on local populations of lemmings or rabbits, even without the extra horror of contagion. For as humankind has multiplied and filled the earth, it has made its home one gigantic city, limited only by time, expense and political conventions. We are indeed all one, both in life and in death.

Although urban growth and crowding is becoming acute in the Third World, the more advanced countries are already almost totally urbanized, their large cities centers of complex problems different from but no less serious than those of their poorer counterparts. And while the situation differs in various parts of the world, the basic problems of urbanization are similar: vast numbers of the poor concentrated in crowded, inadequate slums; deterioration of the heart of the city following the exodus of the middle class to the suburbs; urban sprawl with its massive traffic jams, congested freeways and rush hours; pollution of air and water; stress from noise and delay; and higher taxes without commensurate services. Providing adequate housing is a serious problem for both affluent and less developed countries.

Traffic Woes

The city built the automobile, and the automobile destroyed the city. Urban sprawl has more to do with the mobility of the "car generation" than any other factor, especially in the face of inadequate public transportation systems. In Europe and the United States, the problem is severe, but it exists throughout the world in sometimes worse forms. The U.S. has only the tenth highest mortality rate in the world resulting from traffic accidents.

The car has also created congestion, pollution, noise, space problems, and enormous expense, both direct and indirect—initial cost, maintenance, fuel bills, insurance, fees for licenses, parking fees, etc. It is estimated that to accommodate the automobile, an area the size of the state of Georgia has been paved over with concrete and asphalt. The car industry is nevertheless on the brink of disaster, as more and more cars are manufactured in a world already overcrowded with automobiles. In 1979, over 8.5 million new cars were manufactured in the U.S. where there are already 120,485,000 registrations. With 140,844,000 licensed drivers, we are dealing with half the population of the country. The United Nations reported in 1980 that in the world as a whole, there were in excess of 34 million cars manufactured the previous year.

Another kind of pollution has been introduced into the world with the car, an aesthetic depression which saps the spirit as well as dulls the mind. Not only are city streets generally dirty as well as ugly, the highways linking the inner city with suburban areas and satellite "bedroom" communities are usually lined not with trees and flowers, but with billboards, gaudy plastic and neon signs, high-tension wires and poles, cheap, one-storey commercial shanties, diners, steak houses, filling stations, "adult" bookstores, vacant, weed-infested and trash-filled lots, used cars by the acre and automobile graveyards. But perhaps the most accurate assessment of the problem of the automobile was expressed in a Los Angeles planning report: "The pedestrian remains the largest single obstacle to free traffic movement."

Crime and Grime

Criminal activity and violence demonstrably escalate in cities once they pass the 100,000 population level. Urban crime rates have soared, moreover, in recent years, possibly as a result of greater deterioration in other aspects of city life. It is also demonstrably true that in cities of more than a million, police protection and law enforcement are far less effective than in smaller cities.

A glimpse of the future awaiting us unless we can reverse this process was offered by the science fiction writer Robert Heinlein in his novel, I Will Fear No Evil. He described future cities (not far in the future) in which there were extensive "abandoned areas," whole sections where police surveillance, fire and health protection, sanitation and other services were withdrawn because of violence and lawlessness. Such order as prevailed was enforced by gangs resembling feudal baronies or medieval mercenary companies. Travel through such abandoned areas, Heinlein predicted, could not be hazarded without armed and armored vehicles, security passes and luck. While fiction, Heinlein's apocalyptic vision is hardly less likely than the prognostications of Aldous Huxley, George Orwell or, for that matter, Roberto Vacca.

If overcrowding is the trigger that releases suicidal impulses among lemmings and homicidal inclinations among urbanites, decrowding our cities would seem the logical solution to much of our present distress. But shipping the middle class off to suburbia has demonstrably failed to achieve a balance. Nor has incarcerating the poor in multi-storey incipient slums. However, the "small is beautiful" movement recognized a decade ago by E. F. Schumacher may be becoming manifest in population shifts to and from the city. Kirkpatrick Sale points out in Human Scale that mega-cities of one million inhabitants and larger have shown steady losses in population over the past thirty years. Medium-sized and smaller cities have grown, on the other hand. The greatest increase has been in cities having between 10,000 and 50,000 residents.10/Demographic studies also show that 56% of the U.S. population would prefer living in or near cities of that size.11/ Thus even if Paolo Soleri's creative solution to urban sprawl were widely adopted, we can surmise that the most successful arcologies would also be those which could contain 10,000 to 50,000 people rather than the gargantuan structures in which two or three million could live. Energy requirements and provisions alone will probably limit the optimum size of any future city to less than a million inhabitants, at which point consumption as well as costs take a quantum leap upwards.

Small is Possible

There are several methods by which the size and density of cities could be constructively reduced without further encroachment upon already exhausted land and resources. Failing fuel supplies and the probable demise of the automobile will probably necessitate one or another of them. First, cities can be radically decentralized by urban contraction and the development of more small towns and villages. Suburban "dormitory" communities would simply disappear. People would either live in the city, close to world, or in small towns and rural areas. Second, cities can expand upwards while contracting horizontally, much as sections of San Francisco, Chicago and New York have done. The ultimate expression of the vertical city can be found in Soleri's arcologies and similar designs by Buckminster Fuller, Frank Lloyd Wright and other creative architects. Third, a combination of the two former solutions might well present the most promising and workable method of preserving land, resources and human values.

Upward Bound

By building cities up as well as in, creating a three-dimensional structure, it becomes possible to layer neighborhoods, factories, parks and service areas around a true city center. The distance between the center and the periphery thus becomes greatly shorter, permitting far easier access in less time. Since, as animal and human tests have shown, density alone does not produce stress, it would be possible to include more people in smaller areas without congestion.

The Courage to Build

Solutions do exist and they can be applied. Nevertheless, living humanely in tomorrow's cities will require reserves of spiritual strength we have hardly begun to develop. Presently, many citizens are preparing themselves for anticipated increases in crime, violence, danger and scarcity by stocking up on guns and ammunition as well as food stores and energy supplies. Such remedies are at most a palliative and at worse illusory. Arming ourselves only increases the danger of violence. Survival and, more importantly, humanity will be served far better by acquiring new skills in the civic virtues that have been recognized as the bedrock of civilization since Jericho.

Socially, a return to the medieval ideal of the common good might make the difference between competitive strife and cooperation among the various sectors of the population. More humane (and Christian) than the crude utilitarianism that has provided the customary underpinning of political philosophy in recent centuries, concern for the commonwealth attends to the welfare of the people as a whole rather than piecemeal—i.e., in terms of class interest or personal privilege.

Other spiritual values can enhance as well as empower urban community development: compassion—the capacity to be moved to help those in need, courtesy—that lovely medieval skill in social relations, care—most especially for those most in need, but also for the natural environment, and courage—the will to struggle in order to succeed.

A return to neighborhood pastimes as well as coalitions and other political participation can strengthen people's sense of belonging and sharing. Songfests, bake sales, art fairs, carnivals, street dances, picnics, athletic contests, clean-up campaigns, home visiting programs and "meals on wheels" for the aged and infirm, along with many other humane and celebrative strategies, can vastly improve the quality of life in any urban locale. Similarly, clean air, potable water, safe streets and sidewalks unlittered and in good repair, the presence of flowers, trees and grass where possible, the welfare of urban animals—squirrels, song birds, even the lowly pigeon—can help to make life even in poorer areas more livable.

Cities for the future must be well-planned and well-managed, not for the ease and profit of a wealthy minority, but rather with regard for the highest quality of life for all. As we have too clearly seen, cramming the poor into ghettoes and slums eventually dooms all to deprivation and misery. Even the flight to the suburbs profited few but real estate developers and the construction industry, since the urban decay that ensued in the central city condemned the suburbs themselves to increasing cultural containment, deprivation and tedium.

Thus social justice must be an integral factor in the allocation of urban space as well as of farmlands. Room and resources cannot be earmarked to benefit only an elite, or we will simply repeat the calamities of the colonization of the New World by European commercial interests in the sixteenth century. What humankind must not export to the stars is its tragic legacy of oppression and greed. Urban planning and space exploration both present the coming generation with a spiritual challenge greater than the technological problems awaiting them. Both are fields white for the harvest which only persons of truly humane sensitivities will be able to reap adequately—men and women alive to the mystical, poetic and aesthetic dimensions of experience as well as technical and scientific possibilities.

TWELVE

Spirit and Craft

Our voyage into the past in search of clues to a viable spirituality for the future took us to the Celtic renaissance, long the sole beacon illuminating truly darksome ages. We noted several times the monks' delight in calligraphy, poetry, illumination, sculpture, metalwork and music. At this point in our journey toward a possible symbiosis, we can profitably consider the place of art and especially of handcrafts in an authentic spirituality of sufficiency and human survival. By exploring the varieties of crafts and their role in the evolution of the human spirit, we may in fact discover something of the ancient monastic secret—for the old books tell us very little about why crafts were so important to them. We may also discover something even more important about our own times and the future possible.

<u>Mechanical Man</u>

Over the past two centuries, the industrialized West has evolved into a culture filled with objects made not by human hands but by machines themselves guided not by human hands but by other machines and so on in a continual and ever-increasing regression. Even the words "artificial" and "artifact" no longer adequately describe the synthetic quality of our "goods." For such terms are at least linked to "art" and "artisan" as well as "artifice." And there is little art in most of our plastic possessions.

The economic advantages of mass production are admittedly great—readier access to products such as automobiles, furniture, carpets, radios, washing machines and other appliances (electric can openers, garbage compactors, carving knives, pencil sharpeners, etc.) denied not so long ago to all but the very wealthy. Cheap meat has been made available to all by mechanized agriculture. Health care is now considered a right rather than a luxury. It would still be a mere dream without modern technology. Finally, processed foods and solid state electronics have taken much of the fuss out of our busy schedules.

The economic and ecological cost of increased mechanization has also been great, on the other hand. The use of plastics and other non-natural materials which are cheap and therefore highly dispensable but not biologically degradable has resulted in a growing problem as western societies increasingly suffocate in industrial waste. A host of maladies associated with "artificial" ingredients have cropped up to plague the technopolis—from allergies and lung diseases to cancer. Petrochemical fuels are becoming rarer, more expensive and their use more harmful to the air, water and soil of the entire planet. The bleak spectacles of Love Canal and Three Mile Island continue to haunt us. Roboticization displaces more human workers year by year.

But perhaps the greatest cost of inhabiting a machine-made world is spiritual—the loss of appreciation of making and doing as we blithely accept our decreed roles as consumers of factory items, more often than not shoddily fabricated and hostile to any sense of grace and beauty.

Not everything made by hand is by that fact better or more beautiful than machine-made products. Nor would any intelligent person seriously prefer returning to either the seventh or the seventeenth century, with their recurrent plagues, lack of sanitation and hygiene, primitive transportation and inescapable poverty and misery. Yet that pre-industrialized world of handcrafts and cottage industries seems like a dream of the Golden Age compared to the crammed and littered aisles of today's suburban discount centers. And the survival of folk-arts and crafts from that era—or, rather, their revival—in the post-industrial age tells us something important about ourselves and our world, and it does so far more eloquently than can any mere dip into nostalgia.

The Range of Craft

Recently, the National Geographic Society sponsored a fascinating documentary on public television called "Living Treasures of Japan." These were revealed to be nine craftsmen and women paid a small subsidy but given signal honors as preservers of ancient traditions such as koto playing, puppetry and traditional acting, making paper, papier mache dolls, and swords by hand, firing pottery in a wood-fired kiln and casting bronze temple bells. The artists' main obligation is to hand on these time-honored ways to a new generation in the midst of one of the world's most industrialized societies.

Thus Japan, a nation alive to its artistic and cultural heritage, looks ahead to the future by retaining and enhancing aspects of its past. Other nations honor traditional crafts in similar if less manifest ways. In the United States, we possess no distinctive traditional crafts since, with the exception of Native American crafts (which are highly worth preserving), our craft ways came to this continent with our immigrant ancestors. The American genius in crafts thus seems to lie in collecting a multitude of differing ethnic traditions which thus become available to all.

The Art of Craft

From the dawn of recognizable civilization, the importance of crafts has been evident in the care taken to enhance and preserve craft products, tools and techniques. As we shall see, this holy or numinous attitude toward crafts and craftworkers has a negative as well as a positive aspect, but the origin of both lies in utility. Crafts represent, in fact, a highly developed art form in which the pragmatic, even utilitarian purpose of the product extends the creative impulse directly into the world of action. "Fine" arts, by contrast, arise at a different level of social evolution and provide a medium of communication between the artist and the public which lacks or even repudiates any further use than enjoyment.

Paleontologists generally agree that the emergence of civilization is connected with the appearance of tools— utilitarian creations that manifest an awareness of the relationship between means and ends, that is, which bridge the perceived gaps between the self and the world. The first tools were simple utensils—knives, clubs, bowls, axes, and so forth. While plain in their earliest stages, soon tools and even weapons were embellished with designs, and their value and importance celebrated by elaborate decoration and ceremony. Those who made them and decorated them received honor and praise, especially in more developed societies.

Many proper names in English, German and other languages proudly derive from family craft traditions: Archer, Brewer, Carpenter, Dyer, Fuller, Mason, Miller, Priest, Schumacher and Wright among others. It should also be noted that although the word "craftsman" is almost always employed in standard writings, there have been great craftswomen as well. Arachne was so skilled a weaver, according to Greek myth, that she challenged the goddess Athena herself. Penelope, Ulysses' faithful wife, was also a weaver. In history, Madame Tussaud (1761-1850) was the greatest wax-worker of all time. Grandma Moses earned a lasting place in American art. The greatest potter of our era was Maria Martinez from San Ildefonso Pueblo in northern New Mexico. At the time of her death in 1980, she had received every major award in the world for her work. Maria's pots, now on display throughout the entire planet, not only raised her and her family to prominence in the art world, they also revitalized the cultural and economic life of her people.

Myths and Smiths: The Deeper Dimension

In ancient cultures, the professional craftworker seems frequently to have been handicapped and thus unable to participate in fighting, hunting and agriculture. Lamed warriors, for example, may have become specialists in making weapons and armor. An echo of this double social solution possibly exists in the myth of the lame god-craftsman.

In classical Greek mythology, Hephaestus was the son of Zeus and Hera. Born a weakling, he was cast from heaven by his disdainful father. The child's legs were crushed in the fall, but he was saved and reared by nymphs, becoming a skilled metalworker and jeweler. Later regaining a position among the gods, Hephaestus built the palaces of Olympus and, as god of the forge, created the magical weapons with which the gods did battle. He also made Achilles' armor, Agamemnon's sceptre and the necklace of Harmonia. In some legends, he created the first woman, Pandora, or even the entire human race. Aphrodite, the goddess of love, was sometimes portrayed as Hephaestus' wife—an allegorical celebration of the alliance between art and beauty.

Such myths are a powerful means by which social values and roles are distinguished and sanctioned. Thus the importance of craftworkers can be seen in the part they play in the great legends of most ancient cultures— many resembling the story of Hephaestus the smith. In all such myths there can be found profound psychological and spiritual insights.

In India, the divine smith Trastri forges the weapons by which Indra slays the evil Vritra. In Egypt, Ptah makes Horus weapons to defeat his wicked brother Seth. Zeus kills the dragon-monster Typhon with Hephaestus' aid. Norse saga relates how Sindri forges Thor's great hammer Mjolnir. The Finnish hero-smith Ilmarinen creates the magical talisman sampo. In Irish myth, the smith Goibnu presides over the heavenly banquet. His Norwegian counterpart is Regin; in Japan, Ame No Ma-Hitotsu Kami.

The Roman god Vulcan has much in common with Hephaestus—both were gods of the underworld, of fire as well as craft. Vulcan eventually becomes the Teutonic Volung—also a smith. As Wieland, he forges Siefried's sword Balmung with which the hero slays the dragon Fafnir. In Anglo-Saxon England, Wieland becomes Wayland the Smith, believed to have his forge in a cave near Lambourn, where the great White House was prehistorically cut into the Berkshire hillside. In a district filled with neolithic monuments and burial mounds, Wayland's Smithy can still be seen. For centuries, farmers would leave an unshod horse and a coin overnight there. In the morning, they claimed, the coin would be gone, and the horse would be newly shod.

As at least a semi-divine figure, the smith was often associated with infernal powers—Hephaestus and Vulcan being chthonic deities of fire (hence "volcano"). Such "old gods" were often interpreted by Christians as demons. Devilish or not, even today smiths are regarded as magical persons in many cultures, such as among the Bantu and Masai of Africa, the Yakut peoples and in southeast Asia. We should also remember that craft also means "cunning" and "deceit" as well as "skill." (The word in fact comes from the Saxon kraft, which means "strength.") In its more sinister applications, e.g., "witchcraft," and in its adjective form "crafty," the word can denote a wily, devious, "artful" character.

Biblical Crafts

In ancient Hebrew tradition, crafts were not originally taught to mortals by supernatural beings as in pagan myths and the later Jewish-Christian Book of Enoch. The first craftworker was Tubal-Cain, seven generations after Adam. In a surprisingly accurate synopsis of cultural evolution in Gen. 4:20, we learn that Lamech, Adam's great-great-great-great grandson, had two wives. "Adah bore Jabal; he was the father of those who dwell in tents and have cattle. His brother's name was Jubal; he was the father of all those who play the lyre and pipe. Zillah bore Tubal-Cain; he was the forger of all instruments of bronze and iron."

Here we have a deliberate connection between the emergence of crafts, music and nomadic husbandry. In Exodus 35 and 36, there is a far more explicit sanction of the arts and crafts as God summons artisans to decorate the Tabernacle: "See, the Lord has called by name Bezalel the son of Uri, son of Hur, of the tribe of Judah; and he has filled him with the Spirit of God, with ability, with intelligence, with knowledge, and with all craftsmanship, to devise artistic designs, to work in gold and silver and bronze, in cutting stones for setting, and in carving wood, for work in every skilled craft."1/

The Mystery of Craft

All crafts seem to have been originally surrounded by an aura of mystery, the "secrets of the trade," once carefully guarded and revealed only to initiates in the midst of arcane ritual and solemn oaths. The resemblance to the rites of the ancient mystery religions is · not accidental, at least psychologically. Even today, initiation into a Masonic lodge blends mystical and occult ceremony with craft lore—the compass and the builder's square remaining potent symbols of a once very secret organization.

Preserving "hidden lore" is no longer a characteristic of craft or religion; the occult aspect has largely vanished. The secrets of technique are there for anyone to learn who has the time and patience. But the mysterious aura around the craftsman remains, because the ambivalence toward craftwork has a deeper source than technique. The ancients recognized the power of crafts in the closeness of the worker to the earth itself, from which he drew strength—the fire of Hephaestus. Craftworkers are dangerous, and therefore "holy"—like undertakers and chimneysweeps—because they are in touch with creative energy and unknown forces. Sometimes the village smith was called even in fairly recent times to break magical spells or to "forge" a marriage bond between children of warring families.

This mysterious, "dark" side of craftworkers sometimes added to their sinister reputation. There is something demonic about Hephaestus and the revengeful Wayland. In the apocryphal Book of Enoch, crafts were seen as an endowment of the devil himself: "And Azazel taught men to make swords, and knives and shields, and breastplates, and made known to them the metals (of the earth) and the art of working them, and bracelets, and ornaments, and the use of antinomy, and the beautifying of the eyelids, and all kinds of costly stones, and all coloring tinctures. And there arose much godlessness...."2/

Christian Crafts

To a large extent, this ambivalence continues in Christianity during the ages of persecution. After that, craftsmen were employed to embellish basilicas and churches, a reprise of Exodus 35. In the fifth century, however, we still can find a reminder of the old ways in the prayer called "St. Patrick's Breastplate." In it, protection is sought against "spells of women, smiths and druids." Nevertheless, blacksmiths in England found their patron in St. Clement, third successor to St. Peter, who, according to legend, was banished to the Crimea under the emperor Trajan to work in the mines. St. Dunstan became the patron of goldsmiths. A skilled musician, illuminator and metalworker in the ancient Celtic tradition, Dunstan was a monk at Glastonbury, where he became abbot in 940. Later he was made Archbishop of Canterbury. He was largely responsible in that capacity for the re-establishment of monastic life in England after the Anglo-Saxon conquests.

In Ireland, similarly, St. Colum Cille is often regarded as the patron of artists and craftworkers. And as far as Russia, the ancient Vulcan-like Kuznets was "baptized" into the dual form of Kuz'ma-Dem'yan, otherwise known as Sts. Cosmas and Damian, the patrons of physicians! But the greatest Christian tribute to the crafts (and vice versa) came with the construction of the medieval cathedrals from the twelfth to the fourteenth centuries. Most still stand today, true monuments not only to the faith of generations, but to the skill and generosity of thousands of anonymous craftworkers whose only memorial other than their work can be found in the mysterious mason's marks on certain stones.

However it was conceived and expressed, the mystery of craft was always and deeply a spiritual reality, neither magical nor demonic. And it is in that dimension that we shall find our true clues for a future spirituality.

The Spirit of Craft

Most of our "classical" forms of art originated in folk traditions. Cultural evolution and snobbery notwithstanding, there are differences between crafts and the "fine" arts and it is important to be aware of them. Most important, I think, is the fundamental democracy of the "servile" or folk arts—almost anyone can hope to become reasonably proficient at macrame or decoupage in not too long a time. On the other hand, to become a reasonably proficient ballerina, you can expect to work at it for about ten years—starting at age six!

Receptively appreciating great works of art, music and literature is a spiritual exercise of power and importance. Radio, television, films, the phonograph, tape recorder, high quality prints and art reproductions have made immortal masterpieces available at the flick of a switch and at low cost. But crafts and folk arts are the ordinary ways in which ordinary people actively experience the creative dimension of art. Consequently, they occupy a distinctive and no less important place of their own in spirituality.

The heart of the spirituality of crafts, then, is creativity. But to begin with, as in all spirituality, doing art and crafts exposes us necessarily to the challenge and risk of self-discovery and "purgation" in ways the aesthetic consumer might find surprising.

The Word of Craft: Self-Disclosure

In a small book of exceptional depth and beauty, Carla Needleman has probed the process of craftwork as a journey into the mystery of our own spirit and our relationships to other persons, the world of nature and God. A potter herself, Needleman explores that skill as well as weaving, design, wood carving and teaching crafts in what I can only describe as adventures in spirituality. As a woodcarver, I found her reflections not only accurate but illuminating.

Aware of the current but sometimes ephemeral enthusiasm for crafts, she has little use for the kind of "pop" spirituality based loosely on nevertheless authentic techniques. But Needleman displays both warmth and wisdom as she reflects on the effects of human imperfections such as impatience, pretentiousness and pride encountering the recalcitrance of matter—the indifference of clay, the stubbornness of wood, the bland simplicity of wool. "Craftsmanship," she observes "begins with disillusion."3/

The authentic worker in crafts must acquire the skill of self-knowledge as well as respect for the material at hand. Material means matter, and by means of transforming matter, we gain at least the possibility of a revelation of Spirit. The process in true craftwork is thus twofold—the transformation of matter and, more importantly, the transformation of the worker who, like the ancient alchemist, is the true material. The true process is spiritual development; the objective, a clean heart.

William Ernest Hocking liked to say that we, as creatures, are "apprentices in creativity." Human beings do not create, properly speaking. We rearrange things, we transform. Our creativity is partial and imitative. But it is precisely in art and crafts that we therefore realize one of our closest ties with the Creator, in whose creative image and likeness we, too, have been made. We share in the act of Creation, continuing in our craft the work of the divine craftsman. And in the end, if the worker has been true to the craft, to its work, she will learn the inner mystery of our share in the creative act, "that Form comes from something like 'grace,' although grace is not what we imagined it was, and requires mind."4/

The Carpenter's Son

As we noted earlier, the major biblical tradition regarded craftwork highly, the somewhat puritanical reaction of the apocalyptic period notwithstanding. Thus when it is said of Jesus that he was a carpenter, or the carpenter's son, we can be confident that we are hearing surprise, not contempt.5/ The Greek word for carpenter in these instances, tekton, means something like "artificer." The Hebrew word would have been more concrete—charash ets, "woodcraftsman." (Our conviction that Jesus was in fact a carpenter and a carpenter's son stems as much from tradition as from the Greek words themselves.)

Why a carpenter? A foolish question...perhaps. For just as Jesus' pilgrimage into the mystery of his nature and destiny needed the desert for its completion, the way to the desert must have lain for good reason through the revealing self-discipline of craft. Its schooling was at least appropriate as an echo of the divine craftworker of Genesis whom Jesus came to reveal in his life and work. By the divine irony of a poetic God, it also happens that charash can also mean "gallows-tree." One sad duty of the carpenter under the Roman occupation was the fabrication of the cross-beam used for crucifixion.

206

God the Potter

The spiritual depth of craftwork was not ignored by the biblical theologians who set the foundations of our religious heritage. In Psalm 2:9, the familiar image of the potter's broken vessels repeats a motif that has an ancient lineage. Jeremiah takes up the theme, the smashed pots of wrath appearing in chapters 18 and 19, to be resumed by St. Paul (himself a craftsman) in Romans 9:21.6/ In the writings of Isaiah, however, we come upon a far more beautiful image, and the more ancient one of God the loving potter:

Yet, O Lord, thou art our Father,
We are clay, and thou art our potter
We are the work of thy hand.7/

One of the earliest images of God is that of a craftsman, as found in the Yahwist account of creation in Gen. 2:7 "Then the Lord God formed man of dust from the ground, and breathed into his nostrils the breath of life; and man became a living being." In Gen. 2:22 we read, similarly, "And the rib which the Lord had taken from the man he formed into a woman...."

In both cases, the Hebrew word for "form" is yatsar, which also means "to frame or fashion." Of its twenty-two appearances in the Bible, yatsar means "potter" in fully seventeen cases. When God made man and woman in his own image and likeness, they became creative, apprentices in creativity.

Toward the Future

A spirituality for the future must, I am convinced, encompass the whole person, the whole of human experience. Since crafts and folk arts have an important place in experience, especially with respect to its social dimensions of tradition and celebration, they will occupy an integral portion of such a spirituality, one close to its heart.

Crafts offer a creative holdfast in a world apparently going loose at its seams. Works of craft concretely remind us who we are, where we have come from, what's important. Crafts have an intrinsic meditative and contemplative character—they incarnate a process of self-discovery simultaneous with a respectful, sometimes difficult struggle with the very elements of creation—clay, water, fire, wood, stone, wool, flax and metal. They summon us to patience and perseverance. They require study and experiment. They delight us with unexpected success and dash our foolish expectations against the reefs of failure. They keep us close to the earth and its processes. They are well suited to a sufficiency-oriented lifestyle because of their ecologically conservative nature. They are technologically simple, and thus appropriate in an economy of scarcity. A clay pot is much easier to make—and replace—than an aluminum one.

Crafts open up a truly symbiotic realm to the distracted soul tossed about a fragmenting world by storms of change. And as once they came to symbolize the spiritual achievement of the Dark Ages, they may again offer hope and re-creation in the twilight zone of western, industrial civilization.

THIRTEEN

The Spirit of Music

Nothing so distinguishes the spirit of persons, peoples and epochs as music. In every aspect of our daily life, from the "alarm" which wakens us to the strains which lull us to sleep, music frames our existence. It is not surprising that much of the din over liturgical change in the Catholic Church has centered on it, nor that singing and playing instruments were so important a part of the great Celtic heritage. Nor is it unlikely that music will be a vital component in the future with its power to restore us, to re-create our capacity to live as we struggle to survive humanely and sanely in a world constricting around us.

In the Beginning was the Song

Of all the arts, music seems always to have been perceived as the most spiritual. The Sufi mystic Hazrat Inayat Khan accounts for this connection in psychological terms: "The wonderful thing about music is that through it one can achieve concentration and meditation independently of thought. In this sense, it bridges the gulf between conscious and unconscious, between form and formlessness. If there is one thing that can be grasped by the understanding and is effective, yet at the same time has no form, that thing is music."[1]/

Human musical expression, unlike that of birds, insects and some mammals, is genetically unprogrammed and therefore spontaneous. Such freedom gives human persons an unrivalled power among living creatures, one so close to the essence of spirit that it has been projected onto angels themselves who, from Isaiah to Revelation, chant the trisagion before the throne of God: "Holy, Holy, Holy is the Lord, God of Hosts!"[2]/

For our own time, it is especially significant that a writer of such keen sensitivities as J.R.R. Tolkien has recast the story of Creation in his posthumously published Silmarillion, describing the work of God not in terms of craftsmanship but of orchestration. God appears as a cosmic choir director, the angelic spirits his singers, their music becoming the world itself. But in specifically human experience, the song is the first and foremost perfect musical expression, combining the magic of melody with the logos of mind, the holistic symbion of right and left cerebral hemispheres. All of the earliest religious texts we possess seem originally to have been written down from chants. Many were written to be chanted, partly for purposes of memorization, partly for solemn emphasis.

Musical Tools

From the earliest times, instruments—tools for making music—were invented to accompany the hymn and sacred dance. In all likelihood, drums, rattles and other percussion instruments were developed first, derived perhaps as an extension of rhythmic hand-clapping. Simple reed flutes may have been next—it is hard to reconstruct the evolution of so fragile a phenomenon. And it seems evident from ancient stone carvings from Mesopotamia and Egypt that the harp was one of the earliest complex instruments to appear, the ancestor of all string instruments.

Music and Spirit

Music figures in the development of every religious tradition as both source and tributary. Christianity inherited its "psalms, hymns and spiritual songs"[3]/from ancient Jewish practice.[4]/ Among the Jews, singing and instrumental music were extensively used in both temple service and in the court, as well as informally. The harp (kinnor) is frequently mentioned [5]/ as are the psaltery (pesanterin) and lyre (nebel), which was apparently used by prophets for oracular purposes.[6]/ In Christian usage, the harp (in Greek, kithara) was also favored.7/

Group singing seems to have occupied a special, mystical place in early Christian worship, an echo of which can perhaps be heard in Hazrat Inayat Khan's interesting account of later practice: "In the Middle East it is the custom among orthodox Christians and Armenians not to use the organ in Church. They use a chord, a sound that is produced by ten to twelve people with closed lips. Anybody who has heard it will concede that the sound of the organ is extraordinarily artificial in comparison to this sound. It has a wonderfully magical effect. It reaches so deeply into the human heart and creates so religious an atmosphere that one does not miss the organ. This note is itself a natural, God-given organ...."8/

Cosmic Harmonies

The Church freely borrowed musical traditions from peoples converted during its early expansion. The mystical tradition of music found in Christian spiritual writings right up to the present drew heavily, for instance, on Greek beliefs, especially regarding the celestial harmonies or "music of the spheres" so important in the Pythagorean philosophical system. These resonances created by the revolutions of the planets in their orbits, although generally held to be inaudible to the human ear, corresponded to the fundamental musical intervals. Even though the astronomical system underlying this belief was eventually shown to be mistaken, the ironic fact remains that people still hear "celestial vibrations."

Possibly a psychological rather than acoustical phenomenon, belief in the reality of the celestial harmonies survived in the mystical traditions of the West. From there, they influenced both literature and art, being revived somewhat whimsically, for example, in Holst's tone-poem The Planets. Shakespeare himself used the theme to great effect in Pericles, Prince of Tyre. Long before, however, this experience was known in Christian mystical writings as "the song of the angels." It is mentioned, for instance, by the fourteenth-century English mystic, Richard Rolle. Walter Hilton also devoted a special treatise to help his disciples distinguish true mystical song from merely psychological episodes or delusions. William James observed in the present century that the experience of the presence of God often comes as "a quiet music playing in the back of the mind."

Hearing heavenly sounds or music is by no means limited to Christian mysticism. Sufi tradition also refers to saute surmad, "abstract sound." An entire branch of Hindu spiritual discipline, nada-yoga, is devoted to eliciting and evaluating "the cosmic sound which is perceived inwardly, a continuous, persistent sound which is experienced in the head." 9/ Scott Rogo has collected two volumes of accounts of this experience, NAD-the Music of the Spheres.

In more recent times, this mystical experience of music which seems to emanate from the cosmos itself has been described in detail by both the late English psychic, Rosalind Heywood (ESP—A Personal Memoir), and the South African physicist-mathematician, Michael Whiteman (The Mystical Life). I have personally found it mentioned frequently in cases from files of the Religious Experience Research Unit at Oxford. Whatever it may ultimately be, the Music is there for at least some to hear, and it conveys the unmistakable impression of the presence of a spiritual power far transcending ordinary human awareness.

Making Music

If the reality of the spiritual world can be experienced as music, the human response to Reality has traditionally taken even more musical form. Singing and playing seem to express the sense of God more perfectly than any other medium. Was it Augustine who first quipped, "Anyone who sings, prays twice"?

Perhaps it is the modern tendency toward more passive "enjoyment" of recorded music which has deafened most of us to the cosmic harmonies as well as stifled our efforts to sing and make music. We listen, but do not hear; we try, but, as the holy gremlin Yoda laments in The Empire Strikes Back, we fail to DO.

Canned Music

In 1802, Carl Maria von Weber already regretted what he considered to be over-exposure to music and consequent desensitization. The invention of the microphone and the phonograph by Thomas Edison in 1877 and especially the advent of electricity made a much wider range of "prepared" music available for home listening. Soon professional performances of immortal classics and popular songs began to displace the concert hall as well as the home recital, just as the silent films began shutting down vaudeville. Radio and especially television, and now the video-tape revolution, augmented the trend, hastened by ever-improving technological advances in the communications industry.

Electronic recording and the distribution of tapes and records has undeniably added to the musical education of the public, not least because of the inherent democratic nature of the media. Great performances are ours to appreciate at relatively low cost and the ease of turning a dial or flicking a switch. But canned music has also produced a variety of problems.

Music Consumption: Chambers of Commerce

A most distressing problem involves the commercial expropriation of music—from the classical melodies lifted as "theme songs" for old film serials and radio "soap operas" right up to the travesties of taste in Apocalypse Now and Excalibur. Even sadder was the invention of the "singing commercial" back in the Depression by the father of behavioral psychology, J. B. Watson. Today, thanks to his Pavlovian insights, we are continually bombarded with advertising jingles set to inane tunes on every available channel of communication. (Some, to be fair, are downright enjoyable, such as the Coca-Cola Company's Christmas commercials, but these are by far the exception.) And to make matters worse, we also have to submit to the indifferent sonorities of "Muzak" emanating inescapably from the ceilings of public buildings of all types. The billion-dollar recording and distributing industry also makes sure that there is an incessant stream of acoustical fodder pouring out of radios, phonographs and recorders.

An inevitable response might well be withdrawal from over-saturation by commercialized music. Our sensitivities have surely been blunted, if not eradicated. And with that, we have suffered a collective spiritual loss of vast proportions.

Songs of Revolt

The folk-song movement of the 'fifties and 'sixties seems to have succeeded at first as a kind of protest against commercial exploitation of music. But soon enough, even those prophetic voices were co-opted by the studios. Woodie Guthrie was one of the few authentic artists who escaped appropriation; he died too soon. Today, revolt is in the air again. Alongside the emergence of a new interest in amateur music-making, professional folk singers have begun to hold "acoustic concerts" in which no electronic amplification is used. There is a kind of Schumacher-logic at work. In an age of big sounds, big bands, big promotions, big profits and big headaches, small is suddenly beautiful.

In many respects it is better (as well as harder) to whistle our own tune than always to listen to others' music—whether Mozart, Mangione or Lennon. The best is not only the enemy of the good, it may well prevent us even from attempting to sing our own song, to make our own kind of music. With that loss goes a major opportunity for spiritual expression.

The Amateur Hour

Time was, I am told, both here and in England (and no doubt elsewhere), when our grandparents were children, that guests were asked upon arrival for dinner or a weekend stay which instrument they played. After dinner, violins, celli, flutes, concertinas, spoons and heaven knows what else were produced and a "gather" was held around the family harmonium, harp or piano. Family groups by themselves frequently constituted consorts for the pure sake of entertainment as well as for the sake of a musical education for the children. On a larger scale in the "old" countries and in the hill country of American eastern, southern and south-western states, regular "meetings" and competitions were held in which young and old pitted their musical skills against one another.

Today in Ireland each year a special festival is held which is called Fleadh Cheoil Na H-Eireann or "All-Ireland Competition." There are categories for a huge variety of traditional instrumental playing as well as singing and dancing—fiddle, pipes, harp, bodhran (drum), concertinas, whistle and many more. Besides Ireland itself, the areas for preliminary competition include both Britain and the United States.

More informal gatherings in Ireland and Scotland are called on special occasions (or for no particular reason at all)—the Ceili (or Ceilidh, pronounced KAYlee). The closest American equivalent might be something like an old-fashioned jamboree, hoe-down or perhaps the dance traditionally celebrating the completion of a barn-building, itself a communal event. Ceilis involve singing, fiddling, dancing and, as like as not, an occasional fist fight—all part of the heritage.

In ancient times in the most eastern of the Celtic lands, an annual assembly called an Eisteddfod (pronounced Eye-STETHvod) was held in which poets, bards and minstrels strove against each other artistically. In 1947, the Welsh government reinstituted this musical Olympiad at Llangollen as an annual International Music Festival, which attracts hundreds of contenders from around the world. Regional eisteddfodau are also held at intervals throughout Wales.

Such events, including even the "electric eisteddfodau" of rock concerts such as the famous Woodstock Festival and the jazz festivals at Newport, Rhode Island, and elsewhere, demonstrate the social power of music to integrate peoples of different ages, ethnic backgrounds, interests and economic situations in a remarkable if temporary terrestrial harmony.

Making Music: Instruments

Together with the revival of folk music, the return to handcrafts as an enjoyable and therapeutic reprieve from the stress of technological civilization has generated a growing enthusiasm for making musical instruments, particularly traditional types.

A handful of resolute luthiers such as Richard Brune of Evanston, Illinois, have been hand-making lutes, guitars, harpsichords and wind instruments both in America and abroad for generations. Similarly, Appalachian craftsmen have continued making mountain dulcimers and fiddles as if Fender, Sears and Yamaha never existed. But the appearance of folk-harp crafters, zither-makers and a host of other builders of historical or "elderly" instruments is a relatively new phenomenon. So is the natural correlative—concerts, consorts and solo performers specializing in traditional music. I think there is a lesson here for a more humane future, one I discovered by a circuitous personal route.

Music on the Mountain

The desert portion of my journey into the Southwest took me to the beautiful Laguna Mountains that sweep up from the desert floor a few miles north of the Mexican border in southern California. The purpose of my visit was to meet R. L. (Robbie) Robinson, his wife Phyllis, and their friend and neighbor, Betty Roan Truitt. These are the harp-makers of Mt. Laguna—to give them an adequate title. For they are much more than that.

For several years, a folk-harp movement has been growing in America and abroad. My own interest in the harp stems from my early childhood, possibly a reflection of my Celtic ancestry. But it was not until the late 'seventies that I began to involve myself seriously in obtaining and learning to play the Irish harp. Within a short period of time, I also learned that the center of the new interest in the ancient harp, or very near it, was a man named Robinson.

In 1960, as he tells the story, Robinson "fell in love with the harp and its music" while working with the U.S. Agency for International Development in Brazil. Fascinated by the Paraguayan harp in particular, he began to study "its music, its construction, its history, and the cultures that spawned it."10/

Robinson set up his first harp shop in Uganda. Soon, however, his "obsession" led him to terminate his career with the government. He returned, happy but impoverished, to California, where he set up a new shop. There he not only builds harps, but also supplies other builders' requests for plans, strings and hardware. So far-reaching was his correspondence with other enthusiasts that in 1973, Robbie and Phyllis began the Folk Harp Journal. Through it, hundreds of harpers and harp-crafters exchange news, information and ideas. And today, a steady stream of visitors from all over the world winds up the mountain road to confer with the Robinsons—often to the detriment (kindly tolerated) of publishing deadlines and orders.

The Robinsons embody many of the qualities of the Celtic spirit which seems to offer one of the best tenders of hope for a human future—a sensitivity to nature, animals and friendships as well as the music which so fills their lives and days. Further, they have a keen scholarly interest, not only in the harp, but in all phases of music as well as culture and thought— including philosophy and theology. Nothing about them seems bookish and contrived, however. Their journal is a delight, its poetry, illuminations and letters interspersed with news, construction hints and articles of lasting interest.

Mt. Laguna is the center not only of a modest enterprise but of a true network which now requires a small home computer to operate. These harpers may love the heritage of past ages, but they are certainly not limited by it.

The Romance of the Harp

Besides the intrinsic fascination of the harp (which could be any instrument for that matter), the emergence of a network of enthusiasts struck me as an event of importance to spirituality. The harp is one of the oldest of musical instruments, in its early (i.e., "folk") shape obviously derived from the hunting bow. It was especially beloved of the Celts, and the greatest concert harps which now grace every symphony orchestra in the world are lineal descendants of the elegant lap harps developed in the Middle Ages. At that time, the metal-strung Irish harp was the common liturgical instrument as well as the ordinary accompaniment of bards and minstrels. As we know from Dante, the Irish harp reached as far as Italy by the thirteenth century, and it went north to both Scandinavia and Iceland.

In the twelfth century, the monk Giraldus of Wales visited Ireland in the entourage of King John and wrote of the harp, "Bishops and Abbots and holy men in Ireland were in the habit of carrying their harps with them in their peregrinations, and found pious delight in playing upon them. In consequence of this, St. Kevin's harp was held in great reverence by the natives, and to this day is considered a valuable relic, possessed of great virtues." (St. Kevin died, it is held, in 618.)

The emergence of a new Celtic spirituality would seem a bit flat without the reappearance of the harp, so it was reassuring to discover a growing interest in this instrument throughout the U.S. The Celtic harp has been undergoing a renaissance in Europe as well, its popularity increased by artists such as Mary O'Hara, Derek Bell and the brilliant young Breton harper, Alan Stivell, whose concerts attract tens of thousands of young people. In the best-selling fantasy novels of Anne McCaffrey and Patricia McKillip, harps and harpers occupy .positions of critical importance—a similar, literary testament to their symbolic power among the younger generation.

Musicraft

Making harps, lutes or other instruments involves all the spiritual challenge of craftwork—wood-carving, metalwork, ceramics (bells and stone flutes, for instance), design, decoration and others. Real skill is required to build a good instrument, of course, and acquiring skill requires patience and experiment. Today, fortunately, excellent kits are available for the craftworker unwilling or unready to begin from scratch. These run the gamut from inexpensive to costly—some of the finer instrument kits running into five figures for a double-manual harpsichord, for example. It is wise to begin small.11/

Purchasing finished or semi-finished instruments remains a time-saving alternative. Most companies which sell plans or kits in various stages of completion also sell finished products. The price is also higher, of course.12/ Catalogs for ordering instruments and kits by mail are available from many companies here and abroad.13/

Explorations

By approaching an instrument—a balalaika, a set of Belgian chimes, a mountain dulcimer—especially in its (and your) ethnic and historical context, it is possible to investigate your cultural roots in a richly rewarding manner. It is also possible to obtain access to a different culture through the spirit of its music and instruments, which, like food, convey the flavor of a lifeway more vividly and concretely than any number of books or travelogues.

As a medium of communication, a musical instrument works best in a social context, one reason why duos, trios, quartets and the ensemble are so rewarding to play in as well as to hear. Even the solo performer is engaged in a dialogue, not only with a real or possible audience, but with himself and in fact with God. The choice of an instrument can thus either enhance communication or obstruct it. In either case, it reveals the character of the musician, whose intention as well as image it reflects.

Instruction

Having an instrument is only the beginning. It is also necessary to learn how to play. Here, many introductory books are available. For a simple instrument such as the mountain dulcimer or autoharp, they are adequate. Even in these instances, however, live instruction is not only advisable but probably necessary to develop real skill. For the guitar, banjo, folk harp, mandolin, lute and harpsichord (to name a few), an expert teacher is a requirement, at least at points along the way. Here again, the parallel between music and spirituality is striking.

Folk music is more amenable to self-instruction than classical forms, if only because it is the property, the proprium, of the people, the "folk." But the demands are not necessarily less stringent than in classical training, they are simply less formal. For teaching yourself is really a process of cultural assimilation achieved by imitation and even innovation, but within the continuity of a recognized tradition. Here, the "folk" is the real teacher, the student a good assimilator of ways more felt than articulated.

Harping in the Winds of Change

As we attempt to chart a course into a human future, music will increasingly perform a strategic function with respect to spiritual formation and celebration. What is important here, especially in an age in which advanced electronics have made great performances of many kinds of music (as well as exhibitions of rubbish) instantly accessible at the flick of a switch, is that power of creativity is being returned to ordinary people, the folk.

Having become in large measure passive consumers of packaged music, its quality notwithstanding one way or another, we are now faced with a truly urgent task, that of regaining active mastery of our lives, including the development of music skills as a personal achievement. Such a reactivation might be especially welcome if, as could happen, the switches in our stereos suddenly no longer worked.

In their way, the harpers of Mt. Laguna have begun a task as monumental as the massive structure being built at Arcosanti. And, as with the hermits of Sedona, it was not so much planned that way, but "happened" as the natural outgrowth of an enthusiasm for life cherished by some very attentive spiritual scouts. Out of such events, it is not unlikely that a collective spiritual tradition will someday emerge, fulfilling the dream of an Alcuin, a Brigid or even a Beethoven.

FOURTEEN

Future Friends:
Love, Sex and Intimacy

Two of our chief prognosticators, Aldous Huxley and George Orwell, envisioned vastly different possibilities for love, intimacy, sex and friendship in the future. Brave New World presented a scenario of free but sterile sexual promiscuity in which pregnancy and childbearing were regarded as obscene and nasty. Babies were grown on order in laboratory bottles. In 1984, regulation sex was permitted but only if joyless and especially loveless. Sexual fulfillment was not only obscene and nasty but illegal. Both Huxley and Orwell shared certain themes, however—the divorce of sex, love and procreation; authoritarian control over people's lives exerted blatantly or subtly by government, particularly through the media; and especially the consequent and pervasive loneliness of those unable to find authentic love.

Other popular science-fiction accounts have suggested similarly hard times for love and friendship to come—Ilia's "celibacy oath" in Star Trek—the Motion Picture, the antiseptic asexuality of George Lucas' THX1138, the permutations of loss and frustration in the novels of Robert Heinlein, Ursula K. LeGuin and others.

Reality hasn't lagged too far behind; many of these predictions are paradigms. Soviet totalitarianism, with its state-enforced puritanism, almost mimics Orwell's satire. The swinging American 'seventies had as much in common with Huxley's premonitions. Recent "experiments" in social engineering in India, Africa and Latin America, even in isolated instance in the United States and other First World countries, portend a worse nightmare to come in nations caught between the hammer of rampant over-population and mass starvation and the anvil of involuntary sterilization, abortion and euthanasia.

Whether or not the world's population stabilizes naturally or by force, we seem faced with a future of tension and hardship in the areas of sex, love and intimacy—a multiplex problem arising from a variety of conditions, some of them economic, some political, others agricultural, religious, psychological and humanitarian. The situation is far more dangerous than may seem apparent. For we are not only tampering with the most powerful forces in the world. In terms of procreation, genetics and child-rearing practices, we are tinkering with the very future of the human race.

The Great Divorce

Whether tending toward bleak sexual regimentation or mindless indulgence as extreme possibilities for the future, these and other visions of alternatives presume an accomplishment sought for centuries and realized for the first time on a large scale only in our own time the fission of sex and procreation. Splitting the atom may one day be reckoned as a far less momentous event in human history. Nevertheless, the advent of effective contraception, like that of the atomic bomb, may ultimately have a beneficial effect on the race. For while the Bomb may someday force the nations of Earth to make peace and justice work or else suffer nuclear catastrophe, the Pill (or whatever form the ultimate contraceptive may take) could well bring about by reaction what could be a genuinely novel situation for perhaps the majority of the world's peoples: the deliberate fusion of love and sex...and procreation.

In the meantime, most of us will have to deal with the ordinary problems and promises attendant upon reconciling eros and agape—and some new ones. The recent tendency toward freer sex has begun to give way to what Gabrielle Brown has called "the new celibacy." More seriously, sexual disinterest has emerged as a growing problem among married couples as well as singles. Rape, on the other hand, has increased at an alarming rate. The percentage of divorced couples is rising.

All this may be a result of a economic and social depression or indicate some other factor at work, at least in the U.S. It is too early tell. One thing seems certain: in the coming years, friendship will cease to be a casual aspect of life, even among married couples— perhaps especially so. We will have to work harder at forming, enhancing and preserving our loves, for the hard times ahead will not favor affective relationships, as our scouts have reported.

If any component of human experience embodies the power of symbiosis, it is loving—which brings together different "organisms" for the enjoyment of a mutually beneficial association, frequently a life-long one. Friendship should therefore be a major component in all spirituality—in many respects the central one. For it is our longing for true intimacy that not only brings us together "in one flesh," as members of one Body, as a common family, as friends—it is also the consequence of our deep-rooted openness to others. This openness, properly spiritus, pneuma, is a dynamic capacity resting upon our groundedness in the Other, who has created our hearts restless, longing for the lasting intimacy only God can grant.1/

Present and Future Tense

Within the last few years western society, particularly in the United States, has undergone a profound change consequent upon the divorce of love and sexuality. The so-called nuclear family has exploded, producing a fall-out of increasing numbers of singles and a growing problem of loneliness. There is also an identifiable trend toward serial monogamy as divorce rates soar; toward delayed and childless marriages; toward an ever-increasing number of illegitimate births; toward multiple and replaceable parents for an increasing number of children. Among the effects of this upheaval in family life we can cite a growing sense of social isolation and loneliness, of not belonging to anyone, and a general feeling of rootlessness. We are witnessing the creation of a generation without an integral human past.

The Singles Explosion

A glimpse at population statistics from recent and previous census polls can tell the story briefly. Of the population in this country 14 years and older, between the years 1970 and 1979, there was an 8% increase in the number of married couples, while among singles, widowed partners and divorced persons there were, respectively, increases of 27%, 9% and an astonishing 80%. Between 1970 and 1977, there was 54% increase in the number of divorces, which in that year equalled half the total number of marriages. Between 1970 and 1978, there was a 42% increase in the number of illegitimate births, which reached 543,000 at that time. In 1976, the number of illegitimate births exceeded that of legitimate births in the city of Washington, D.C. In 1979, 11.6% of the total number of households in the U.S. were single-parent homes. These 8,974,000 represented an 83% increase over 1974 figures. Commenting on these trends, Dr. James Lynch says, "Popular magazines and books regularly discuss the possibility that the very notion of marriage and family will soon be outmoded. Marriage by contract, renewable every three to five years only upon the mutual consent of both partners, is seriously predicted by many." He goes on to note, importantly, "Even more remarkable is the way in which books on health used daily in our high schools and colleges remain blind to the fact that divorce, infidelity, and marital swinging may have detrimental effects on health."2/

Heart Trouble

Recently I participated in a psychiatric symposium on loneliness held on St. Valentine's Day. The irony was heightened by the traditional association of love, loneliness and the human heart, often portrayed on cards as pierced by the arrow of love. Similarly, the breakup of a love relationship is symbolized by a heart cracking in pieces. Such images are not idle decorations. Dr. Lynch's now classic book The Broken Heart demonstrates quite clearly that "loneliness is not only pushing our culture to the breaking point, but also pushing our physical health to the breaking point, and indeed has in many cases already pushed the human heart beyond the breaking point."3/

Loneliness exerts a tremendous strain on health and life, especially with regard to heart disease. Singles, moreover, seem to experience not only more loneliness than married persons, but more heart problems. The leading cause of premature death among U.S. adults between the ages of 24 and 65 is heart disease. It is also demonstrable that married couples outlive single persons. Bachelorhood can be hazardous to your health. Dr. Lynch observes, "The mortality statistics for heart disease among those adult Americans who are not married are striking—a death rate from heart disease that is as much as two to five times higher for non-married individuals, and those who are divorced, widowed or single, than for married Americans."4/ The same holds true for other diseases as well: cancer, stroke, cirrhosis and even accidents.

Aloneness and Loneliness

Each of us faces inevitable aloneness at some time in the future. Patrick Kerans stated it simply when he wrote, "To me the most mysterious part of the marriage vow is that after a lifetime at loving, each spouse undertakes the risk of burying the other."5/From all appearances, the future is liable to be a more lonely time for most people than the present or the immediate past, moreover. The fact that population rates are growing so rapidly that shortly after the turn of the century there will be twice the number of people on this planet increases the prospect of loneliness for many. For most of these people will be crammed into cities—perhaps the loneliest places on earth.

Population density created loneliness by restricting the degree of significant time and space that can be spent with a number of persons well enough to be part of one's personal system of reference. The Lonely Crowd by David Riesman and Philip Slater's The Pursuit of Loneliness still appropriately describe the behavioral constraints self-imposed by modern urbanized people. Our activities themselves militate against familiarity: commuting, especially in single-passenger automobiles, waiting in lines, hospitalization and other forms of institutionalization—in schools, universities, prisons, factories, offices, day-care centers, nurseries, convalescent and retirement homes, "asylums" for the mentally disturbed, etc.

Loneliness and Networks

Loneliness refers to discomfort or anxiety that accompanies aloneness. It is a longing for significant contact with others, that is, with people who care about us. The subtitle of an early study of loneliness aptly defined it as "the experience of social and emotional isolation." For the lonely person, the social network which supports, heals and enhances human life has been broken—not merely temporarily disrupted, but severely and apparently permanently severed. Milton Mayerhoff has described this feeling as a sense of being "out of place" rather than being "at home" in his superb little book On Caring.6/

In a recent article, the Jesuit psychiatrist James Gill employed a psychosocial network grid developed by Dr. E. Mansell Pattison in order to discuss the anxiety problems of celibates, among whom loneliness is often a paramount concern. "A normal network is one in which a person has ongoing relationships with 22 to 25 persons, with five or six in each of four subgroups (family, relatives, friends/neighbors, and social/work associates.) An individual who has such a network around him, Pattison found, has frequent contacts with and a positive and strong emotional investment in most of these people. The relationships are valued and reciprocal, and those involved provide one another with concrete assistance when needed."7/

The "neurotic-type" network, by contrast, "includes only about 15 people, with fewer relatives, friends and co-workers, and a higher reliance on a person's own nuclear family. There are frequent negative and weak emotional interactions, and many of the 15 persons are seen infrequently or not at all. The individual within this network interacts with only half as many persons in each subgroup...as does a person in a normal network."8/

The result of such a disrupted style of life characterizes loneliness and in many respects indicates the negative side of single life: "Living in an impoverished and isolating neurotic network results in a person's investing too much interest in himself while failing to interact vitally with persons in his environment. Real-life interaction is limited by avoidance of contact and by a weak or negative emotional quality in relationships that are characterized by expectations and obligations that make the easy give and take of emotional and helpful interaction difficult. And, finally, there is no reliable set of social norms and expectations either to guide behavior or to correct distorted behavioral responses."9/

Single persons, including celibates, risk finding themselves in such a neurotic-type network, particularly those who experience a total break between work relationships, recreational pursuits and family ties. This seems especially true of the "swingers" who frequent singles or gay bars after work hours or at night, but would be distressed to be discovered there by their professional colleagues. At worst, such a situation can take on the sordid hues of "Looking for Mr. Goodbar."

The Quest for Intimacy

As a host of psychological writers have argued, one of the greatest needs—and most difficult goals for modern people to attain—is intimacy, by which I mean, simply, honest emotional closeness with others. Singles are understandably less likely to develop true intimacy for the very reason that they are single. Dr. Jack Dominian has argued very persuasively, I think, that true intimacy involves "the interaction of whole persons encountering mind, body and feelings in each other."10/

Normally, a permanent relationship such as marriage is the most likely situation for the cultivation of intimacy. For, as Dominian observes, "Once a person has involved the whole of our being, it is natural to wish to continue that relationship, and commitment means continuity, reliability, predictability and responsibility for each other."11/

The single person runs the risk of partial involvement or episodic relationships—whether as a result or as a cause of the single state. According to Dominian, "The crisis of love lies in the fleeing from one human being to another in an attempt to find wholeness and fulfillment instead of engaging fully and overcoming the obstacles of relationship through commitment, faithfulness and permanency."12/

The deliberate espousal of relationships devoid of exclusive involvement, commitment or responsibility for the other can be taken as a definition of promiscuity.

Casual sexual encounters with willing partners picked up at bars are frequently justified on the grounds that in such instances no one gets hurt. There is little risk of rejection since there is no expectation of commitment or continuity. Such relationships are intended to be brief, fun and functional—a sexual release and social diversion. But it is just the momentary, disconnected and superficial aspects of such encounters that over the long haul are most destructive of psychosocial health. The incorporation of a casual pick-up, a "trick," into a supportive network is precluded from the outset. A multitude of such isolated encounters fulfills Pattison's neurotic grid perfectly.

From a moral viewpoint, I would here agree with Dr. Dominian: "The real evil of our age is not the permissiveness of sexual pleasure but the impermanence of relationships whereby, through transience and divorce, human beings become stepping stones of temporary exploitation where the whole is never engaged and the depths are never touched."13/

The motivating factor behind a pattern of such behavior may well be anxiety at being lonely. Much so-called "promiscuous" conduct is likely to be a form of avoidance which masks the very fact it tends to create. As an emotionally vicious circle, the "swingle" scene may preclude the possibility of insight until a person is approaching middle age, when a point of diminishing returns may elicit a crisis.

Singled Out: The New Celibacy

The new celibacy heralded by Gabrielle Brown and others could in this respect by just the old sexual disinterest. The swinging life does reach a point of diminishing returns, when the hollowness, futility and repetition of casual encounters leads to a withdrawal from the quest for intimacy. The danger is that rather than adopting a more constructive approach to human relationships, the ex-swingle will retreat from even superficial involvement into a state of narcissistic self-absorption. Such a radical disengagement can tempt other singles besides the swinger, however: the recently divorced, the widow or widower, the celibate sister or priest or brother who may in effect despair of ever finding a human friend in whom they can place their trust, confidence and love. Whether by intention or effect, for such lonely people other persons exist mainly as clients or servants. The selfless altruism of the lay or religious celibate can also be a covert dodge away from human encounter, a way of avoiding intimacy by playing a game of Sacred Rescue.

The Varieties of Love

As "crazy" behavior is a disturbed person's attempt to behave sanely, so also loneliness and its masks bespeak an inescapable capacity and desire of the human heart for love. Yet despite the incorrigibly disparate forms our quest for love takes, poets, theologians, philosophers and the adolescent burgeoning with new-felt emotion who carves "Wilfred loves Ambrosia" on a maple tree, have all tended to betray a peculiar attitude toward this phenomenal experience. They presume that love is a unified phenomenon—that, like weather, there is basically one type of love, although it may admit of varying degrees of intensity, from steamy to frigid.

A few wise observers have realized that common opinion is wrong. There are many types of love, depending in large part on the character and temperament of the persons in love and on the nature of the relations between them. The most fundamental division has been into "carnal" love and charity, eros and agape. A generation ago, lengthy debate resulted from the efforts of Swedish theologian Anders Nygren to pit these "loves" against each other—to the detriment, need it be said, of eros. Much of the discussion was moot, of course, not the least reason being the unrealistic simplicity of a two-member typology for a reality as complex as human love.

The Four Loves

The first recent writer to develop a usable typology of love based on shared differences and similarities was C.S. Lewis, who in The Four Loves added affection (storge in Greek) and friendship (philia). Lewis' book became a minor classic, but as a classic is less indebted to the facts of life than to literary tradition and his own rather narrow brand of Christianity. It is still worth reading, however.

More Loves

A typology of love styles more encompassing of the diversity of human personalities and temperaments, as well as experiences, was devised and empirically tested by Dr. John Alan Lee, a sociologist at the University of Toronto. Accepting three of Lewis' "four loves," eros, agape and storge, Lee added six others. A typology of behavior rather than personality, Lee's The Colors of Love 14/ categorizes styles of relating and therefore of the spirituality of love, however implicit.

According to the test schedule, handily found in Lee's book, the basic love styles are called mania, eros, ludic-eros, ludus, storgic ludus, pragma, storge and storgic-eros. Finding one's own favorite love-style is a rewarding task (most of the time) and enjoyable. It is important to recall, however, that even with comprehensive theories and tests such as Lee's, each of us remains different and each of our relationships is unique. Even a relationship with the same person will change over time—as Lee well knows. Fortunately, he allows for a profile rather than a single score. The most important thing to remember is that there is no one single type which is somehow best for everyone. All of us can do well with our own style if we attend to its shortcomings as well as its strengths.

Love in the Future

Assuming that many of the predictions we have been considering are to some extent likely models of the future, we can try to envision possible modes of living in terms of a situation of greater scarcity, stress and social disintegration. One thing seems certain from a study of the place of love and friendship in hard times past—how well we love may determine how well we survive the Coming Dark Age.

The Celtic monastic settlement presents a model in which storge and pragma, even eros, are not absent, being a heterogenous community of married, single, religious and lay, male and female persons. But the bond which united these people was first of all, agape—the desire to live together in a symbiotic relationship with nature and other persons and so be open to the free gift of God's love—"the bond of completeness." Worship and ministry were primary motives for gathering together, but the solidarity of friendship, philia, gave the settlement much of its distinctive character. Regarding eros, the presence of married couples in the monastic settlement suggests its presence, perhaps in modes now lost to western spirituality. Today we tend to believe that eros must be "sublimated" or transformed into agape to be Christian. I suggest that this is not in fact true and never was. Agape is the divine eros, and our participation in God's love will always evoke erotic spiritualities. Further, my hunch is that agape is somehow compatible with all the love-styles Lee evolved, at least in their nobler aspects.

The real challenge of the future (as it has been of the past and present, I might add) will be how to integrate eros and agape, storge and ludus, both individually and collectively. Without eros, the other loves lack force. Unbridled, eros becomes demonic mania.

Societies of Friends

Even without the severe shocks to civilization many expect, the sheer intensity of life as we have known it, both its pace and the density of human population, will demand a health-giving cultivation of friendship. Recalling the psychosocial grid developed by Pattison, it seems to me that networks of friends can provide the support and celebration we will require in the coming years. Such networks can be structured in a "formal" sense such as in a Celtic settlement like that we have been viewing as a paradigm. Alternatively, they can be structurally "informal"—a real bond among persons separated by space or work. In either case, the network would be limited to about 20 to 30 major friends, each having a sub-group of further "acquaintances" or "buddies" which provide a wider reference group without the intensity or commitment of the network.

The "Celtic" network would also be <u>heterogenous</u> or mixed—women, men and children, young and old, married, celibate or single, straight and gay, blood-related as well as chosen. Members would represent different approaches to life, possess different talents and skills, but all would share a common vision of life's value and meaning. Some networks could specialize as agrarian cooperatives, others as urban centers. Some would be more religious in tone, others more secular. Most, I think, would probably share common spiritual activities of some kind. Such networks would also probably be as diverse politically as they will be religiously and professionally.

A Celtic settlement and the network envisioned at its core, as well as those in non-settlement alliances, would also permit a maximal exercise of personal initiative and freedom. Rules would be minimized and non-coercive. Social control mechanisms would be recognized and avoided as much as possible. Informal consensus rather than parliamentary procedure or other formalized modes of decision-making would be favored if for no other reason than that it requires total participation, trust and honesty to work effectively. Without such qualities, it is doubtful whether a network would survive in the first place. Call it a "latitudinarian" politic.

Therapies

Even if such settlements and networks come to pass, there will be inescapable aloneness ahead for all of us, as there always has been. The intensity of the future may make loneliness more pervasive, however. Then, as now, two courses of action are open to us to prevent aloneness from turning into loneliness: the development of self-fulfilling talents and capacities, and the cultivation of interests in the wide world outside. The exploration of nature and the inner self by engaging in arts and crafts, especially with their release of the pent-up abilities of our holistic "right-brain," is a potent preventative for self-pity. The experience of creativity in any of its forms is liberating.

An interest in literature and music will likewise open up the world inside us as well as that "out there." Similarly, developing hobbies such as gardening, animal care, sports and leisure activities can be refreshing and expanding, especially for those advanced in years. Growth and encounter groups are available in larger metropolitan areas, and even small communities are always eager for volunteers to help with day-care centers, "Meals on Wheels," visits to shut-ins and so on.

A sovereign remedy for the sense of social and emotional isolation that so easily dulls our lives is also prayer, including the art of meditation. With God present, we are never alone, much less lonely. We so easily forget the most basic thing of all, however, that those who abide in God abide in love.

FIFTEEN

Death and the Future

One way or another, mortality has been a strong thematic undercurrent in most recent considerations of the future, including this one. Of course, death is an inescapable fact of life itself. The "great mortality" of the Dark and Middle Ages, plague, reached so great a height that the Black Death alone, a recurrent epidemic which arrived in Europe in 1347, carried off at least a third of the entire population by the end of the century. In our own times, we have seen natural disasters as well as human slaughter under Stalin, Hitler, Pol Pot and other tyrants which have killed tens of millions of people. We may yet see even greater casualties resulting from worldwide famine, disease, war and want. The difference between our era and the Middle Ages is that we seem strangely capable of denying the reality of death.

In past ages, death understandably figured as a prominent component of both lay and clerical spirituality. Sometimes morbidly so, as in the wake of the Black Death. At other times, the contemplation of inevitable death served constructively and even correctively as a goal-directing exercise. Even in their later secular form, the little bedside books called Ars Moriendi (The Art of Dying) were ordinary spiritual resources for well-educated persons right up to the Enlightenment. Eschatology, the closing section of systematic theology, appropriately begins with the subject of death. Thus, personally to ignore death as the spiritual finale of life short-circuits the development of an authentic spirituality. To deny death collectively falsifies the meaning and value of experience in general—which has been the ordinary stance of western industrial society for well over a century. In attempting to outline a spirituality for a possible future, a symbiosis, we must therefore deal with death and dying, first as an inevitable biological fact of existence, but also as a dimension of spiritual development.

The Quality of Death

Where there is life, there is death—nature's law. And where life has been abused, death abounds. Naturally, death leads to a renewal of life on another, simpler plane of existence. But when it exceeds the natural order, death spreads its sway too rapidly to allow for new life to appear, and all life becomes endangered.

The spiritual task of this and coming generations must be to restore death to its proper station in order to ensure a new beginning of life. That is, we must not only recover a sense of life's worth, we must prevent the power of mortality from maintaining or increasing a demonic hold upon the majority of humankind through injustice, ignorance, poverty, disease and war. We must refuse to flee from death, but we must also consider the possibility of life beyond death, if only to enable us to assess the value of living in terms of its lasting personal and social consequences.

Cheating Death

One of the oldest human hopes, if a futile one, is to cheat death. A few are held to have escaped, including Enoch, in the seventh generation after Adam, and Elijah—two examples from the Bible.1/ Thus avoiding death seems to have been a special favor from God, however, if indeed the whole business is not, after all, mythic symbolization. For Moses, the beloved of the Lord, died as had Abraham and the Patriarchs. David died, as did the prophets. Jesus, too, died—a fact of history which is half our Easter hope. Ultimate liberation therefore seems to be won through death, not around it. Thus also the Buddha, Lao Tzu and the Prophet.

Still, the possibility of cheating death has perdured as a lure for speculation and occasional practice, sometimes leading to lurid instances of black magic and alchemical experimentation. The quest for the Elixir of Life and the Fountain of Youth attracted many a brilliant mind and courageous soul over the ages. And if all else failed, a Faustian bargain with the devil remained as a kind of short-cut, a belief that still survives to haunt us.

Achieving even relative immortality would, however, be a hollow victory at that. John Boorman's whimsical film Zardoz explored the issue of immortality as boredom. A generation or two before, the novels of H. Rider Haggard proposed the same theme, as did Walter Miller, Jr. in A Canticle for Leibowitz with the character of Benjamin, the Wandering Jew.

Faust 1984

Today, and more likely tomorrow, people will turn to science rather than to magic for immortality. There have already been several technological attempts to outwit death. Of these, cryogenics and artificial organs seem the most promising.

By super-freezing the human body, some scientists believe that it may be possible to preserve life indefinitely in a state of suspended animation, as with Han Solo in The Empire Strikes Back. Fish and some insects seem able to survive being frozen for short periods of time, and rapid, deep cooling of human tissue has been used surgically to slow down metabolic processes in order to obtain needed time for medical treatment. For persons suffering from incurable diseases for which an eventual cure is likely, such a procedure could easily seem to be a last, desperate chance for life. But unlike Han Solo, those who have already been frozen are, at today's level of technological expertise, almost certain to be very old corpses when they are eventually thawed. For at present, we cannot super-freeze a whole organism without lethal damage to its cells. And even if we become able someday to cheat death by temporary freezing, the client, like Lazarus, would eventually face death anyway after a very expensive detour.

Bionic People

Not unlike Mary Shelly's Dr. Victor Frankenstein, many proponents of artificial replacements for vital organs believe that they might thus be able to prolong life greatly if not indefinitely. As long as there are biological organs at work, however, death will eventually claim even a 60-Million-Dollar Man. Mechanical parts will also wear out. Still, there are undoubtedly great numbers of people who would consider the vast expense of time, resources and money well worth the effort to gain a clock-work heart or plastic-and-metal pancreas. Indeed, one can sincerely hope that a relatively inexpensive, long-lasting artificial kidney will be developed soon, so that those with kidney diseases, for instance, rich and poor alike, could add even a few years to their lives. In fact, new surgical methods are being developed now to facilitate biological organ transplants, a procedure which despite its present cost does provide a measure of hope for those suffering from defective body parts.

But as a way of indefinitely avoiding death, such "high-tech" solutions are an affront to the value and meaning of life. They mock hope and deny the universal human condition, rather than acknowledging and affirming our truly "humble" station. For we are of the earth, humus. Death is our earthly destiny.

In this respect, we can far more appropriately turn to the Celtic monks or the American Plains Indians for inspiration. Their simple acceptance of death as the end but therefore a part of life, led them to return simply to the earth. Whether by inhumation or exposure, their bodies were abandoned to the gentle, rhythmic processes of nature, literally to be recycled.

The Necessity of Death

Still, for many reasons—psychological, religious, perhaps philosophical, there is a deep-rooted tendency in human beings to regard their death as a superfluous evil to be postponed as long as possible.2/ Christian belief includes the notion, introduced by St. Paul, that death is somehow redundant and punitive: through sin, death entered the world (Rom. 5:12). But even Paul was aware, keenly so, that although Jesus overcame the power of death by conquering sin, he did not eliminate it. We all still die.

From a symbiotic viewpoint, death is not only inevitable, but necessary. More, it is a blessing. The God-willed order of Creation itself depends upon death for its regeneration. Without death, populations of animals and plants would quickly reach maximum size and begin to stagnate. Evolutionary adaptation and development would be impossible. Resources needed for life processes would be consumed without being adequately replenished. The world would become a vast, overpopulated and quite impossible desert.

The late Dr. Kit Pedler presented a strong case for the biological place of death in his challenging and important little book The Quest for Gaia. He suggested, contrary to our contemporary cultural bias, that we realize the deep truth of the paradox "Decay is beautiful."3/ Artificial preservation, whether of food or of bodies, is an affront to Creation and thus to the Creator.

With respect to the human race, the necessity of death is also indicated by the developmental aspects of culture. Unless death created opportunities for new generations of youth, there would be little if any growth in society. Innovation would be impossible. Human life would stagnate spiritually as well as physically. Given the fact of evil in human experience, hope belongs to the young. For evil can never be overcome completely in any single generation. Age, further, brings weakness, sickness and fear. As long as we are embodied in time, the need for youth is a natural function of the cycle of life. Death permits renewal.

Death's Sting Rethought

We might welcome death, then, not only as a release from the debility and suffering of old age, but also as the condition for the possibility of new growth and development. But what then of Christ's victory? Has death retained its sting?

Once we recognize the biological necessity for death as a part of the natural order, we can begin to see in it an aspect of the gift of life itself. And even Paul longed to die so that he could be with Christ (Phil. 1:23). By interpreting the sad fact of death in the light of hope, therefore, especially in terms of the early mystical notion of Christ's restoration of all things, the apokatastasis, we can begin to understand that through Christ's death and resurrection and ours, death is being restored to its rightful place in the natural order.

Death, then, is "merely" a necessary biological function which has value and meaning in terms of conditioning the appearance of new life. Faith tells us, however, that our acceptance of this biological necessity as an aspect of the full human condition taken up by God in the Incarnation becomes an opportunity for new life on a wholly different level of existence. Death in Christ becomes our entrance into Life itself.

Life Beyond Life

Such mystical paradoxes abound in the gospels and other New Testament writings about life and death. They are not merely riddles or exaggerations intended to shock us into recognizing the precariousness of our situation. They express a truth so profound that its full grasp exceeds the possibilities of ordinary language and experience.

We cannot transcend the mortal condition of humankind by rejecting it in some mad flight from death or any other aspect of our embodied existence. We can, however, surpass even the further reaches of human nature by a total abandonment of ourselves to the demands of the human condition, a full acceptance of our nature as earthly creatures in imitation of Christ (Phil. 2:8). This entails accepting death as the God of Creation intended it—a phase in the natural rhythms of life, not as a penalty for sin. In Christ we can choose to die freely, not as slaves condemned to execution. By so humbling ourselves, we can at last obtain a glimpse of the "hereafter"—the life Jesus called eternal which comes to us not as our due, but as God's gift.

Chastening Death: Four Encounters

In the early 'seventies, several unexpected meetings led me to a profound reconsideration of the possible place of death and dying in a truly human context. Battered spiritually from reading Jessica Mitford's The American Way of Death and Evelyn Waugh's The Loved One, I met, first of all, a remarkable woman during a seminar at the University of Chicago. Her name was Dr. Elisabeth Kubler-Ross. This was shortly before the publication of her revolutionary book On Death and Dying.4/

Dr. Kubler-Ross' work with dying patients and minis- terial students at Billings Hospital had convinced her that much of the ministry that involved death and dying withered at the stem because of the ministers' fears and ignorance as well as doubts. In addition to helping the clergy confront their own anxieties on the way to helping others cope with their own or a loved one's death, she also formulated what has become the classical account of the various emotional states both the dying and the bereaved pass through en route to a mature acceptance of death. In more recent years, Dr. Kubler-Ross has begun to explore further dimensions of death and dying, investigating phenomena usually within the scope of psychical research.

Visits from the Dead to the Dying

Another encounter came at a conference on para-
psychology and religion in the form of a lecture by Dr.
Karlis Osis, the director of research for the American
Society for Psychical Research. For ten years, and now
for much longer, Osis had been collecting deathbed
observations from physicians and nurses who had attended dying patients. These reports concerned only
persons who were lucid in their last moments, free from
drugs and delirium.

Osis' findings are remarkably consistent overall, even
when compared with similar cases from India—a later
phase of his work. In many instances, the experiences of
the dying corresponded closely with the "death experiences" of persons who have been revived following
clinical death. Even more fascinating than reported
encounters between dying and their loved ones and old
friends who had previously died (some of whom were
not known to have died by either the dying person or
those in attendance) were the recommendations Osis
made on the basis of the research. His most revolutionary suggestion, given present hospital procedures,
was that special areas or environments be set aside for
the dying and their families and friends, especially in
hospitals, so that the experience of death could be as
constructive as possible.

Friends and family would attend the dying person until
death had occurred. They would have been prepared for
this great event by specially trained assistants, probably volunteers, ideally ministers of the same faith as
the dying person. The physical setting would be pleasant
and even cheerful—with bright colors, flowers and
suitable music if possible, and as little like a hospital as
possible, under the circumstances. Medical equipment,
uniforms, and other paraphenalia associated with professional methods of physical healing would be gone.
The dying person would lie in an ordinary bed, able to
receive encouragement and reassurance by those present (and perhaps to offer both in return). Eventually,

the "celebrants" of this mystery would "hand over" the care of their loved one to the "helpers"—invisible to all but the dying person—who inevitably seem to show up during the final moments as "escorts" into the next phase of life.

Such procedures strike many people as artificial and even threatening. Compared to current practice in hospitals, where most people die unattended in their final moments, frightened and unprepared, often in the dark, silent hours of early morning, they are both wise and compassionate. If anything, they recall the deathbed customs of monastic communities and families of by-gone eras, in which the death of a loved one would be accompanied by prayer and song on the part of relatives and associates, who delivered over their brother or sister to the communion of saints.

Death Experiences and the Hospice Movement

In 1974-75, I spent an academic year studying reports of religious experience submitted to the Religious Experience Research Unit founded by Sir Alister Hardy at Oxford University. Many of the thousands of reports were concerned with death experiences—usually those of other persons, but occasionally of people who had "returned" from death following an accident, illness or operation. Again and again, I was struck by accounts that seemed to match reports cited by Drs. Kubler-Ross and Osis. One of the most typical results of these experiences was the complete absence of fear, together with an unmistakable conviction, sometimes on the part of a declared atheist, of the immortality of the human spirit.

Toward the end of my stay in England, I had the great satisfaction of spending a day observing the first hospice for the terminally ill, St. Christopher's in Sydenham, near London. Founded by Dr. Cicely Saunders in the late 'fifties, and financed by the Church of England, St. Christopher's is technically a center for the treatment of chronic and terminal pain. Most of the patients there are cancer victims, the majority of whom die within a year. Some of these men, women and children recover, however, for reasons not always evident. Others return to their homes to die in the midst of their families and friends.

Beyond helping terminally ill patients cope with terrible and incessant pain without resorting to the extreme narcotization widely practiced elsewhere, helping them and their loved ones meet the challenge of death with courage and faith undoubtedly represented a major breakthrough in humane health care. Here, the work of Drs. Saunders, Kubler-Ross and Osis coincides.

Today the hospice movement has spread from England around the world. Perhaps the nearest equivalent would be the heroic work of Mother Teresa of Calcutta and her followers among the destitute and abandoned in the great cities of the world, those without loved ones to care for them or the means to provide for any health care until they die. To face death with dignity among a caring human community may not be a legal right. Nevertheless, it is a human right.

Such encounters, and others like them, have helped me recognize the depths of the mystery of death, though I am sure that I shall never understand it until I undergo that baptism myself. Nor do I have a comprehensive theology of the afterlife. But in an era in which abortion, euthanasia, assassination and mass murder in Cambodia, Uganda and El Salvador have risen to the level of journalistic commonplace, some effort at a synthesis is called for in terms of a future possible for belief and sacrifice. The following reflections are offered then as hints and suggestions, plausible and perhaps otherwise.

The Other Side of Death

In the crude burial pits of the paleolithic era, over 10,000 years old, archeologists have found bones painted with red ochre—perhaps the first human attempt to affirm the primacy of life over death. Primitive burial customs still testify to a strong belief in some kinds of survival of the human spirit beyond the grave. Today, we citizens of the industrial state are perhaps unlikely to accept unquestioningly the existence of a distinct entity called the soul, a kind of shadow-self independent of the body which somehow survives the ordeal of bodily death. Theological skepticism as well as widespread materialism have probably laid the "ghost" theory of the human spirit to rest—if not permanently, at least for the foreseeable future.

Yet the obvious materiality of the body is not in itself sufficient reason to conclude that death is the complete and final end of the human personality. I can switch on a flashlight and then totally destroy the instrument. Its beam will nevertheless continue to travel through space at 186,000 miles per second, apparently forever. (Similarly, much of the starlight we see at night undoubtedly came from stars which ceased to exist aeons ago.) As a powerful energy field generated when the appropriate constitution of matter is achieved, the human spirit or soul could similarly survive the dissolution of those elements. Given the sophistication of the system of material ingredients—particularly the brain and nervous system—I believe that this is in fact a likely account of what happens. However, this need not guarantee the indestructibility of the soul. The flashlight beam will in fact eventually dissipate because of entropy—(i.e., energy loss) even if it is not intercepted and terminated by some opaque object. The soul, too, unless it were endowed with a new supply of energy, could also dissipate in time—if it indeed exists in time as we know it. Hence, it is not idle to speak of the gift of life everlasting.

Similarly, the resurrection of the body (or, more properly, the resurrection of the dead) must be viewed as a mystery of God's loving wisdom and omnipotence. Conversely, it is also conceivable that for a variety of reasons, a "separated soul" could refuse or resist the gift of life and thus come to a complete and final end. Perhaps this is the ultimate meaning of damnation.

All this is, of course, theoretical. What of experience itself? Hamlet describes death as "the undiscover'd country from whose bourne no traveller returns..." (Act III, i). But such an account is not exactly accurate, as Hamlet himself should have known, having received several visits from the ghost of his murdered father. Do apparitions, "death experiences" and similar events have anything to tell us about life beyond death?

In the late nineteenth century, the founding members of the Society for Psychical Research initiated a scientific study of apparitions of both living and deceased persons. One result of these surveys was a remarkable two-volume study, Human Personality and its Survival of Bodily Death (1902) by Frederick W. H. Myers, a remarkable scholar whose work on the unconscious antedated Freud's. Other works followed and are still forthcoming, such as the study by G.N.M. Tyrrell, Apparitions.5/

What such responsible research has produced in the field of psychic studies, now including the justly famous study by Dr. Raymond A. Moody, Jr., Life After Life,6/ Osis' books, and the further writings of Kubler-Ross, is at least this: we cannot rule out a priori the survival after bodily death of the human personality or some aspect of it, which in thousands of well-documented cases has appeared to living persons. Many of them did not even know that the person whose apparition they were experiencing was in fact deceased.

The evidence does not necessarily support the thesis that these surviving aspects will endure indefinitely. Nor have we learned very much from such cases about the nature of life after death. It seems likely, however, that at least for a while the post-mortem self remembers previous experience, recognizes friends and loved ones in both this world and the "other" one, and is aware of other dimensions of the spiritual life presently beyond its capacity. Customary notions of heaven, hell and purgatory, on the other hand, do not seem to be borne out.

Death and the Future

What bearing does all of this have on the future? It seems to me that even the likelihood of some form of post-mortem survival entails several practical implications. For one thing, it reinforces the case urged by Osis and others for death counseling both for dying persons and those about to be bereaved. This would at least make the passage from "here" to "there" less traumatic for all concerned. Similarly, hospices and the heroic work of Mother Teresa of Calcutta and others like her warrant additional support. Another issue that will require serious attention concerns the disposal of dead bodies, particularly with respect to embalming procedures and the possibility of "recycling" organs and bodies.

To begin with, much of the considerable cost of funerals is devoted to providing illusory consolation to the bereaved—expensive coffins, complete with adjustable, cushioned mattresses; new clothes for the corpse; costly embalming procedures; vaults to protect the loved one from the "assaults" of moisture, worms and roots; mounds of flowers; a long automobile cortege, etc, etc.

Artificially preserving a corpse in order to allow for public display and viewing, except possibly for important public personages, is also a wasteful and unnecessary extravagance. It will certainly become more so in the future. Moreover, pumping a body full of preservatives disrupts the natural processes of cyclic renewal. By cosmetic artifice, we in effect attempt to cancel the simple statement of fact we have heard so often on Ash Wednesdays: "Dust thou art and to dust thou shalt return." Fortunately, alternatives do exist.

Personally washing and laying out the body of a loved one is not only a final opportunity to express love and respect, it is as experience has shown, a powerful therapeutic experience for the bereaved, a constructive outlet for grief. This is especially true in the instance of parents who have lost an infant child. Societies have been founded, further, which help people arrange their funeral activities in ways which are dignified, humane and inexpensive, while conforming to health codes. For instance, it is possible to be buried in a plain pine box, even one purchased long beforehand for use as a trunk or even a coffee table for those with a sense of humor.7/ Cremation is being sought by increasing numbers of people as a simple, inexpensive and ecologically more conservative way of "returning to dust." No disrespect to the body is thereby shown, as was once feared by Catholics. And for the future, it is more likely to be warranted for reasons of monetary and spatial economy, especially among the poor and dispossessed. Cremation could be an especially symbolic ritual for deceased bishops, priests and religious as a gesture of humility and poverty.

Spare Parts

Other options emphasize our social connectedness—for instance, donating one's eyes, kidneys (and possibly heart) as transplant organs for those who need them. (Organ donor cards can be obtained from your local Kidney Foundation.) The body itself can be donated to science or medicine for purpose of learning—another, final opportunity for offering oneself for others' welfare. Truly a Christ-like act.

However we deal with "this body of death" in the future, I think it safe to suggest that the traditional funeral ritual from mortuary to mausoleum will resemble that of the recent past far less than the simpler rites of the so-called Dark Ages. Then, cremation and simple inhumation were the ordinary lot for rich and poor alike, whether clerical and lay. Our sensitivities may have become more delicate. We are not by that fact necessarily nearer the Kingdom of Heaven.

SIXTEEN

Conclusion:
Simple Gifts

Looking ahead is necessary if you don't want to stagnate in a cowardly and comfortable way in the present, waiting passively for the future.

—Karl Rahner 1/

We begin this trek through the present critical moments of western civilization, in fact of the world as a whole, by projecting ourselves backwards as well as forward in time and space, following the counsel of those two imaginative Frenchmen, Louis Pauwels and Jacques Bergier, in The Morning of the Magicians. For as they reminded us beforehand, "Only a contemporary of the future can truly be of the present. Even the distant past may be conceived of as an undertow tending toward the future."2/

We have met optimists and pessimists along the way, those who view the impending months and years ahead with grave concern and evident despair, and those who look forward to a bright new renaissance after the "coming dark age." Like the hero of H.G. Wells' novel, The Time Machine, however, as like as not we will be surprised by the eventual shape of things to come. We may well be horrified, too.

As Wells foresaw even as a young man, the forces that can rend humanity into irreconcilable branches are industrial technology fired by greed and fear on one hand, and humanism itself on the other, but an irresolute variety which cherishes but has forgotten how to strive. Between them lies a way of life committed to human dignity, freedom and truth, committed as well to the arts, literature and science, but also bold enough to create ways and means of enhancing life on earth from the resources truly at our disposal.

Such a "middle way" between exploitation and indolence is what I mean by a symbiotic spirituality.

The seeming triumph of the technological system over more humanitarian concerns may be reversed by a series of disasters which could throw much of the world back centuries in terms of the development of civilization. But at present, we must reckon more with the loss of a sense of value in life as a whole, the subjugation of everything to monetary equivalence. Perhaps the chief casuality in this respect has been the capacity for reverence. Even in a religious context, true respect for the great mysteries which we claim to honor has apparently evaporated along with our instinctive sense of awe in the presence of the Holy.

Little seems holy today. Our experience of awe is more than likely an emotion engineered by special effects artists and a booming soundtrack, as in Carl Sagan's pretentious and shallow Cosmos series. It is ironic that an almost religious sense of majesty and vastness permeated a program designed to reduce God to a pre-scientific superstition. The irony lies in the evident need to fill that perceived longing of our imagination and desire with pseudo-religious electronic glitter.

A New Cosmology

But even as the media high-priest of popular science busily dispensed with God on television and with the entire record of humankind's religious history in the data sent to the stars in the Voyager rockets, a surprising shift occurred in the attitude of many other, perhaps more thoughtful scientists, particularly physicists. Volume after volume by Robert Jastrow, Fritjof Capra, Gary Zukav and Douglas Hofstadter have stretched concepts of the cosmos into shapes that would fit the mind of an Aquinas (or an Einstein) rather than that of an agnostic astronomer or a Soviet Cosmonaut who finds his unbelief fortified because he can't "see" God in outer space.

The Spiritual Dimension

Environment has become the touchstone of a holistic, symbiotic spirituality which can usher us more safely through the Coming Dark Age. But attention to the total context of our lives, like the total context of matter and energy, requires changes in our attitudes on every level of experience, from the psychological and spiritual dimensions of our inner environment, to the social and natural dimensions of the outer environment.

Thus, we launched our investigation of a spirituality for a possible future with an examination of environmental issues. A clue for integrating these manifold elements of life into a more meaningful whole in the future came from a glimpse ahead through the eyes of a generation of literary prophets. We then looked back to a previous dark age when the light of learning and love of God illuminated Europe after the barbarian invasions and the collapse of the Roman Empire.

Hoping to find something like a contemporary Celtic spirituality, I began an actual search in this country and abroad. One of the most encouraging signs, I found, was the movement toward smallness and appropriate technology pioneered by E.F. Schumacher and others, a way of dealing with the natural and social environment which respects both life and intelligence. As we draw our considerations to a close, we would do well to review the penetrating appraisal of industrial society made by these prophets. Schumacher's own indictment is even more pertinent for spirituality today than it was a decade ago:

"Why should industrial society fail? Why should the spiritual evils it produces lead to worldly failure? From a severely practical point of view, I should say this:

"1. It has disrupted, and continues to disrupt, certain organic relationships in such a manner that world population is growing, apparently irresistibly, beyond the means of subsistence.

"2. It is disrupting certain other organic relationships in such a manner as to threaten those means of subsistence themselves, spreading poison, adulterating food, etc.

"3. It is rapidly depleting the earth's nonrenewable stocks of scarce mineral resources—mainly fuels and metals.

"4. It is degrading the moral and intellectual qualities of (the human race) while further developing a highly complicated way of life, the smooth continuance of which requires ever-increasing moral and intellectual qualities.

"5. It breeds violence—a violence against nature which at any moment can turn into violence against one's fellow human beings, when there are weapons around which make nonviolence a condition of survival."3/

That Schumacher's assessment of economic industrialism has not been mitigated by recent developments can be easily seen in other, similar estimates of world problems. A few years ago, Michael Merrien identified the following issues of concern to current writers on the global situation: 1) the arms race; 2) population growth, resource depletion and environmental deterioration; 3) global economic collapse, including an 85% chance for a second Great Depression; 4) the evident decline in the quality of life on a world-wide basis.4/

At the present moment I would cite the following as the five most serious challenges confronting this generation: 1) the likelihood of nuclear war in the near future—the most dangerous; 2) overpopulation—the most difficult; 3) increasing world-wide hunger—the most widespread and immediate; 4) growing economic disparity—the most fundamental and cruel; and 5) environmental deterioriation—the most destructive in the long haul, barring all-out nuclear war. To these, a sixth might be added—political terrorism—the newest and perhaps most dehumanizing of all.

Room for Hope

Signs of positive change can be found at the grass roots level in the United States and elsewhere—the alternative technology movement, communidades de base, pressure toward nuclear disarmament, ecological and food programs. There are even techological factors at work which Merrien and others see as promising enough to lend a sense of restrained optimism: 1) the development of new energy sources; 2) biomedical research, including the development of new species of edible plants, new uses for bacterial agents, and new means of promoting health and extending life; 3) new developments in communications; and 4) civilian activities in space.

Similarly, Gerald K. O'Neill, one of America's foremost space scientists, identifies five "drivers" of social change which will greatly influence culture and civilization for the better in coming years: computers, automation, space colonies, energy developments and communications.5/

Such technological developments alone cannot constitute fundamental reasons for hope. They may in fact exacerbate present difficulties. For their very expense and inaccessibility to most of the world's peoples limit their effectiveness to those countries already in the process of industrial deceleration or those "developing" countries attempting to follow them along that woeful route. A more fundamental reason, as Schumacher tirelessly insisted, is because the real, bottommost cause of our global malaise lies in our deviation from the most cherished spiritual values of the race. We have in fact turned our feet from the way of peace, and set them on a road of greed and envy, corporately and socially. We have not hesitated to stoop to violence, deceit and coercion in order to attain our economic goals or power—whether on a personal, corporate or national level. It is with a pang of nostalgia that we hear the narrator in the new Superman films speak with pride of "Truth, Justice, and the American Way of Life."

The crisis of the modern age is a crisis of spirit, and only a spiritual revolution will lead us back to the way shown us so long ago in the Book of Deuteronomy: "I call heaven and earth to witness against you this day, that I have set before you life and death, blessing and curse; therefore choose life, that you and your descendents may live, loving the Lord, your God, obeying his voice, and cleaving to him; for that means life to you and length of days." 6/

The Politics of Reconceptualization

Even were our intentions as clean as our looks, prior to the application of new technological solutions to world problems, we would still need to change our way of thinking. In a large and fascinating work on the demise of economics as a science, Hazel Henderson, herself an economist and a disciple of Schumacher, calls for a thorough reconceptualization process. She rightly maintains that our solutions will continue to fail, as is so painfully clear as we watch the evening news broadcast day after day, so long as we persist in thinking about global issues in the bankrupt concepts of the late nineteenth century—whether capitalistic or socialistic. According to Henderson, we are entering a post-economic era, not merely a post-industrial age. It is therefore wrong-headed to think any longer of industrializaiton as a true criterion of progress. And thus the need for reconceptualization.

Such a project of "cleansing the doors of perception" through which we envision the economics of world process is no easier, individually and socially, than the parallel process in the spiritual order. But it is no less necessary for planetary adulthood. "Together, we must demystify today's counterfeit priesthood of 'puppet' leaders, and map and align our own energies with these larger-field forces and the energies that, in reality, drive our planet: the daily solar flux, which in turn drives our planetary weather system; the cycles of oxygen, of nitrogen, and of hydrogen, and the plant photosynthesis that is our primary economic system."7/ And this, for Henderson, is what she means by "the politics of reconceptualization": "We can see ourselves and our diverse social-change activities as part of a living orchestration, generating larger patterns, out of which grow new paradigms of knowledge, policy, and personal behavior."8/

The evidence that such an alternative economy might work on a global scale is found in the fact, obvious to many, that it has already worked and for centuries, long before the existence of the monetarist "industrial" economy. Henderson identifies this age-old system as a "shadow" or "informal" economy. "It is based on our traditional heritage of cooperation, reciprocity, barter, and use-valued (rather than market-valued) productive activities. It includes home remodeling and fix-ups, mechanical repairs, home-workshop and craft production, furniture refinishing, food growing and canning, and all the vital community-based voluntary and unpaid household production (including parenting children, caring for the old and sick, ameliorating the stresses of the marketplace competitors, and cleaning up the messes left by careless production and consumption)."9/

Toward Voluntary Simplicity

This kind of "folk" economy, essentially no different from what the Celtic monks developed or what would be necessary in at least the early stages of a space colony, has been growing for some time in the United States, even in the heart of urban centers. Neighborhood technology, cooperatives—whether for food distribution, day-care, or "meals on wheels" for the sick and elderly, etc.—flea-markets and barter all evince an alternative economy which is not part of the Gross National Product, and therefore not reckoned in terms of its real contribution to human life and welfare. As a result, the "leading economic indicators" may well be a false barometer of the real situation. For instance, over 40 million Americans are now engaged in growing some or all of their ordinary vegetables and fruits. All this is not officially counted, however, as "produce" but regarded as hobby-gardening.

Such a trend toward self-sufficiency is not likely to be a mere fad as long as the price of super-marketed produce continues to climb. Other alternatives for conventional "consumer" items are also part of a new way of relating to nature and society. And, I would argue, because of that, a new kind of spirituality has begun to emerge—a cooperative, life-affirming, symbiotic spirituality. Nowhere is this more evident than in the movement called VS—voluntary simplicity.

The concept and practice seem to have been identified some years ago by Richard Gregg. More recently VS has been subject to study at the Stanford Research Institute by Duan Elgin and Arnold Mitchell. In their article in The Futurist, they describe it as "living in a way that is outwardly simple and inwardly rich."10/

Similar in concept to the lifestyle espoused by such outstanding spiritual leaders as Thoreau, Emerson, Gandhi and Jesus (not to mention Francis of Assisi and the Buddha), the elements of VS, according to Elgin and Mitchell, are 1) material simplicity, 2) human scale, 3) self-determination, 4) ecological awareness, 5) personal growth, and, it could be added, non-violence. As a distinct code of values and behavior, VS has much in common with the Shakertown Pledge and the notion of "creative simplicity" associated with it.11/

Elgin and Mitchell caution against misconceptions regarding VS. Among other things, it is not cheap. Exchanging hand-made durable goods for mass-produced, plastic disposables may, in fact, be expensive, at least in the short haul. It is not a "back to nature" movement, rejecting urban life and issues. It does not mean embracing a life of poverty, but of sufficiency. It is not a phenomenon limited to the United States, nor is it a fad.

Voluntary Simplicity and Christian Tradition

Primarily, simplicity of life-style cannot be evaluated in terms of material comfort, wealth, efficiency, hygience, possessions or any other indices of the standard of living enshrined in our social institutions. Rather, simplicity must be recognized foremost as an attitude, an approach to the whole of life, a quality of mind and spirit. It is not essentially a quantitiative factor, although quantification has a large role to play with respect to sufficiency.

With that, we find ourselves squarely in league with St. Paul and his master, Jesus. Paul's straightforward account of his lifestyle neatly summarizes much New Testament teaching on "spiritual poverty": "I have learned, in whatever state I am, to be content. I know how to be abased, and I know how to abound; in any and all circumstances I have learned the secret of facing plenty and hunger, abundance and want. I can do all things in him who strengthens me."12/

The key notion here is, ultimately, sufficiency—but coupled with an outgoing sense of responsibility for others, especially the poor and dispossessed. There is nothing self-serving about Christian economics. It is not hard to imagine how Jesus and Paul would have responded to the current cult of "survivalist" or "life-boat" ethics with their emphasis on withdrawal, hoarding and armed defense.

Practically, voluntary simplicity is not equivalent to a wholesale repudiation of every kind of "convenience" as a way back to some presumably simpler life-style. Truly time and labor-saving devices should contribute toward appropriate simplicity, and many do just that. Using an elevator to avoid climbing one or two storeys is just laziness for a healthy person. But having to mount sixty storeys is quite another matter. (Of course, why we need sixty-storey buildings is also another matter.) What Schumacher, Henderson and other perceptive critics have called for is the construc-

tive employment of such instruments of human liberation.

More importantly, we should question whether the time
and labor undeniably saved by automobiles, computers,
jet aircraft, high-speed trains, telephones, satellite communication (as opposed to trinkets such as electric can-
openers and pencil-sharpeners) are in fact being made
available for properly human activities. Or conversely,
are they being co-opted by trivial preoccupations such as
computerized pin-ball games, or, even worse, just "waiting time" vacant of any constructive content at all? A
case in point would be the inescapable traffic jams
involving aircraft as well as automobiles and other
transportation and communications systems in our under-
planned, over-developed megalopolises.

Agenda for the Future

Whether considered under the rubric of voluntary
simplicity or Celtic spirituality, a lifestyle dedicated to
the preservation of human values and achievements in
the coming age will and must include an action-
component. Examples have been mentioned in previous
chapters with regard to food, conservation, art, music,
even dying. Overall, I would identify the following areas
as needing immediate and continual action:

(1) Nuclear disarmament—working to outlaw all nuclear
weapons and to dismantle existing stockpiles.

(2) Reforming agricultural practices on a world-wide
scale, beginning with the preservation of small farms
along with the development of organic methods of weed
and pest control.

(3) Developing alternative sources of energy, particularly passive solar radiation and wind power.

(4) Voluntary but real limitation of industrial growth on
a national and international scale.

(5) A massive clean-up campaign with regard to industrial pollution of gulf areas, inland waterways, and urban air.

(6) Stopping the operation and construction of all nuclear power plants of whatever kind.

(7) World-wide conservation efforts to preserve woodlands, grasslands and all existing wilderness areas.

(8) A personal effort to recover the humane elements of civilization by involvement in art, craft, music or literature.

Embarking on such a program without seriously arranging priorities would be foolhardy, of course. But that is the primary task of a true spirituality. No one can do everything. But it is necessary to do something, even indirectly. There are, for instance, many organizations dependent on financial contributions which can accomplish collectively what individuals cannot singly, some of them being the Sierra Club, Friends of the Earth, Bread for the World, Food First, the Center for Science in the Public Interest, Greenpeace, the Environmental Defense Fund, the National Wildlife Federation, as well as more traditional welfare organizations such as the International Red Cross and CARE, the United Fund, etc. Volunteer service for these and similar organizations is, further, a contribution that far outstrips monetary concerns.

The Unlosables

When we think of civilization, I believe that we tend to conceive of it as a single package, one enormous collectivity representing the achievements of all bygone ages toward creating "the good life." In fact, civilization is probably a great deal more particular than that...and more fragile. More than forty years ago, William Ernest Hocking wrote of "the unlosables"— those aspects of civilized life without which existence as we know it would be greatly injured, if not virtually unthinkable. They are not many, and in this nuclear world, I am less optimistic than Hocking about their possible loss. We are living, after all, in an era in which a sufficient number of nuclear weapons are already poised to kill every living person on earth sixteen times over.

I was particularly struck by the poignantly fragile character of civilization when living in England at Christmastime in 1974. As the great feast drew near, it seemed that every town and village in the Midlands had at least one church where a surprisingly fine performance of a Bach Christmas oratorio or Handel's Messiah could be heard. I am sure that something irreplaceably unique would be missing from Christmas without them.

More recently, I witnessed a striking example of the effects of industrial society in Dublin, once one of the most beautiful cities of the West. Now, whole city blocks once graced by wonderful old Georgian flats are being razed to make room for soulless brick and concrete tenements to house the urban poor. Nor do I take it as progress that these Dubliners, who once might have peopled the stories of Joyce and Gogarty, now prefer the doctored strains and bathetic lyrics of American country and western music to the great songs of their own rich heritage. The less prosperous Dublin I had first met and loved ten years ago seems to exist now only in pockets of cultural resistance. And in the protected ruins of the great monastic settlements at Glendalough, Cashel and Clonmacnois, the tourist arrives at the gate by passing through booths filled with cheap plastic souvenirs and decaying "refreshment" stands. The struggle for a human future goes on.

At the end of George Pal's wonderful film version of Wells' Time Machine, the hero returns briefly to his study in Victorian England to retrieve five books to take "back" with him to the distant future, which has lost all continuity with past history and civilization. Pal leaves the viewers to answer for themselves which books were chosen of all the thousands of possible volumes. If you were given that opportunity, which books would you select? How would you wish the previous history of the world to read for the first time to your remote descendants? If you could take "back" five objects of art, what would they be? Or five paintings? Or five musical instruments or compositions? Or five scientific treatises?

We cannot know the future, except imaginatively, in the projections of artists, writers and the occasional prophet, who as always offer us possible futures which we can work to attain or to avoid. Our spirituality is the form our response takes, for wittingly or not, it is our way of building the future. It is the way we live the future in the present, whether grace-fully or to our ultimate condemnation. The stakes are that high. Thus we return to our brother, Paul, who urged us: "Do not conform yourselves to this age, but be transformed by the renewal of your mind, so that you may judge what is God's will, what is good, pleasing and just."13/ Such sentiment is not far different from the advice of Pauwels and Bergier with which we take our leave: "Those concerned with the domain of the interior life and its realities are in step with the pioneering savants who are preparing the birth of a world that will have nothing in common with our present world of laborious transition in which we have to live for just a little while longer."14/

Footnotes

Foreword

[1]*The Body, A Study in Pauline Theology*, Philadelphia: Westminster Press, 1977, p. 8.

Chapter One

[1]Carl Sagan and others, *Murmurs of Earth*, New York: Ballantine Books, 1978, p. 143.

[2]Ibid., p. 88

[3]Ibid., pp. 34-35.

[4]Louis Pauwels and Jacques Bergier, *The Morning of the Magicians*, trans. by Rollo Myers, New York: Avon Books, 1963, p. xxiii.

Chapter Two

[1]Carl Sagan and others, *Murmurs of Earth*, New York, Ballantine Books, 1978, p. 11.

[2]Harold Bloomfield, M.D., "Holistic—the New Reality in Health." *New Realities*, 11, 1 (April, 1978), pp. 14-15.

[3]J.A.T. Robinson, *The Body*, p. 19.

[4]J.A.T. Robinson, *The Body*, p. 7.

[5]Ibid., p. 8.

[6]Thomas Aquinas, *Summa Theologiae*, I. Q. 63, A. 1 ad 2.

[7]Louis Savary and Patricia M. Berne, *Prayerways*, New York: Harper & Row, 1980, p. 56.

Chapter Three

[1]Aldous Huxley, *Brave New World*, New York: The Modern Library, 1932, 1946, p. 10.

[2]George Orwell, *1984*, NY: Harcourt, Brace and World, 1947, pp. 270-271.

[3]Roberto Vacca, *The Coming Dark Age*, Garden City, NY: Doubleday Anchor, 1978, pp. 210-211.

Chapter Four

[1]See Richard Woods, *Understanding Mysticism*, Garden City, NY, Doubleday, 1980, pp. 247, 319, 321.

[2]New York: International Universities Press, 1952.

[3]These and related materials have been compiled into the series *Arthurian Sources* and *The Age of Arthur* by the late John Morris, London: Phillimore & Co., 1977 and following.

[4]See Richard Barber, *King Arthur in Legend and History*, London: Cardinal Books, 1973, pp. 58-67.

[5]Pauwels and Bergier, p. 210.

[6]Proinsias MacCana, *Celtic Mythology*, New York and London: Hamlyn, 1970, p. 11.

[7]John T. McNeill, *The Celtic Churches*, Chicago: The University of Chicago Press, 1974, p. 92.

[8]Kathleen Hughes and Ann Hamlin, *Celtic Monasticism*, New York: Seabury Press, 1981, p. 50.

[9]A delightful account of the art of Irish malediction is found in *The Book of Irish Curses* collected by Patrick C. Power, Springfield: Templegate, 1974. A counterpoint of rare beauty was compiled from the incantations, blessings and hymns of the Scots by Alexander Carmichael in *Celtic Invocations*, Norton, CT: Vinyard Books, 1972.

[10]New York: Harmony Books, 1980.

Chapter Five

[1]Berkeley: The University of California Press, 1977.

[2]Paul Freudlich, Chris Collins, Mikki Wenig, *A Guide to Cooperative Alternatives*, New Haven, CT: Community Publications Cooperative, 1979.

[3]See Richard Woods, *Mysterion*, ch. 17.

[4]*Desert Call*, Vol. 15, No. 1 (Spring, 1980), p. 11.

[5]Ibid., p. 10.

[6]Ibid.

[7]June, 1980.

[8]March, 1981.

[9]Cambridge: MIT Press, 1973.

[10]Ibid.

[11]Ibid., from the 1973 preface.

Chapter Six

[1]Marshall McLuhan, *Understanding Media: The Extension of Man*, New York: New American Library, 1964.

[2]Jacques Ellul, *The Technological System*, New York: Continuum, 1980.

[3]R. Buckminster Fuller, *Utopia or Oblivion: the Prospects for Humanity*, New York: Bantam Books, 1969.

[4]Cf. Barbara Ward and René Dubos, *Only One Earth*, Baltimore: Penguin Books, 1972.

[5]E.F. Schumacher, *Good Work*, (with Peter N. Gillingham), New York: Harper & Row, 1980, p. viii.

[6]An early effort at a philosophical appraisal of Schumacher's philosophy as found in *Small is Beautiful* is "The Metaphysics of Hierarchical Order" by Paul G. Kuntz, *Ethical Wisdom East and/or West*, Proceedings of the American Catholic Philosophical Association, Vol. 51, Washington, D.C.: ACPA, 1977, pp. 36-46.

[7]E.F. Schumacher, *Small is Beautiful*, London: Abacus, 1974, p. 69, American edition: New York: Harper & Row, 1975.

[8]Ibid.

[9]*Small is Beautiful*, p. 121.

[10]*Small is Beautiful*, p. 130.

[11]Ibid., p. 131.

[12]See especially *A Guide for the Perplexed*, pp. 71-88.

[13]See Ibid., pp. 91-92.

[14]See in this respect Richard Woods, *Mysterion*, ch. 20.

[15]See especially pp. 78-82.

[16]*Good Work*, p. 65.

[17]Rom. 12:2.

[18]Eph. 4:23.

[19]At least one magazine, *New Age*, is devoted to publicizing such movements at present. Another, *Communities, A Journal of Cooperative Living*, is published periodically to provide up-to-date information. Other journals such as Stewart Brand's *Co-Evolution Quarterly* and the *Fox Fire* books have also stimulated interest in alternative societies.

Section Two

[1]Garden City, N.Y.: Image Books, 1980, p. 86.

Chapter Seven

[1]Roberto Vacca, *The Coming Dark Age*, pp. 58-59.

[2]Ibid., p. 59.

[3]William Ophuls, *Ecology and the Politics of Scarcity*, San Francisco: W.H. Freedman, 1977, p. 147.

[4]See Erik Eckholm and Lester R. Brown, *Spreading Deserts — The Hand of Man*, Worldwatch Paper 13, Washington, D.C.: The Worldwatch Institute, August 1977, pp. 30-34.

[5]Lester R. Brown, *The Twenty-Ninth Day*, New York: W.W. Norton, 1978, p. 51.

Chapter Eight

[1]London and New York: Granada, 1979, p. 25.

[2]William Irwin Thompson, *Passages about Earth*, New York: Harper & Row, 1974, p. 101.

[3]Robert Stobaugh and Daniel Yergin, eds., *Energy Future*, New York: Random House, 1979, p. 11.

[4]Ibid., p. 12.

[5]Gerard K. O'Neill, *2081: A Hopeful View of the Human Future*, New York: Simon and Schuster, 1981, pp. 75-76.

Chapter Nine

[1]*The Raw and the Cooked*, New York: Harper & Row, 1969, p. 65.

[2]*The Supper of the Lamb*, Garden City, NY: Image Books, 1974, pp. 51-52.

[3]New York: Harper and Row, 1971, p. 48.

[4]Frances Moore Lappé, *Diet for a Small Planet*, N.Y.: Ballantine, 1975.

[5]Published by MIT Press, Cambridge, Mass.

[6]The latter three may be obtained either free or at minimal cost from the Superintendent of Documents, U.S. Government Printing Office, Washington, DC 20402.

[7]New York: Warner Books, 1976.

[8]A valuable chart comparing the sugar content of over 75 breakfast cereals prepared by the American Society of Dentistry for Children is available from the Hyperactive Children's Institute, 2610 W. Evergreen St., Chicago, Il. 60622.

[9]Cited in *Eating in America*, p. 48.

[10]*Eating in America*, p. 55.

[11]Michael Lasky, *The Complete Junk Food Book*, New York: McGraw-Hill, 1977, p. xvii.

[12]Lasky, p. 24.

Chapter Ten

[1]Edward T. Hall, *The Hidden Dimension*, Garden City, New York: Doubleday Anchor, 1969, p. 16.

[2]T.A. Heppenheimer, *Toward Distant Suns,* New York: Fawcett Columbia, 1979, p. 176.

Chapter Eleven

[1]Emrys Jones and Eleanor Van Zandt, *The City Yesterday, Today and Tomorrow,* Garden City, New York: Doubleday, 1974. p. 11.

[2]Ibid., p. 168.

[3]See Rev. 21.

[4]Cf. Is. 24:10.

[5]Cf. Lk. 9:51.

[6]Cf. Lk. 13:34.

[7]Cf. Heb. 13:12.

[8]Rev. 21:2.

[9]Jones and Van Zandt, pp. 7, 165.

[10]Kirkpatrick Sale, *Human Scale,* NY: Coward, McCann & Geoghegan, 1980, p. 206.

[11]Ibid., p. 205.

Chapter Twelve

[1]Ex. 35: 30-34.

[2]Enoch 8: 1-2.

[3]Carla Needleman, *The Work of Craft,* NY: Alfred A. Knopf, 1979, p. 49.

[4]Needleman, p. 141.

[5]See Mk. 6:3, Mt. 13:55.

[6]See also Rev. 2:27.

[7]Is. 64:8.

Chapter Thirteen

[1]Quoted by Peter Michael Hamel in *Through Music to the Self,* Boulder: Shambala, 1979.

[2]Is. 6:3, Rev. 4:8.

[3]Eph. 5:19, Col. 3:16.

[4]Cf. Mt. 26:30, Mk. 14:26, Heb. 2:12, Rev. 5:9, etc.

[5]Cen. 4:21, Ps. 33:2, Dan 3:5, etc.

[6]Cf. I Sam. 10:5, I Chr. 25:1.

[7]Cf. I Cor. 14:7, Rev. 5:8, 14:2, 18:22.

[8]Hamel, p. 213.

[9]Hamel, pp. 191-192.

[10]*Folk Harp Journal*, Sept., 1978, p. 13.

[11]A good selection of kit-makers, catalogs, supplies and manuals can be found in the *Next Whole Earth Catalog* (pp. 472-484). For anyone interested in the folk harp, excellent blueprints and supplies for a variety of harps can be obtained from Robinson's Harp Shop, P.O. Box 161, Mt. Laguna, CA, 92048. I'd also recommend Gildas Jaffrennou's little book *Folk Harps*, Hartfordshire, England: Model and Allied Publications, Ltd., 1973.

[12]Shops such as Hobgoblin (659 El Camino, South San Francisco, CA 94080) also sell used instruments as well as new ones, specializing in those of Celtic persuasion.

[13]The Early Music Shoppes in London and York rank among the best (28 Sunbridge Rd., Braford, Yorkshire BD1 2AE.) Be sure and request a price list.

Chapter Fourteen

[1]See Richard Woods, *Mysterion*, ch. 9, "Mysticism and Sexuality."

[2]James J. Lynch, *The Broken Heart*, New York: Basic Books, 1979, p. 10.

[3]Lynch, p. 11.

[4]Lynch, p. 35.

[5]Patrick Kerans, *Sinful Social Structures*, NY: Paulist Press, 1974, p. 42.

[6]Milton Mayeroff, *On Caring*, New York: Harper & Row, 1971.

[7]Dr. James Gill, S.J., and Linda Amadeo, R.N., M.S., "Celibate Anxiety," *Human Development*, Vol. 1, No. 4 (Winter 1980), pp. 6-17.

[8]Ibid.

[9]Ibid.

[10]Jack Dominian, *Proposals for New Sexual Ethic*, London: Darton, Longman and Todd, 1977, p. 55.

[11]Ibid., p. 56.

[12]Ibid., p. 70.

[13]Dominian, p. 65.

[14]John Alan Lee, *The Colors of Love*, New York: Prentice-Hall, 1976.

Chapter Fifteen

[1]See Gen. 5:22 and 2 Kings 2:11.

[2]See in this regard the brilliant chapter "The Terror of Death" in Ernest Becker's *The Denial of Death*, New York: Free Press, 1979.

[3]Dr. Kit Pedler, *The Quest for Gaia*, London and New York: Granada, 1979,

p.57.

⁴New York: Macmillan, 1969.

⁵New York: Collier Books, 1963.

⁶New York: Bantam, 1976.

⁷See Ernest Martan, *A Manual of Death Education and Simple Burial*, Burnsville, NC: The Celo Press, 1980 ed.

Chapter Sixteen

¹"A Conversation with Karl Rahner," Teofilo Caestrero, ed., *Faith: Conversations with Contemporary Theologians*, N.Y.: Orbis Books, 1980, p. 139.

²Pauwels and Bergier, *The Morning of the Magicians*, p. xxiii.

³*Good Work*, pp. 34-35.

⁴"The Good News and the Bad News," *The Futurist*, XIV, No. 3, June, 1980, p. 3.

⁵*2081: A Hopeful View of the Human Future*, NY: Simon and Schuster, 1981.

⁶Dt. 30:19; 20.

⁷Hazel Henderson, *The Politics of the Solar Age*, Garden City, New York: Doubleday Anchor, p. 5.

⁸Ibid.

⁹Ibid., p. 9.

¹⁰*The Futurist*, August, 1977, p. 200.

¹¹See in this respect *No More Plastic Jesus: Global Justice and Christian Lifestyle* by Adam Daniel Finnerty, New York: Orbis Books, 1979.

¹²Phil. 4:11-13.

¹³Rom. 12: 1-2.

¹⁴*The Morning of the Magicians*, p. xxiii.

Meditations with™
A FEW WORDS WITH MATTHEW FOX, O.P.

"Bear & Company is publishing this series of creation-centered mystic/prophets to bring to the attention and prayer of peoples today the power and energy of the holistic mystics of the western tradition. One reason western culture succumbs to boredom and to violence is that we are not being challenged by our religious traditions to be all we can be. This is also the reason that many sincere spiritual seekers go East for their mysticism — because the West is itself out of touch with its deepest spiritual guides.

Meditations with™ Meister Eckhart
by Matthew Fox

For Eckhart to be spiritual is to be awake and alive — Creation itself is sacrament. The spiritual life begins where life does — "the spring of life...the heart."

Reflections of Meister Eckhart with an Introduction and versions by Matthew Fox.

"Spirituality begins with humanity's potential to act divinely in the ways of beauty-making, compassion, and sharing."

0-939680-04-1 128 pages **$6.95** with ART

Meditations with™ Julian of Norwich
by Brendan Doyle
with foreword by Patricia Vinje
and preface by Matthew Fox

Julian's spirituality is based in acknowledging God where God is. Her creation-centered vision — God-with-in-us — was the basis of her meditation. Brendan Doyle presents this feminist mystic's words in the context of her capacity to find meaning in creation. A treasure house for meditative reading.

0-939680-11-4 128 pages **$6.95** with ART

Meditions with™ Hildegarde of Bingen
by Gabriele Uhlein
with foreword by Thomas Berry and Preface by Matthew Fox

Sharings from the 26 "vision" of this ageless Benedictine of Medieval Germany. Visions which this "new age," this age of alternative, holistic spiritualities is at ease with. From this famous Benedictine sharings of her 26 "visions"...

Gabriele Uhlein selected these messages from a woman of profound prayer and insight — Hildegarde of Bingen.

0-939680-12-2 128 pages $6.95 with ART

Meditations with™ Mechtilde of Magdeburg
by Sue Woodruff
Foreword by Matthew Fox

Like so many women of the middle ages Mechtilde was a prophet who loudly decried the abuses of organized religions and its priests in her day. While she made enemies this way, she did not cease composing this beautiful poetry of the soul for those who live very much in the world.

In this book, the author, Sue Woodruff, brings together, in moving drawings, and well chosen verse from Mechtilde a beautiful meditation experience — one based in God's beauty in creation, and humanity's dignity in God.

0-939680-08-8 128 pages $6.95 with ART